CW00958025

Just About Coping

DR NATALIE CAWLEY

Just About Coping

A real-life drama from the
psychotherapist's chair

PICADOR

First published 2024 by Picador
an imprint of Pan Macmillan
The Smithson, 6 Briset Street, London ECIM 5NR
EU representative: Macmillan Publishers Ireland Ltd, 1st Floor,
The Liffey Trust Centre, 117–126 Sheriff Street Upper,
Dublin 1, DOI YC43
Associated companies throughout the world
www.panmacmillan.com

ISBN 978-1-0350-1180-3 HB
ISBN 978-1-0350-1184-1 TPB

Copyright © Dr Natalie Cawley 2024

The right of Dr Natalie Cawley to be identified as the
author of this work has been asserted by her in accordance
with the Copyright, Designs and Patents Act 1988.

The author and publisher are grateful for the reproduction of
the Paranoid Scale and the Holmes and Rahe Scale.

Paranoid Scale: Green, C. E. L., Freeman, D., Kuipers, E., Bebbington, P., Fowler, D.,
Dunn, G., and Garety, P. A. (2008).
'Measuring Ideas of Persecution and Social Reference:
The Green et al. Paranoid Thoughts Scale (GPTS)', *Psychological Medicine*, 38, 101–11.
Holmes and Rahe Scale: Holmes, T. H., and Rahe, R. H. (1967).
'The Social Readjustment Rating Scale', *Journal of Psychosomatic Research*, 11(2), 213–18.

All rights reserved. No part of this publication may be reproduced,
stored in a retrieval system, or transmitted, in any form, or by any means
(electronic, mechanical, photocopying, recording or otherwise)
without the prior written permission of the publisher.

Pan Macmillan does not have any control over, or any responsibility for,
any author or third-party websites referred to in or on this book.

1 3 5 7 9 8 6 4 2

A CIP catalogue record for this book is available from the British Library.

Typeset in Dante MT Std by Jouve (UK), Milton Keynes
Printed and bound by CPI Group (UK) Ltd, Croydon, CRO 4YY

This book is sold subject to the condition that it shall not, by way of
trade or otherwise, be lent, hired out, or otherwise circulated without
the publisher's prior consent in any form of binding or cover other than
that in which it is published and without a similar condition including
this condition being imposed on the subsequent purchaser.

Visit **www.picador.com** to read more about all our books
and to buy them. You will also find features, author interviews and
news of any author events, and you can sign up for e-newsletters
so that you're always first to hear about our new releases.

To Jared and to all of my patients
who have taught me about resilience
and the joy of connection

Contents

A note on the text

To respect the privacy of friends and colleagues, I have altered various personal details. All characters, both patient and personal, are composite characters. To maintain patient confidentiality, I have anonymized names and changed demographic information, clinical details, dates, times and places.

ONE

The activating event

The Attachment

I cross the room in the dark and perch on the corner of the bed, too exhausted to look for the light switch. This tiny room attached to a hospital somewhere on the outskirts of London is my new home, but this is not where I am supposed to be. I am supposed to be moving into a riverside flat in Manchester, with cream carpets, a double bed piled high with throw pillows, and bespoke ceramic tiles in the kitchen. The only tiles here are four cracked white squares above a corner sink – my new bathroom – and the bed is sadly single.

I prepare dinner, a bag of Quavers I bought on the train. Bursting the packet open sends a cheesy-smelling plume into the air and its familiarity brings a little comfort in this alien space. To try to stay strong, I remind myself I was lucky to get this free accommodation and the chance to work as an assistant psychologist earning the living wage – well, the minimum wage. Well, the minimum wage *eventually*. I am starting on an honorary contract, meaning I won't get paid until I prove myself.

I eat the last Quaver and my thoughts return to the event that propelled me here.

I noticed him at a party in Leeds. We were first-year students navigating the world away from home. He was in a group of boys identically dressed in white shirts, striped ties and cream chinos, all gliding into medical school from public school. I was fascinated by their behaviours. No one in my family went to public school. From a distance, clutching my warm Prosecco, I watched them compete in drinking races then gaffer-tape bottles to their wrists and shout, 'Amy Wine-hands!' As they erupted into laughter, I crossed the room and, emboldened by booze, lifted his shirt and suggested a new competition based on physique. For this medical-school rugby team 'shirts off' was a welcome challenge, and I met his gaze with an approving smile while the others rushed to strip down.

He introduced himself as Steve, then introduced his friends by their nicknames. 'This is Oinko,' so named because at school he looked a bit like a pig. 'And this is my friend, Fish,' because he once had his hair cut like a monk, which evolved into Monkfish, which devolved into Fish. The guy called Burger, it turned out, had once eaten five burgers in one go.

This was seven weeks in at university and my inferiority complex had been peaking. Apparently, my Manchester accent made me difficult to understand, with one student even calling out 'Alreet duck!' – something I have never said in my life. I wasn't an all-right duck, more a fish out of water, and on top of this I was studying psychology, which in the eyes of the medics was a 'soft' science, the 'clown school' of medicine, and of little significance to patient care outcomes. I was desperate to be accepted, but now I had got myself noticed by a medical student, a public-school boy, destined to be a doctor.

Placing doctors on a pedestal is common. The distance makes it acceptable for them to put their hands on our chests and cut into our flesh. At times of deep distress, we don't want to think of them as mere mortals; we need to believe they can fix us. Once, when I saw a surgeon struggle with the ring pull on a can of Diet Coke, I had to look away. The deification worked both ways, with constant deference towards the junior medics fuelling their confidence. Steve's self-assurance was magnetically attractive to me, and we soon became a couple.

During our first year together, Steve's parents separated, and we spent long nights sitting up in my student digs, talking things through, over and over. While I built my ability to comfort him and empathize, he grew more detached and began to focus on his work. He stopped texting in the daytime, seemed less open to humour, grew harder at the edges, more rational, and less available in every sense. Over time, I accommodated these changes. My identity became bonded with his and I began to hold his victories as my own. In my vision of our future, never far from my thoughts, his career took priority and my own took a back seat.

After graduating, I moved back to live at my parents' house. Sleeping in my childhood bedroom, with its pink colour scheme and a line of toys along the bed, I told myself this was for two years only, while I waited for Steve to finish his degree, and then we could move in together. To earn some money, I got a job as a care assistant on a psychiatric ward, supporting a psychologist called Dr Macklin and her eighteen male patients who all had frontal-lobe damage.

One of the patients, Adam, was six foot six inches tall, with treatment-resistant schizophrenia. He was experiencing regular delusions, sometimes thinking he was Pegasus. He arrived on the ward after throwing himself from the top of a two-storey car park, believing he would fly. The fall broke Adam's arms so badly they had to be pinned back into place, stuck out in front of him and bent at the elbow, giving him the look of a T-Rex. Periodically, Adam would run at the concrete pillar in the middle of the ward and, when appropriate, we needed to physically restrain him to keep him safe. Each member of staff was assigned a specific part of his body, and I was charged with Adam's head. But I was swiftly discharged when he simply lifted his head into the air, and with it my whole body, making his way to the pillar unfazed.

The work was demanding, with long shifts and a wide range of jobs assigned to us daily on a whiteboard. One morning, the instruction next to my name read simply, *Find out who did the poo*, and it was this humour, along with the kindness and camaraderie, that helped us cope. I started to get the feeling I was in the right place, but I was too intimidated to see myself as anything other than a junior. When a frustrated patient challenged my boss, Dr Macklin, saying, 'Fuck you and your fucking little sidekick over there!' I inexplicably performed a small wave, as if to say, *Yes, it's me. I'm the fucking little sidekick.*

High alert

At long last, Steve graduated, and we put a deposit on a rental flat in a small market town on the outskirts of Manchester. It would be a reasonable commute to his first hospital job and easy for me to catch the train to London, where I had finally found a part-time post as a trainee psychologist in a hospital. As the move-in date approached, my future looked secure.

Then suddenly Steve stopped texting.

Before we form any conscious thoughts about an unusual situation, we have an unconscious awareness: a 'gut feeling'. This comes from the subconscious. Our brains are constantly scanning the environment for cues of safety or danger. This scanning process is called neuroception, and the gut-feeling sensation happens even before we have a conscious thought. But it is a relatively blunt instrument. We feel the same physiological arousal whether we are nervous or excited. The only difference between feeling nervous and excited is the story we tell ourselves. When Steve went quiet, I was quietly thrilled. Yess! This must be the build-up to a proposal, I thought.

Finally, Steve messaged.

I can't do this.

With a shaky hand, I put the phone on the floor, face down, and pushed it away, as if the distance would make me safer. Shrinking to a crouch, I held my stomach. I noticed the sounds coming towards me were the voices of my parents, but they seemed muffled and incoherent. I was acutely aware of a pungent chemical smell from the dishwasher which was making me nauseous. My senses were all mixed up as I reached for the phone to look again and saw the three bubbles that told me Steve was typing. My heart stopped. The bubbles went away. Then came back. I held my breath and flooded with hope until the message eventually appeared.

Do you need me to come and break things off to your face?

I repeated the four words Steve used to end our six-year

relationship, trying to make them lose potency. Repetition can make words become blurred and disjointed until they begin to sound strange and lose their meaning, a phenomenon known as semantic satiation. I tried saying them in another voice to create an observing stance, pretending that they belonged to someone else, a cognitive behavioural therapy technique which can be helpful when we feel overwhelmed. It helps us detach a little. But this time it didn't work. I went to my room and looked into the mirror, framed with joyful pink glitter, and searched my face for the flaw – the reason he didn't want me.

It feels strange to inhabit a person who now feels like a different version of me, a version I feel disconnected from. The person looking back at me in the mirror feels distant, yet desperate. They are in pain.

What now?

I didn't know whether to take up my new trainee psychologist job in London or stay at my parents'. How could I travel across the country, away from friends and family? I couldn't even face the local shops. The pull of familiarity was magnetic. Maybe I could stay and start a new life on the couch . . . I was paralysed with uncertainty, a sign of acute anxiety, unable to make any decisions, right down to still or sparkling water. I couldn't trust myself and I couldn't trust the world. Logically, this makes sense. Why should you be able to trust your thoughts and feelings when you just got it so horribly wrong? When you couldn't tell love from betrayal and that has meant the loss of your future and your sense of identity. In this state, the nervous system puts you on high alert to protect you in case it happens again. It makes you hypervigilant, interpreting every-thing as a potential threat. A napkin flung down on a table by a waiter triggers a scream.

And break-ups leave you anxious. Anxiety is the friend who takes up an entire evening talking about that guy who stopped texting back, seizing every opportunity to return the conver-sation to themselves and their unrequited love, no matter how tenuous the link. 'Pizza! Oh, Steve ate pizza once. Let me tell you about him. He left me . . .' In the throes of anxiety, we desperately seek reassurance from those around us, but how-ever much we receive, it can never be enough. The exercise is exhausting for everyone involved and, sadly, people often grow tired of it. But anxiety is self-indulgent, pursuing people even as they pull away.

Hypervigilant, anxious, indecisive – the perfect trainee psychologist. I can't see this working.

Reset

I tried refocusing my brain using a method I'd learned from Dr Macklin, who, whenever I was stressed, would set me the simple repetitive task of data entry to calm me down. I dragged my case from under the bed and started placing items inside, very deliberately, ticking them off a mental list. Simple, meth-odical activities can restore our ability to think clearly. They engage the rational, executive part of our brain, and relieve the emotional part that is feeling overwhelmed. It's the reason we have *aha* moments when we start to wash the dishes. Clarity returns. The answer arises in our consciousness just when we are least expecting it and don't have a pen to write it down.

Before I knew it, my case was packed, but mentally I was still not ready. I had two days to make sense of what had happened and imagine a new future. I started mapping out what had taken place. Traumatic memories are laid down differently in the brain. Intense emotion can make it difficult to assess them correctly and may even make them seem worse, which can slow down the process of recovery. Events become imprinted on the memory with the intense emotion experienced in the moment, rather than with a time stamp. Think of memory as a patchwork quilt and each patch as a lived experience; the memory incorporates new patches in a way that fits with its past, its present and the representation of the self. But, if something painful or shocking happens, that little patch won't fit with your sense of the world and who you are, so it can't find a place to fit in seamlessly. Instead, it sits outside and keeps popping up, trying to attach and make itself part of the quilt. Every time you have a flashback, an intrusive thought, a nightmare or a re-experiencing, it's the little patch still trying to knit in. It has stayed the same, unprocessed and just as painful. If we ignore it, it won't stop, so we have to make sense of it, make it part of our narrative and a small, manageable part of ourselves.

I thought about my patchwork quilt and the trauma I didn't want to keep or amplify; I didn't want to keep recycling this painful patch. I needed to look after future me.

I started recording my story, adding the time stamps.

Tuesday: I received the text from Steve, marking my descent into dissociation and panic. Dissociation is a common experience, often not too troubling. It's something many of us encounter while driving – we arrive at a familiar destination safely and we know we haven't mown down anyone on the way, but we can't recall any details of the journey. But dissociation can also be very scary, leading to a sense of unease, panic and disconnect.

A few days of feeling total disconnect from reality and blurred attempts to function followed.

Thursday night: I was driven around by Dad (dads need to do something action-y in times of crisis) to look for pharmacies open late enough to sell me a sleep aid. Sleep seemed like something I would never have again and, like food, a silly thing to 'need'. We got a McDonald's. I managed a few chips.

Saturday: A few hours of sleep brought some clarity; I wanted something else to focus on. I decided to have a go at my new job.

Sunday morning: Dad drove me to the train station. On the way, he helped to ground me by breaking down the rest of my journey. 'Just get on the train, find the Tube thing, get the next train. If you get lost, ask a train man. One step at a time.' The prospect of London's transport system felt daunting, the Tube map just a mess of colours and lines. After finding a seat on the train, I started to panic, so I pulled out my laptop and opened up an old data spreadsheet, and the repetitive task calmed me down.

Writing the events down like this, as my train sped to London, helped me make sense of where I was. Emotionally, still shaken and shocked. Physically, alone, 200 miles from home, perched on the end of a narrow bed, eating Quavers in the dark, about to start my new life.

Monday

Monday morning, my first day in my new job. I try out a strategy borrowed from one of Dr Macklin's patients, Rob. He would initiate a dissociative experience by staring at himself in the mirror until his reflection became completely disconnected, a stranger. He was then able to give this person more objective advice. Desperate, I try Rob's trick. I start with a firm greeting: 'Hello, it's me.'

After an awkward silence in which I stare back at myself, I respond: 'I know, I'm here too.'

I try to sound stern, when really I'm shaky and nervous, as if I'm meeting a stranger at a party. I find myself using a phrase I didn't even know was in my repertoire: 'Ah, bingo!'

I try to give myself a pep talk: 'Just aim to get through the day. You can do this; you can do this!'

A terse male voice calls out, 'No phone calls in the mornings!' followed by the bang of a fist on my door.

I shift back into reality: I am standing at the foot of a tiny single bed in a bare room, staring into a mirror.

After a solitary breakfast in the canteen, I walk down a corridor looking for the location of my first meeting. The distinctively rigid figure progressing towards me from the opposite direction is Dr Weller, the head of paediatrics.

He greets me with a cold, 'Good morning, Natalie, how are you?' as he stretches out an arm to open one of the doors.

Now, when you're very much not all right and someone asks you how you are, there's something about it that makes the mask slip. In my vulnerable state, I read the outstretched arm as a signal to come in for a hug and throw my arms around him. For a moment, time stands still.

'What are you *doing*?' he says, looking alarmed.

And this is how I begin my new career.

The inner worlds of others

Thankfully, there is little time for reflection. Thrown into my role, I barely have time to think about Steve or leaving the familiarity of home. As I step into other people's lived experience and walk them through their emotions, I have less room for my own, which I am grateful for. I feel an intense pressure to offer something helpful, so I am hyperfocused and listen intently to each person who sits opposite me.

Dr Macklin taught me that, as a therapist, you have to learn to track the lived experience of others – to be empathetic. This requires that you step into their world and, ideally, leave your own behind. It's a skill that takes honing, resilience and boundaries. Dr Macklin taught me this so that I could protect myself from absorbing each and every patient's pain. It is currently serving to protect me from my own. Here, in the therapy room, I can leave my own world behind, and I do so willingly.

In the social world, when someone tells us their deep feelings about something, we try to relate. We scan our memories in an attempt to find a time in our own lives when we felt a similar way. We enter our own story and feed it back, instinctively trying to understand, connect and bond through shared experience. Of course, some of us do this better than others. We show that we understand without hijacking the other person's narrative – it's a careful balancing act of give and take.

As a therapist, however, you retrain your brain to stay in the other person's story and avoid linking back to yourself. This is their experience and theirs alone.

At work, I have to step out of my own experience, but it's equally important to carefully package the empath away at the end of the working day and remove the therapist's air of *Tell me what you're feeling*. But it is easier said than done.

At the end of the day, at the gym, I go to the steam room to relax, but the other occupant, a man in his mid-fifties, begins an intense comprehensive trauma history. His dad never loved him. His wife never touches him. And even his much older cleaning lady has rebuffed his advances. I take in his torment as I rub the sting of sweat from my eyes, and he goes on to express his ambivalence towards life and his thoughts about taking his own.

I don't usually last long in steam rooms. I find the heat over-powering. But I am trapped. Who gets up and leaves when someone is telling you they feel suicidal? But, at the end of a long day spent tracking the challenging life experiences of others, I am struggling to tune in. I respond with as much compassion as I can muster, while contemplating my own suf-focating death in the steam room or having to live out the rest of my life resembling a small raisin.

It is time to sort out my boundaries. Enter my new super-vising psychologist, Dr Lane.

Boundaries

Dr Lane has tiny hands that are always struggling to carry an overstuffed colourful diary with Post-it notes that spill out of it, while clutching biscuits or other little treats she thinks I might like. With her gentle looks of encouragement and support, her blatant compassion, she begins to draw me out of myself.

The purpose of this supervision for trainee psychologists is not just to talk through patients and plan interventions, but also to discuss the impact our work is having on us. It's designed to be a space to offload and to gain tools for reflection and resilience, to help us to be 'the strongest person in the room' with any patient. The idea is that supervision prevents us from taking any of our 'issues' into our work with patients.

Dr Lane and I work together with all manner of patients; she is a rare breed in that she specializes in both adults and children. Sometimes I get to shadow her sessions, and this is my favourite time with her. I savour every moment, even when patients become argumentative or sullen; I watch her navigate through each feeling and micro-expression with strength and compassion, unfazed. At the end of each session, she nods towards me and asks if there's anything I would like to add or share. Knowing she is going to ask me this, I usually spend the full fifty minutes trying to think of something electrically powerful or moving to say, as if I am the cherry on Dr Lane's expertly iced cake. Rarely do I achieve this. Usually I just thank the patient for allowing me to hear their story. I really am grateful for these insights into their experience.

Other times, Dr Lane listens to my work with patients and observes my attempts to show empathy. She is thoughtful and encouraging in her feedback, always constructive and hopeful. I admire her can-do approach; Dr Lane and I opt to view the person not the label, stretching our expertise to the limit.

We also put in the work to skill ourselves up, reading articles, research papers and subscribing to therapists' magazines to prepare for whatever is thrown at us.

I tell Dr Lane about the man in the steam room who held me hostage emotionally, and she listens with a chuckle before suggesting I adopt a ritual at the end of each day that marks my 'shedding' the role of therapist, allowing me to step out of 'rescuer mode'. Taking this advice on board, as a practical solution I bring a different jacket to work to help me switch roles. Off with the psychologist, on with Natalie. The structuring of my day helps me to maintain the balance of my mind. But, of course, I can't tell her this because I am convinced it will make her doubt my ability to do my job. I don't want it to change her view of me, as I am gaining her confidence through the quality of my work.

Kiwi

As a trainee psychologist at the hospital, I am often treated like a second-class citizen by the consultants, when the truth is that, despite my relatively junior status, I often represent the entire emotional health and well-being service, and I have just one hour a week with Dr Lane to help me 'manage' my caseload. I am given the title of 'assistant psychologist', which means most patients walk in believing I am the assistant – there to make the tea and arrange the biscuit plate for someone more superior and capable. They often seem disappointed when they realize that I am the start, the middle and the end of their treatment plan, which typically extends across just six sessions over a few weeks.

The activating event

The hospital has a room shortage, especially for me. But one freezing morning I arrive to the announcement of a miracle: they have found a permanent room for me. The rooms are all named after fruits and, on a list of allocated rooms, next to my name it says, *Kiwi*. But, when I check all the doors around the ward, the word *Kiwi* isn't on any of them. I am about to ask when I spot something vaguely resembling a picture of a kiwi fruit that has been scrawled in black biro onto a life-sapping piece of grey A4 printer paper and crudely sellotaped to the door of a store cupboard. I step inside.

Kiwi's walls, I discover, have been painted a sickly grey, not even a kiwi green, and there is one stark, cold ceiling light dangling from a central cable. The room is bare apart from a small wooden desk facing the wall, with a chair tucked neatly beneath. When I pull the chair out, it leaves just enough space for me to sit down. A second chair fills the only remaining space between the table and the door, so that the second chair has to be moved each time the door is opened or closed. There is no natural light.

Psychologists and therapists are taught how to place the two chairs in their room. The patient's chair and the therapist's chair should face each other, but at a slight angle rather than head on. This is to make the sessions feel gentler, less confrontational. In Kiwi, my patients will need to sit just centimetres from my face, a set-up which I can immediately see will generate an initial unease. It is claustrophobic, to say the least. The therapeutic effect of my new room is comparable to that of standing on a drawing pin.

After a few sessions in Kiwi, one of my youngest patients

15

brings me a drawing of a window to stick on the wall, concerned that I might 'get sad'.

Kiwi becomes my home, and my days develop a frenzied structure: session with a patient, run to grab a coffee or breather in the staff break room, session with a patient, and so on.

Dr Lane says to another colleague in the break room, 'You can send Natalie anything, nothing fazes her,' and I start to believe in myself. I don't want her to know I've spent some of the morning breathing into a paper bag, a technique which has become a handy tool. I discovered it following one of my first Kiwi sessions, after which I'd hidden in a maternity-clinic room, hyperventilating into a sick bag that I found by the bed. Watching the paper rise and fall, and hearing the scrunch-unscrunch sound with, eventually, increasingly long intervals, helped me to visualize my panic and take enough control to slow my breathing down. It worked.

While Dr Lane isn't aware of my interludes with a paper bag and other aspects of my life and self, sometimes when we laugh together I get the sense she's holding my gaze for a little too long – whether to stay in the moment or maybe to check the sincerity of my amusement or just to hold the connection, I don't know. In this way, I sense there's also more to her life than I am aware of, but I don't ask.

Moving on

After three months I move out of the hospital accommodation into a house-share with my best friend Alex, which I can just about afford now I have a living wage. Alex and I were put in rooms next door to one another in university halls when we were eighteen. I didn't care for her much at first. We were from different worlds. She was a trilby-wearing indie kid from the Midlands and I was a woefully mainstream Mancunian. I think we each found the other a bit cringe, but we quickly realized we were both trying a little too hard to have an identity, to reinvent ourselves, and we soon bonded over a love of comedy. Now, we share the same world.

Three other girls join us in the new flat to start our adult lives in north London. Our flat is next to a busy bus stop and above a chippy, the smell a surprisingly welcome new friend, and we sit on a precarious little flat roof at night, looking out over the busy road, and share chips and Diet Cokes. Alex is such a familiar comfort and an eternal optimist: 'At least we will never miss the bus again,' she exclaims, as the roof of a bus almost scrapes us off our perch.

It is not the domestic bliss I had once envisioned for myself, but I like it. I think I am making progress.

Back on the bike

Just as I see patients swap alcoholism for gambling, sex addiction for binge eating, or cocaine for addictive shopping, I too need to replace Steve and fill the emotional void. This means I am on the hunt for a romantic attachment. The compulsion is to avoid pain, distract myself from it or morph it into something more tolerable. But transferring pain from one thing or person to another creates neurotic suffering. When we replace the truly painful thing with something more tolerable, on repeat, we never get done with it; we never address the underlying issue. It lives on, just manifesting in different ways.

Moving from one person to another, or being 'on the rebound', has many negative consequences, but I don't want to accept that this is the real reason for my romantic desire. Rebounds are frequently unsuccessful, I know that. And yet here I am.

Several patients have worked hard to convince me that their new rebound relationship is in fact true and pure love. They cite examples of shared intimacy or familiarity as evidence: 'But I go to the toilet when she's in the shower, so we do really know each other.' Or, 'It's only been a few weeks and I've already started clipping his toenails.' And, although it is true that intimacy is inversely related to disgust, it doesn't always work the same when intimacy is synthetically created. You have to feel known, seen and heard, deeply and intrinsically, which typically takes time.

When relationships begin, the first stage is the fusion stage, which involves lust, attraction and desire, all good ingredients to distract us from anything else that's going on in our lives. But, when we attempt to transfer loss and grief from a break-up into a new relationship, we try to rush through to the next stage – the development stage of the new relationship – to make it feel safer, more established, more of a like for like.

Even while there's an element of danger, some psychologists claim rebounds can actually be helpful and adaptive for those who have a tendency to focus all their energy on one other person, forming an intense fantasy bond with them. A rebound renews hope that other relationships can be forged, and offers a sense that all hope is not lost, that the original significant other is not the whole world. This is something I clearly need reminding of in my own anxiety-ridden state.

My potential rebound is with Tod, a musician – not the type of musician who sleeps on his mum's sofa, but one from a world-famous band. I am not a person who typically goes on dates with world-famous musicians; I currently feel like an imposter who is working out of an office that is really a cupboard. I don't even really know the band's music, having barely moved on from being the woefully mainstream Mancunian, but Alex thinks they're cool. At least I can legitimately have etched on my tombstone, *Here lies the woman who once had a vodka tonic with a famous musician.*

Is the date ill-advised? Yes. Does it represent the catalyst for a spiral into what might be clinically described as 'absolute fantasist lunacy'? Well, in part, but some of it – if I am being kind to myself – is down to the circumstances. Being new to London, the romance of the city catalyses my falling for this man almost immediately. He seems to pick up on this as we walk over a twinkling bridge after dinner, taking in the scene. We are in the process of waving goodbye – to both my logic and my sanity – when a man falls and loses consciousness right in front of us.

Tod and I snap out of whatever is going on between us and spring into action. He pulls the man from the road and calls an ambulance as I comfort his partner, who is having a barely suppressed panic attack. We wait with them until the emergency services have done their job, and then we are thanked and sent back into the night like a version of Batman and Robin – if Batman had become sexualized and the subject of Robin's infatuation.

Because of all of this, I feel Tod and I have a unique connection. Or maybe I am just scrambling for a connection (with anyone) and the conditions are met by the unusual intimacy-inducing situation, if not by us personally. While the latter may be closer to the truth, I decide to run with the former. I am fully aware that I have entered into de Clérambault's Syndrome, characterized by the delusional belief that one is loved by another person, generally of a higher social status. I have de Clérambault's Syndrome all right, and it is chronic. I have become the anxious person at the party, bringing Tod up in any way I can, as if we are really part of each other's lives. 'Oh, I see you've got legs; Tod has legs.'

I create a whole narrative around me and Tod. I have a new storyline, finally, but I soon discover that I am being 'breadcrumbed'. I have learned this term in my work with adolescents. Breadcrumbing is the act of luring someone in by maintaining a surface-level flirtation, while avoiding any level of commitment. In the context of breadcrumbing, my fictitious courtship with Tod would be more accurately categorized as him 'flouring the surface'. There are sporadic text messages, which hold me in constant and relentless hope and maintain the illusion, just enough. To mask my feelings of humiliation and abandonment, I have created a fantasy world, entering the exquisite and surprisingly tolerable torture of unrequited love. This is the very epitome of neurotic suffering.

Clinging on to the fantasy that there is a 'me and Tod', while also knowing deep down that it isn't real, creates an uncomfortable sensation known as cognitive dissonance. And yet I can't stop the fiction playing out in my mind. The irresistible, obsessional narrative takes over. Thankfully my self-awareness is intact enough for me to realize this means I am not quite coping; I am just about functioning by creating an alternative reality to anaesthetize my pain and carrying around a paper sick bag to breathe into when panic takes over.

It's time to follow my own advice and seek support. The next step in my psychology training will mandate that I have therapy anyway, so there's no harm in getting a head start. I opt to choose a private therapist, as I don't want to run into any NHS colleagues in waiting rooms. The cost means I will have to forgo my weekly Prezzo ritual, but the need for therapy feels almost urgent.

Meeting Kelli – my psychoanalyst

It is surprisingly embarrassing to tell my therapist, Kelli, about my fantasy life. She is a classically Freudian psychoanalyst, which means I lie on a green velvet chaise longue as she delves into my subconscious. But that's where the clichés end; Kelli is not what you imagine when you think of a Freudian psychoanalyst. Kelli is young, vibrant and looks more like a bohemian free spirit. She wears floaty fabrics and bright lipstick. Her compassionate expression, framed by soft auburn curls, emanates warmth. She has a casual laid-back energy to her, and I like her instantly. She is slightly older than me – old enough for me to assume she has more wisdom than me, but young enough to still 'get it'. I realize this might be something my own patients think about, but thankfully most of them are currently children who guess my age as being anywhere between eighteen and fifty-five. I am now accustomed to being on the other side of the exchange, with patients opening up to me, but I find that I love the chance to switch the roles. I sign up to see Kelli once a week. Freudian analysts often prefer more frequent sessions, with some patients going three times a week, but my purse strings dictate how much I'm able to be healed by the talking cure.

Kelli allows my own fantasies, secret thoughts and wishes to come forward in a safe space, which is more adaptive than pushing them down or numbing them. She hears me without judgement and validates each of my feelings, which is at the core of my own job, and which I know leads to shifts and breakthroughs. However, I have learned that, when it comes to validations, checking the patient's understanding is key. I asked one patient, Joey, to access his rage and, at the opening of the next session, he began, 'You know how you told me to start hitting people again . . . ?'

Despite Kelli's support and my own understanding of what I'm experiencing, in the privacy of my windowless cupboard, I still find respite in creating my fantasy bond and story with Tod. I have been taking a little more time getting ready in the mornings, energized by the hope that he might message me and suggest an impromptu after-work drink, or a late intimate dinner. The hope of this endures throughout the day and I play it out step by step, imagining what I will order, how I will flirtatiously gaze at him over a vodka martini or spaghetti vongole. In reality, when he does text, which is rare, I am so filled with adrenaline and the pressure to seem aloof yet bold, flirtatious yet intelligent, that the texts read as overly familiar and odd, or like the transcript of a TED Talk. I think I prefer pretending that he has texted me rather than when he actually does, because then I am in control of the narrative. It's an effective tool for regulating my emotion, enough for me to be able to get on with my job and do it well.

I am using a lot of cognitive behavioural therapy, or CBT, with my patients. CBT seeks to identify and interrogate hard-wired cognitive distortions and thinking traps such as negative biases, catastrophizing and all-or-nothing thinking.

One strategy I start to apply is 'chaining', a useful visual example that also breaks the tension with new patients, as it's widely relatable. It happens to many of us several times a day. This 'if, then' chain works as follows. If I can't find my car keys, then I will be late for work. If I am late for work, then I will likely be sacked. If I am sacked, I won't be able to pay my bills. If I can't pay my bills, then I will be homeless. If I am homeless, then I will be a failure left to wander the streets.

This all happens at the speed of striking a match, or perhaps lighting a fuse, and with varying degrees of rationality and severity. One patient who came to see me had 'if, then'ed himself into believing he was personally responsible for a major paedophile ring because he had left a catalogue in the local Argos open on a page of children playing on climbing frames. This sort of catastrophic thinking genuinely plagues many of the adult patients I am seeing. The worst version of any lived experience can be visualized and felt in very real ways through our imagination. And mine is vivid.

My own 'if, then'ing goes on deep into the night and usually involves the same theme: professional failure and complete humiliation. If I left those patient notes out, then someone he knows might read them. If someone reads his confidential notes, then they might ridicule him. If someone ridicules him, then he might not be able to cope and his trust in me will be broken for misplacing the notes. If he can't cope and he has no support, then he might do something terrible like hurt himself. If he hurts himself, then an investigation will find me to be incompetent. If I am found to be incompetent, I will be sacked and everyone will know – everyone will know I am hopeless, including Steve.

Thinking outside the box

I am working with a little boy who has needle phobia. As a type-1 diabetic, this profound fear creates a daily nightmare, leading to tension-filled hours and parents who now see themselves – and are seen by their own son – as torturers. I have tried multiple strategies, including naming the needle 'Wriggle' to make it seem less threatening, while providing him with control and autonomy by characterizing him as the superhero 'Wriggle Boss', the bravest boy in the universe. I have used timers, rewards, placebos, numbing cream . . . the list goes on. But eventually we land upon a solution: watching YouTube videos of men running at full speed into cacti, with the little boy shouting, 'At least that's not me!' This seems to do the trick.

I got the idea from an article I read in Kelli's waiting room about a model of therapy known as dialectical behavioural therapy, or DBT, which is having a resurgence. The article advised that, when teaching patients skills to tolerate acute distress, therapists should have them think about comparisons, either to people who are less fortunate or to themselves when they were in a worse state. I circled this tip in the article and thought, What could be worse than a daily needle? Lots of daily needles, I suppose.

I am not entirely sure that managing your own pain by watching others experience worse pain is recommended in any textbook, but Dr Lane has taught me to think outside the box. Patients are individuals, not a tangled bunch of symptoms that can be 'fixed' with a 'one size fits all' philosophy. Treatments need to be nuanced, imaginative and personal.

Ridicule

With all this in mind, I go about my sessions with a patient who has a paralysing fear of fainting in public places. I have tried all manner of strategies to help her. One day, I try desensitizing her to what happens when people faint by taking her to witness me falling to the ground in the hospital canteen, my intention being to demonstrate the care and non-judgemental response of the people who are witness to it. I glide onto the floor at the tail end of a busy lunch service and, as I wait for a helpful medical professional to run to my aid with orange juice, a reassuring arm and a kind word, Dr Weller looks down at me with disdain, clearly assuming I am hung-over or playing a practical joke.

'I understand that you have just moved to London, Natalie,' he says, 'and it must all be very exciting for you, but *please* maintain a basic level of professionalism.'

My patient looks on, trying to conceal her laughter.

At our next session, she says that if I can return to work

after that embarrassment, then she can risk a legitimate faint. And from that point on, she stops fearing ridicule.

In the spirit of full disclosure, I tell her about the accidental hug with Dr Weller on my first day, which also seems to help.

I am glad this story brings some relief to someone, as it continues to fill me with intense and crippling embarrassment. Dr Weller has come to parallel Tod in some ways; the more I try to prove myself to be 'normal', competent, together and capable, the more I seem unhinged. I try reading up on his research papers and opinion pieces, referencing them in meetings and quoting them as 'best practice'. But instead of seeming knowledgeable and interested, I come off as an urgent, obsessed people-pleaser.

The same is happening with Tod and I know I am really losing my grip on the very thin, pretty much transparent thread that holds us together. The message chain between us is just wave after wave of long blue boxes of text from me trying on different personas and possible openings. In between the crashing waves is the odd little white box with a one-liner reply from him, lost like a buoy in a vast sea.

In the eyes of both Tod and Dr Weller, I am a maniac.

Self-care

In Kiwi, I talk numerous patients through anxiety and its impact. It is so difficult to put into words what anxiety feels like, especially to people who don't suffer from it. Let's say it's a bit like the feeling you get as you're hurtling towards the floor when you've tripped over, but experienced chronically, not momentarily. Anxiety narrows our focus into a hyperfocus on tiny negative details or mistakes we've made. We then use these mistakes and negative details as tools for berating ourselves, losing sight of the bigger picture and the positives of our lives.

I gently reassure my patients that a sense of crushing internal anxiety does not show to the outside world. There is no neon anxiety sign flashing above one's head, and thus no cause for shame. The fantasies we generate about others' thoughts and perceptions of us are an extension of our own persecutory fears and misplaced self-beliefs. The point of therapy is to look at the dark places within ourselves, places we don't like or don't want others to see. We look at our shadow. I want to ensure that, at the very least, my little office represents a safe space where all thoughts, feelings and fantasies are permissible without judgement. Hopefully patients can then take some of the caring conditions of this room home with them and engage in better self-care.

Self-care is also an important part of what I offer to patients. We focus on meeting basic care needs and using routine and structure to feel less chaotic and less out of control. Basic care needs include sleep. I often discuss 'sleep hygiene' tips such as reducing stimulants and screen time before bed, as play on phones and iPads keeps the brain in an active state. I also suggest using weighted blankets or vests, and white noise. I am building a toolkit to skill up my young patients to help them manage their bundles of emotions.

Now, I just need to learn how to manage mine.

Curating the pamphlet

Despite building my knowledge and confidence at work, I am constantly seeking reassurance from the people around me in my own world and it is wearing thin, especially when it comes to posting photos on Instagram. Alex, who is now unwittingly my therapeutic support companion, breaks one night after I have spent an inordinate amount of time panicking about my nose looking out of focus on my latest Instagram post. 'Remember that people *do* know you have a nose!' she shouts. The photo has been posted entirely to gain the attention of one man and one man alone: Tod. My Instagram is less a documentary of my life and achievements and more a carefully curated pamphlet invisibly captioned, *Will* this *make you love me?*

I can't focus on anything else for the entire evening. I ruminate and catastrophize as I work my way through a multipack of Diet Cokes. Overstimulated, my heart is beating so fast it feels like it might escape my chest. I slope off to bed too late, flooded with adrenaline, unable to sleep. I swipe on dating apps late into the night, staring at the bright screen, keeping my mind alert, before finally losing consciousness, my 'sleep hygiene' documents scattered around the floor.

I lose count of how many mornings I wake with a sweaty phone lodged under my chin, a car-horn alarm shocking me out of a restless sleep. It seems so easy when I tell my patients what they should be doing.

I pour out all my fears and anxieties to Kelli: the corridor hug which I've reframed as mild physical assault, the fantasy life which is driving my best friend to distraction, and my acute adrenaline. I need validation – that hit of reassurance from her that this is OK, that this is normal. I try to justify my insatiable need to comfort myself in tangible ways. I check the Holmes and Rahe stress scale, which lists the forty-three life events considered stressful enough to negatively impact your health.

The Holmes and Rahe Stress Scale

- Death of spouse (100)
- Divorce (73)
- Marital separation (65)
- Jail term (63)
- Death of close family member (63)
- Personal injury or illness (53)
- Marriage (50)
- Fired at work (47)
- Marital reconciliation (45)
- Retirement (45)
- Change in health of family member (44)
- Pregnancy (40)
- Sex difficulties (39)
- Gain of new family member (39)
- Business readjustment (39)
- Change in financial state (38)
- Death of close friend (37)
- Change to a different line of work (36)
- Change in number of arguments with spouse (35)
- A large mortgage or loan (31)
- Foreclosure of mortgage or loan (30)

- Change in responsibilities at work (29)
- Son or daughter leaving home (29)
- Trouble with in-laws (29)
- Outstanding personal achievement (28)
- Spouse begins or stops work (26)
- Begin or end school/college (26)
- Change in living conditions (25)
- Revision of personal habits (24)
- Trouble with boss (23)
- Change in work hours or conditions (20)
- Change in residence (20)
- Change in school/college (20)
- Change in recreation (19)
- Change in church activities (19)
- Change in social activities (18)
- A moderate loan or mortgage (17)
- Change in sleeping habits (16)
- Change in number of family get-togethers (15)
- Change in eating habits (15)
- Vacation (13)
- Christmas (12)
- Minor violations of the law (11)

A score of 300 to 600 suggests you have a high or very high risk of stress-related illness and you are advised to seek professional input. But the Holmes and Rahe stress scale does not include 'Dumped after six years'. Why does this not count as a 'major life event'?! Not only dumped, but dumped by text. That's more points, surely.

To the rescue

I have seen Max a few times at social events with mutual friends, but despite his striking good looks – at least six foot two, a chiselled face surrounded by boundless blond curls and vibrant blue eyes – I haven't really registered him. Until now. We are at a gig, and I notice him trying to reason with a girl who seems excessively excitable. He is her caretaker for most of the evening and he's distracted by that role. I am watching closely, while pretending not to watch at all. At one point, she grips his plastic tumbler of beer and throws it into the crowd. He looks less than pleased. She must have taken something, I think, as I drink my beer on the sidelines. For a brief moment, I think of Tod, what it must be like to be on the other side of this, to be the spectacle the crowds are drawn to. Despite the seduction of this thought, I am not drawn back into the fantasy of him; I have let go of the non-existent thread between us just enough to re-enter the real world.

Post chippy dinner, Max and I find ourselves in an old pub with our mutual friends in north London, and something shifts between us. Nothing actually happens, it's more that there is a sensation to it. Something has changed. My neuroception has returned, this time signalling a cue of safety, unspoken and unconscious. He holds my gaze longer than anyone ever has before and, when he speaks to me, I feel he is truly engaged and connected. We enter a state of shared intimacy, almost like the one I feel in the consulting room when I am truly attuned to my patients.

But there is more to it. I don't hold back like I usually do in social situations these days, thanks to my state of heightened self-consciousness. Most of the time, I still feel like half a person and I am still a little unsure of myself. With Max, however, I feel more comfortable, partly because I already sort of know him – he's a friend of a friend of a friend – but this unexpected level of intimacy between us is new and thrilling. Like Kelli, he gets me talking and I enjoy the role reversal.

Following loss or trauma, some patients find it impossible to talk, to put their terror into words. This is not simply resistance or a choice, it is a response in the brain. Calling a traumatic memory to mind can incapacitate an area of the brain known as Broca's region, the bit in charge of creating expressive speech. This makes the trauma literally unspeakable. This fact comes to mind during the week when I see Jude. Jude is a seventeen-year-old boy struggling with anxiety and finding it impossible to articulate his suffering. 'I just can't say it,' he keeps repeating. To reduce the pressure, I suggest we play a game and pull out my trusty pack of felt-tip pens. This is a game my dad taught me when I was little, to manage my own impatience when waiting for food in restaurants. My dad would close his eyes and scrawl something on the paper tablecloth in our local Italian, and my job would be to turn the scrawly scribble into a picture. A curved line would become a giraffe's neck, a jagged edge would become a spiky spine for a dinosaur. It took my mind off things. Drawing often gets people talking and also engages their imagination. A powerful imagination can be a blessing and a curse; the ease with which rich imagery comes to mind about feared outcomes, and the speed at which the brain can access this, contributes to higher levels of anxiety.

The activating event

Jude begins to make pictorial sense of the lines and marks I make on the page and, as I watch, I see how he can make anything into a detailed and beautiful flower or figure. As I compliment him, Jude explains that tattoo design is his passion and side project, so I suggest he draws a tattoo that he would design to symbolize his feelings. He carefully draws out an incredible hummingbird. I ask him about the picture and what it brings to mind. He pulls back for a moment, looks at his sketch and then underneath writes, *I'm sorry I flapped.* We explore this, gently. Jude is able to share that he stood still and frozen to the spot as he watched his girlfriend's handbag be ripped from her hands by a mugger who appeared to have a weapon. Jude is carrying a lot of shame for this. We talk it through and we think about fear and risk, how acting may have increased the risk to both of them, given the weapon. We end by discussing how he kept his girlfriend safe emotionally afterwards and what his shame says about him as a person – that he cares deeply for her and wants to protect her. Jude says he feels lighter and takes the picture away with him.

Shame often makes us hide things; it is my job to create the conditions that allow for shame to be overlooked or disempowered. On our first date, Max creates those conditions for me. He takes me to an outdoor market with twinkling fairy lights framing little stalls that sell a dizzying array of cocktails, with dizzying prices to match, as you'd expect in a gentrified area of east London. Max brings an element of old London with his strong cockney accent and attempts to haggle down the price of everything. I find it charming. And, bathed in the glittering lights, Max's intense gaze is irresistible. It's not just the gin speaking; his blue eyes hold me in the moment and I feel special. It's something everyone finds seductive, let alone someone who has been feeling emotionally ignored for some time now.

Our conversation reaches exposing depths when Max senses that I am not 'fine'. He wants to know all about me, fascinated even when I am telling him about Steve leaving me via a text after six years together. He listens without judgement or ridicule. Then he leans in to kiss me and I feel myself actually swoon. We go on to drink our way through the cocktail menu, and the wooziness and the romance of it all propels me even closer to him. I let him rescue me and allow myself to escape from being alone.

Reward cycles

The nurse at the sexual-health clinic looks up at me between my legs. 'And have you been having oral and/or anal sex? How many sexual partners have you had and do you have a regular partner?' she asks.

I wonder if this questioning is more or less exposing than sitting with legs in stirrups while being asked if I 'mind' a student taking a look. But, after having had one sexual partner for six years, the world of sexual activity with others frightens me. And so, I am here, facing the music.

The sexual-health nurse glares at me, waiting for an answer. 'Natalie, if you give me the same answers as last week, I will have to cut you off from sexual-health screens,' she says.

What began as the act of a responsible adult has mutated into a classic OCD-like reward cycle – the same cycle I have been teaching to a patient only this morning. We have personified

OCD so that we can look at 'him' objectively and start a dialogue with 'him'. The patient has chosen the name 'Woody' because OCD 'pecked at the inside of his head'. It's a very insightful name from a seven-year-old.

We figure out that Woody's beak pecks at a scary thought that flies around the boy's mind with the intensity and panic of a bird who has flown into a room and can't escape, so stuns itself by flying at a window. The only thing to settle Woody down is for my patient to climb the ladder to his bunk bed and back down again, over and over. With OCD, it often starts with a magic number. At first, the magic number for ladder climbing is four. This works for a while, but, after a time, four isn't enough. Woody is currently insisting that the ladder be climbed for hours and hours at a time, without stopping, making my patient fall asleep in school and pull away from friends, games and anything other than sitting and waiting for the ladder time to begin. Woody needs to be stopped and together we tell him so in no uncertain terms. Trouble is, Woody teaches us about the deep reward of the feeling of relief, a way to control and counteract our inner panic and fear – albeit momentarily.

Now, I have my own Woody, as it were. The resources and amenities of the sexual-health clinic at the hospital have become a playground for my neurosis. The first time, I wanted to be sure I was safe. I felt the anticipatory anxiety before going in, then the relief wash over me when it was over, then the peak of arousal and fear again as I waited for the result, followed by the relief and release of the all-clear result. I repeat the process, without a real need to. And now I have become addicted to the anticipatory anxiety and the rush of endorphins you get when told you're fine.

Crucially, there is also the reward of someone paying close attention to me when asking about my life, general health and well-being, in a safe space. There is a lot to be said about health professionals becoming pseudo-carers. The nurse and I are both aware that I am using the sexual-screening facility too often and for no reason, as I have started dating a single regular partner. I am seeing Max.

The nurse asks me again about my sexual activity and I have a smug feeling as I reply, 'Just one regular partner.' For me, it feels considerably better than, 'I haven't had sex in quite a while now . . .' But this feeling doesn't last very long, since this time she goes on to diagnose a slight allergic reaction to semen. I have never considered what would happen if it wasn't good news at the clinic and I didn't get my relief hit.

The doctor writes out a prescription for antibiotics, and rattles off the warnings on the label, like the terms and conditions squeezed in at the end of a TV ad. All I hear is '. . . and you can't drink alcohol for a week.'

'But it's pancake day on Tuesday!' I splutter.

The doctor and the nurse both look at me blankly. But, if they met Max, they would immediately understand.

TWO

Seeking distraction

A balancing act

I have entered a whirlwind of impulse, unpredictability, passion and hedonism. Max lives with several young aspiring actors and models in a cavernous, dilapidated house-share in north London. He sells it to me as a converted loft. 'Like in Manhattan,' he says. In reality, it's more like an abandoned warehouse for squatters. Still cool, though. There is no distinction between day and night in this world, and there is always someone ready to party or otherwise lose control. Max himself is working for a start-up, an ambitious company trying to make retro, slightly camp drinks, like the Shirley Temple – the current 'It' drink of the London hipster. Max's hours are loose and often include lengthy 'product analysis seminars', which seem to me to just be sessions of drinking as much alcohol as possible. Nevertheless, I keep to my structure and routine as best I can, not least because my commute to the hospital is an early-morning drive. And it's handy to have my wits about me when I'm with my patients.

Max's housemates are lovely, open and non-judgemental,

just the sort of antidote I need for my internal critical voice and feelings of residual despair, which I can't yet slough off. It feels freeing and reparative to be in this house. I start not to notice people having Bloody Marys on a Tuesday morning as I sling my NHS lanyard around my neck and grab a coffee. At the hospital, I am more alive, more engaging, with Max always at the back of my mind.

'Are you on new meds?' Ethan, one of the trainee psychiatrists, asks gleefully as I pour hot water into chicken-flavoured powder in the staff kitchen.

I always think there is something a little off about Ethan – plus, he has an air of superiority about him. Over 'lunch', he begins to ask my views about a patient he is seeing that afternoon. She experienced sexual abuse by a teacher in her childhood and remains hypervigilant to threat, all these years later. He says this as if he is irritated by it. He explains he is feeling stuck with her. I ask him how he thinks he might be contributing to the 'stuckness'. He is male, after all, and in a position of power. Maybe she feels unsafe – triggered, even – in the room. I wonder aloud if Ethan has asked her this. He seems to ponder my thought, then brushes me off.

At around 3 p.m., I hear a commotion in the waiting area and rush out of Kiwi to see what's going on. Ethan is shirtless, crouching over a patient who seems to be having some sort of fit on the floor.

'What on earth are you doing?' a nurse shouts.

'Well, I had to use *something* to protect her head from hitting the floor,' he replies, pointing at his balled-up shirt beneath the patient's head.

Later, in the staff debrief meeting, we are told the patient was having a pseudo-seizure (now known as psychogenic non-epileptic seizures), and that she is OK now, but was very distressed afterwards. I circle back to what Ethan feels he might be doing to re-traumatize a patient who has been sexually assaulted. The rest of the staff group confirm the need for this question with nods and eyebrows raised towards Ethan. For once lost for words, he looks down at his notepad.

Unpredictable

Like Ethan, we are not always aware of how we are contributing to a situation or a relationship. I have decided not to dwell on this when it comes to Max, and try to just go with what comes, never knowing what will happen when I meet up with him – where we will end up or how. We go out for a late breakfast and, before I know it, I am thrust into a parade of Hare Krishnas, banging a tambourine and sipping rum from a hip flask, Max beside me carrying a man on his back. We meet many colourful and interesting people along the way and sample all the craft beers north London has to offer. At every pub, staff greet us with a warm smile and Max is offered his 'usual'.

One weekend, Max takes me out of London for what I think will be a romantic couple of days, just the two of us, getting to know each other better. We are sitting in a quaint little pub in a picturesque city when we bump into an old friend of his, Dylan, and his girlfriend, Beth. She appears quiet and timid and sugary sweet, and he is continually twiddling her plait, which is the length of her back and tied with a ribbon. It's all so . . . nice. I spend most of the evening chatting with

Beth while Max talks to Dylan, but Max briefly stops at my chair on his way to the toilet to whisper into my ear, 'We don't go back to their house, OK?' – which I dismiss with a tipsy wave of the hand.

Soon after this, we are seated in a modest semi-detached somewhere in the suburbs, remarking on the feature walls and the many window boxes sprouting tiny plants, each labelled with a handwritten note: *Good Thymes* and *Parsley? Sparsely!* and *Botany new plants lately?* The #LiveLaughLove energy is strong, here. Then, without warning, the lights go out and dry ice billows into the room. Open-mouthed, I glance at Max and try to get to my feet, confused, but Beth enters with a tray of shot glasses, changing colour in the rotating disco lights which have sprung into action.

My last cogent memory is of Max mouthing, *I told you.* I wake up lying next to him in the spare room, on top of the covers, both of us fully dressed and with our shoes still on.

Max's eyes shoot open a second after mine. He grabs my hand and bundles me down the stairs, but the front door won't open. We are locked in the party house, scared it is about to start all over again. I watch Max scramble through drawer after drawer in the kitchen, looking for a key, breaking off briefly to throw up in the sink. Finally, he finds a key, jiggles it in the lock until it clicks open, and hurries me out of the door.

I ask Max, based on his warning, 'How many times have you been suckered in by these two?'

It's clearly a long story.

'Another time,' he says, with a shake of the head, avoiding all eye contact.

Kelli's confrontation

'Tell me about missing the last session.'

Kelli addresses it head on. I feel awkward, as though I have stood a friend up on a coffee date; the therapeutic relationship can feel like a real-world relationship in these moments. My excuses are weak. I try to move on and talk about anything else. Kelli says nothing and I drown in the silence.

'What are you *not* telling me, Natalie?' she asks.

A prickle of heat creeps up the back of my neck.

For my homework, Kelli asks me to think about avoidance – its power and what happens if we split off from feelings or emotions. As I drive home, I think hard about what I am not seeing or accessing. I try to focus, but it slips quickly from my mental grasp.

Painful reality

So engulfing is Max and his chaotic lifestyle that our micro-adventures go a long way to distracting me from my internal turmoil and the pain of heartbreak. But Kelli is right. Acutely painful reality surfaces when you're least expecting it. Mine intrudes when I pause for a moment to boil the kettle in the hospital staff room or when I'm waiting at a roundabout on my drive home, and I'm reminded that my relationship with Max isn't real and maybe, one day, like Steve, he won't want to be with me. I remember that I am alone.

Doing the washing-up in the kitchen of my shared house, which I am often acutely aware is not my marital home, my anxiety spikes, gripping my throat. The fear is that I could be abandoned again and flung off this new merry-go-round with Max, and where will I be then? What will I do?

I know deep down that Max is really a coping mechanism. I am focusing all my attention on him and his world, a hyper-focus that is a dissociation from pain. We all do it. We zero in on one thing to block out all the rest. We can lose track of time and fall into an almost dreamlike state, distanced from reality. Psychologists call it 'flow'. Flow acts like a little holiday for the brain. It offers respite when we are feeling overwhelmed. In my case, I am using flow to mask the pain of rejection which I still feel despite the time passing and new lovers taking up space in my imagination. Maybe I am more sensitive to rejection than others, or maybe I attach too much meaning to it.

I have researched how to cope with rejection or reduce its potency. One article suggested that we put down, devalue and diminish the qualities of the person who rejected us. This is said to help, and this I have tried – I have looked at Steve more objectively and acknowledged his flaws and failings. In doing so, I realized that I often found the relationship itself quite mundane. I was so desperate to play at being an adult, my focus and preoccupations were for people to see my relationship as legitimate, grown up and important, and I tried to achieve this with milestones, playing house in teenage soft play.

Since Steve, I have come alive, if only in my imagination and in my terrified yet curious excitement of new possibilities with Max. Chaos, in its way, is thrilling. Yet, the pang of rejection remains. I continue my Google Scholar search for reasons why, and an article suggests that, on average, people report feeling better from rejection after eleven weeks. Six months in – twenty-four long weeks – and I am definitely bumping up that average as I fail to move on.

As the anxiety rises, I look for a repetitive task. I polish our cutlery in hot vinegary water, using the monotony of my actions and the visual progress of the mounting clean pile to bring me back to earth. I now regularly suggest such step-by-step strategies to patients to counteract the fact that the traumatized brain keeps us stuck in the moment of trauma, recycling it over and over so that we re-experience it in the present moment and feel as if it is happening again, now. The feelings, images, sensations and even the muscular responses and movements are re-engaged, and the body responds as if we are reliving it. The body holds a blueprint and follows it exactly. The brain hasn't been able to process or integrate this blueprint response and so it remains permanently active, preventing us from achieving a psychological sense of safety and contentment.

When working with trauma patients, I seek to physically ground them in the here and now. With the little ones, I like to use the five senses.

'Name three things you can see.'

'I can see my bedroom and my blanket and my toys.'

'Name three things you can touch or feel.'

'I can feel the mattress under my legs, the fluffiness of my pyjamas against my skin, my hair against my neck.'

'What can you taste?'

'I can taste the water next to my bed. I can taste the air.'

'Name three things you can smell.'

'I can smell my covers, my teddy bear and my pillow.'

Now, I use the practice on myself. As my thoughts dart around, I try to focus on one sense at a time.

What can I smell? *I can smell the vinegar used in the water to polish the cutlery.* What can I hear? *I can hear the whirring of the extractor fan.* What can I see? *I can see the clean pile of cutlery growing.* What can I feel? *I can feel the warmth of the water against the rubber of the Marigold gloves.*

Once grounded, I usually then have patients ask themselves, 'Am I safe?' and get them to take some deep breaths. Even the most reluctant of patients will engage in deep breathing if you get them to measure their own pulse as they do it, so they can physically feel their heart rate reduce.

Standing at the kitchen sink, I take off the Marigolds and put my fingers to my own throat, breathing deeply, feeling the pulsation slow a little. Despite this evening's anxiety, I am having to rely on my own grounding techniques less and less as Max is such a whirlwind of distraction. But the truth is it is difficult to balance a life with Max and working full time in a job which requires me to be fully present and engaged at all times. A wandering mind can jeopardize a relationship with a patient. Any lapses can re-traumatize them if they have suffered from neglect, been unheard or ignored at home. A distracted therapist can reinforce a patient's belief that they are unworthy and will always be ignored by others.

No matter how I feel, I can't allow my patients to feel re-traumatized.

Grounded

I try the grounding exercise with an adult male patient when he starts hyperventilating, interjecting my question into his fear: 'Tell me one thing you can see.'

And through his panic he shouts, 'I can see her. I can see her moustache!'

He is pointing to the medical student sitting with me, squashed up against the wall in the corner of the room, observing as part of her training. The social faux pas has us all hyperventilating, but it is at least effective at bringing the patient back to the present moment.

Reward centres

Heartbreak creates adrenaline because it leaves us in a vigilant state of searching. When we are in the loving relationship, the reward centres in our brains are activated and stimulated to the extent that brain scans of those 'in love' mirror scans of those with alcohol- and drug-abuse disorders. The brain is rewarded, then motivated to re-seek the reward, which is readily available when you're in the relationship, so the brain is sated again and the cycle continues. Disaster strikes when the rewarding loved one leaves, is removed, is ripped from us. The brain panics. It is highly motivated to seek out the reward again or to replace it. This is why, during heartbreak, people often rely more obsessively on alcohol, food, promiscuity or other vices to light up the reward centres of the brain in a synthetic way.

Heartbreak also causes the brain to be activated in a way that matches the experience of acute physical pain. In fact, opioids like morphine can regulate both physical and social pain. But, although social pain usually takes longer to heal, we don't prescribe morphine for a broken heart. All the more reason to reach for things that are numbing or able to shift our emotional state into something more manageable, less painful.

I am receiving my rewards through Max, through the giddy excitement of romance and the immediate feelings of desire, the tactile contact with someone else, drinking lots of mimosas, and the novelty and freedom of all the new experiences. Novelty also happens to be rewarding for the brain – it activates it to seek out *more* reward.

All of which is to say that my brain couldn't be more activated or motivated than it currently is to seek pleasure, and that's what is keeping me moving forward and keeping me energized with Max and with my demanding job. Much more astonishing is Max's level of energy and output, since he isn't recently heartbroken. I am impressed. We should all be more Max, I think.

Shutting down

In contrast to Max's high energy, my new patient, Steph, is struggling with chronic low mood and loneliness. She has started to feel hopeless, scoring high on the hopelessness inventory. This is a worry, as high levels of hopelessness correlate with suicidal ideation. We start with loneliness: Steph explains that she can't get past three dates with a man and she has started to feel that she lacks value and is a hopeless case. The first two dates seem to go brilliantly well, and she is confident they will follow up, but after the third she never hears from them again.

In our first two sessions, I connect with Steph; she is engaging and sparks my interest. By session three, I feel my mind wander and am glancing at the clock, disconnected; she has little energy or spark and leaves me feeling flat.

On the drive home after the third session, I am struck that I have followed the same pattern as her dates. After the third meeting with Steph, I too have lost interest. I have to address this with her. As therapists, we have to talk about what's going on between us and the patient, because the patient's behaviour towards us is usually an enactment of how they engage in external relationships. Therapy is reparative because the response the patient receives in this room is different – for instance, a chronic people-pleaser may get on fine with others in the world, but in here their passivity and superficial responses will be pointed out and challenged, the social facade is chipped away to get to their own needs. Similarly, a patient's resistance, rage or stonewalling will be met with patience, curiosity and compassion, rather than withdrawal or conflict. Even the best practised defences eventually melt away and the false self is replaced, if they are brave enough to stick around. Therapy is not for the faint-hearted.

I share this with Steph, wording it carefully, 'It takes a lot of courage to come here today and share this sense of failure and longing.' Together we draw out the cycle of her most recent romances, searching for the subconscious goal of her losing her vivaciousness after two meetings. We slowly trace back through her life, until we're talking about how, as a child, Steph was supposed to have supervised contact with her father every third Saturday of the month. But her dad was inconsistent and sometimes didn't turn up. For the first two weeks of each month, Steph held out hope that he would show up for her – hope that was dashed by week three, when she would go into shutdown mode. The fear of being rejected made her close off and she is enacting this now, building up to the third meeting with such anticipation and fear that the default shut-down system steps in. Steph becomes struck by disconnect, she becomes monotone and switches onto autopilot.

Steph and I look at why this might be adaptive, a learned response, a survival mechanism that worked in one environment, at one point in her life.

'I guess they aren't rejecting the *real* me, if it's just the shell of me,' Steph says eventually. Her self-preservation is working too hard for her and, paradoxically, isn't working for her at all. But this realization is progress.

Warning signs

I too experience a mini shutdown as I start to feel a tinge of burnout with Max. He clearly doesn't share my exhaustion. He bounds into the room one evening and suggests we take a stroll around central London at midnight, taking in the views from various bridges while drinking Prosecco. This time, I don't feel an immediate leap of excitement in the pit of my stomach, but rather a sinking feeling and more than a slight tug towards getting into bed with Netflix. I set a boundary, but carefully, not wanting to hurt his feelings. 'It's not a *no*,' I say, 'but it's a *not tonight*.'

Another boundary I've set myself is to drink less, limiting myself to one glass from the bottle, without making it noticeable, and then suggesting pizza on the way home a little earlier than if it were up to Max. I decide it is time to temper things in order to sustain both him and my job. I draw back a little, take myself away for some early nights and some yoga classes followed by chats with the girls at home.

As I take a step back, I start to notice patterns in his behaviour that have been presented as spontaneous but are in fact more predictable than meets the eye. Rather than feeling it's exciting when he says, 'Let's go out and do something tonight; who cares that it's only Tuesday?' I realize that every Tuesday for the past four weeks we have 'spontaneously' walked around town before landing in the same place that does two-for-one on red wines. It's in my sobriety that I'm able to notice that Max isn't as impulsive as I once thought. In fact, I find that, once Max has enjoyed something novel, he will seek to repeat it, almost with precision, over and over again. Why have I not noticed before?

Battling addiction

As I try, somewhat unsuccessfully, to ignore Max's chaos, fixations and repetitions, at the hospital I begin working with a few patients struggling with addiction. Mike is a police officer who is proving hard to connect with. He seems stand-offish and resistant. He doesn't say too much, but, when he does, he is very keen to let me know about all the skills he possesses and how many high-risk, high-speed, high-octane incidents he has exerted his power over. And I use the word *power* very deliberately.

I stay with him as he takes me on this self-congratulatory journey. I validate him and reflect back to him how important his role is. I also comment on the other roles in his life, his clear ability as a father and as a dutiful son to a mother who has become hostile and aggressive towards him in the late stages of dementia.

After several sessions, however, I asked Mike why it is so important for him to share his successes as a police officer with me and if there is anything he feels is less admirable about himself that he would also like to share.

Mike shifts in his seat. There is a long pause.

He tells me that he has recently been let go from the police force. I do my best to hold a soft expression as I feel compassion, but I also feel deceived and confused. This is an incredible loss for him. He doesn't know who he is outside of his job.

'My shocking secret has finally taken everything,' he says.

My response is to be gently curious about what this secret is. I offer that anything kept secret automatically shrouds it in shame, perpetuating its potency. Mike says he feels too self-conscious to tell me, and I'm reminded of the snugness of our shared space in Kiwi, so I suggest we move the positions of our chairs a little. We stand up and awkwardly shuffle around to adjust the chairs to even more of an angle, so that Mike is almost parallel with me. This way, he can avoid all eye contact.

Mike tells me that he was called to a dispute outside a brothel, late one night. He acted accordingly and did his job to the highest level; however, he couldn't help but return to the brothel later, despite still being on duty and with his radio on. When he missed a call-out, the station located him there and he was caught 'making use of the facilities' while on shift. I can feel the burning heat of his shame.

He goes on to say that the urge to have sex has taken over his life. He is addicted to watching porn for up to seven hours a day. While he is watching one video, he is thinking about search terms for the next. One of the culprits for this is, again, novelty. Novelty-seeking activates the same neural pathways that mediate the rewarding effects of drugs, and, like any addiction, when thresholds are met, Mike is compelled to seek more and more novelty, and thus more and more strange and/ or repugnant porn.

Mike says this is why his marriage has broken down, telling me that he cannot have sex with his wife, he feels resistant to it, and yet he needs his 'fix'. Research shows that those using online porn very frequently report abnormally low libido and sexual desire. I try to share this with Mike to normalize his loss of arousal. Mike shares back that he recently shut down sexual advances from his wife in bed, and she later found him frantically watching porn in his study and felt bitterly rejected.

Mike looks at me in desperation. 'Why would I rather watch some stranger's amateur hour than have the real thing? I need answers!'

I slow things down and offer concrete responses which I hope Mike can relate to. I talk to him about the three different ways we connect to others: attachment, romantic love and sexual desire. Attachment is your blueprint for relationships; the way you bond with your parents demarcates how you connect with the world and people in it. Romantic love is what you have with your wife, I tell him. And sex drive or desire is what has taken over. I share that there are different neural pathways in the brain for each one and that his brain is addicted to the sex-drive pathway. We tend to respond to ideas when we are given a neural or a physical basis, not least because there still seems to be a stigma around mental ill health not being 'real' or being 'all in the mind'. So, if we can see its physical basis, we feel less ashamed and more valid in our suffering.

Mike seems to settle as I distance him from the problem, referring to mechanisms in his brain, and his distress seems to lessen. My initial goal is to reduce the chronic shame, which is so debilitating. Mike asks me how he could have got into such a mess – a mess only a teenager would get themselves into, he thinks. I explain how all brains are responding unhelpfully to technology, how technology is overriding our natural drives and keeping us hooked in our compulsive pursuits. I tell Mike about the theory that the internet is creating 'supernormal stimuli' – stimuli that are synthetic but irresistible to our brains. I tell him about a scientist who created mock birds' eggs that were bigger and more vibrantly colourful than natural eggs; they then found that mother birds would hop off the eggs containing their own offspring in favour of the bigger, better, imposter eggs. This is like us with reality versus the vivid stimulation of the online world. I do my best to remove blame.

Blame removed, Mike looks me in the eye for the first time and agrees to come back to see me.

The same song

Waking up at Max's, the house is quiet, and I wander into the kitchen to find the winter sun streaming through the open windows. Jazz is playing on the stereo, and I sit at the counter and watch adoringly as Max makes us smoked salmon and scrambled eggs – a treat usually reserved for Christmas Day, back home with my parents. I feel completely content clutching my chipped coffee mug and bathing in the warmth of Max's sun-like presence.

But this soon turns into every Sunday – the same song, the same breakfast – as he tries to recreate that initial energy. As the weather turns colder, and the mornings more grey and chilly, it is particularly difficult to conjure the same ambience. The whole thing now feels more like a laborious ritual. The novelty has worn off for me. I get sick of the song and – something I never thought I'd say – I get sick of smoked salmon.

I try to rationalize the ritualistic act, to make sense of it. I have worked with neurodiverse children who hyper-fixate on what they eat, narrowing their palate to one or two specific foods. The sensory properties of certain meals have brought me comfort – chips on the roof with the girls, and my afternoon energizing sugary coffee at the hospital – so who am I to judge? Max seems to be trying to get all the conditions just right in order to feel content and at ease; he is chasing peace as some people chase a high and, as with most things with Max, this feels extreme.

As Max becomes more fixated on repetition, I instinctively start to withdraw further. Up until now, I have remained quite passive; I don't feel I can match his energy. While he is so full of life, I feel deflated and so my strategy is retreat. This in itself is restorative for me. I am starting to reconnect with myself, even if just on the primitive level of trusting my gut. If something's not quite right, you have to be able to trust yourself to pull away.

My mind has circled around the word *addiction* in relation to Max, but I haven't been ready to give it much thought, not wanting to spoil things. But it's now very much on my mind, and I'm just not sure what to do about it.

So, for now, I do nothing.

They f*ck you up

I begin seeing another new patient, who also has an addiction to porn. Roman is nineteen and desperately seeking to connect with his dad. Mostly estranged from his cruel mum, he idolizes his dad, despite being offered the bare minimum in return. This sometimes happens when one parent falls short and is neglectful; the child subconsciously sees the other parent as perfect. For the subconscious, something is better than nothing.

Roman began watching porn, as this was modelled to him by his father; he later learned that his father was also seeing high-class escorts using an exclusive boutique website, and this too is a behaviour Roman is now mirroring.

I feel deep discomfort as I notice Roman's enjoyment when he tells me about his sexual experiences with these women; I have to regain control of the session, so that I am not another 'female commodity' for him to control.

'Tell me, Roman, how do you feel about women?'

Roman looks irritated by the question, but I see some fear in his micro-expressions, so I begin to think he is scared of women, or scared of women leaving him, and thus he seeks to take control of any interaction with them.

As we discuss his involvement with the escorts, it seems to dawn on both of us that Roman and his father have each encountered the same women, as the pool at this boutique agency is so small.

Roman looks horrified. He is speechless. He almost gags. Seemingly this hadn't occurred to him before. I glimpse the same shadow of terror that I saw when he mentioned his mother.

In the evening, I ring my dad, who often serves as my Samaritans line, day or night, when I need reassurance and grounding because I'm suddenly gripped by a catastrophic fear or a rambling existential dread. My dad has clocked up many hours. Sometimes he lets me talk, taking all the messy thoughts and helping me organize them, or he interrogates them until they show themselves for being foolish. But sometimes he cuts me off. He tells me I can have ten minutes to dwell in the self-loathing and disaster thinking, and then I can't mention it again. This also works. It stops perpetuating the energy I am giving to anxiety and cuts it dead.

I tell my dad a skeleton version of Roman's situation, being careful not to give away personal details and giving him a fake name, Patient X. My dad trained as a psychologist later in life, at night school, when I was just a toddler. Naturally, he credits himself with my fascination for the profession and, to be fair, I do regard him as my inspirational mini encyclopaedia on trauma.

He ponders Patient X and tells me about the importance of parental dynamics and the power of the parent–child relationship. 'Everyone is reduced to their most seminal experiences as a child,' he says, 'you only have to look around the table when they bring out a birthday cake to know that.'

'I'm going to need a little more detail, Dad,' I reply.

He explains that, when a birthday cake is brought out at a party and everyone starts to sing, the ritual of it all, the smell of the candles being blown out, the sound of the song and the slightly frenzied charge in the room can all be an incredible sensory trigger. This trigger transports people back to their own experiences of birthdays throughout their childhood. 'Watch people's faces at parties,' he says, 'and you might get a glimpse into their past.'

Never alone

I tell Max I need a night alone in my shared house, to decompress from the week, catch up on a few things and have some chips on the roof with the girls. He seems unfazed. However, as 8 p.m. rolls around, he rings to say he happens to be in the park near my house, so may as well come and stay the night. I am ambushed. I try to dissuade him, but he sounds frantic. 'But I already bought you snacks and that beer you like,' he says, and I capitulate.

This turns into a frequent occurrence, until eventually I am never alone.

I enjoy going for a run in the evening before dinner. Exercise helps with my anxiety and I like the feeling of accomplishment. As I return to my flat, red-faced, with endorphins coursing through my body, Max is there to meet me. He hugs me a little too tightly and says, 'Do you go on runs to get away from me?'

I feel a tightness in my chest, as though I am trapped in a vice. A sense of suffocation creeps in and I take a deep breath.

Feeling good

I ask Mike what porn does for him.

He stammers over the answer, but then says, 'It's the place I feel good.'

It's not what he's seeing or engaging with that compels him, it's the state that's being produced in him. I ask him about other places he feels good about himself, and he falls silent.

After a while, he says, 'I told you all that stuff about how good I am at my job and how I save people. But, really, I'm not very good. I hang back.'

'It sounds like you see yourself in an inferior position at work, so you don't feel good at work,' I offer.

Mike nods.

'What about at home?'

Mike says he married a very passive woman, so he has been able to assume a more dominant role in the marriage, which initially made him feel good. But over time his wife has become very critical and negative, so he doesn't feel good at home any more.

I feel a great deal of compassion as he paints a picture of a life where he always feels inferior.

I book to see him again at the end of the week.

Transactions

As he enters Kiwi with a bold brashness, I am struck by the powerful scent of his aftershave.

'Twice in one week, hey?' Mike says, and leans towards me in his seat.

I sit stock still.

'I looked up what it means when a therapist fancies a patient. *Erotic* transference,' he proclaims, raising his eyebrows and emphasizing the 'erotic'.

'What it means when a therapist fancies a patient,' I reflect back to him, careful to remain neutral in my tone. I need to draw a firm boundary and reinstate the nature of the therapeutic relationship, while not being critical or shaming. A difficult balance. 'Is that how you have interpreted my responses to you in our work together?'

I wait. Silence.

'As I stated at the start of the sessions, this is a professional endeavour and boundaries must remain in place at all times. It was not my intention to cross any boundary and I must reinstate them now.'

Mike apologizes. He then says this is the reason he likes it to be transactional with women, so he can't get it wrong. 'When I buy them, there's no guesswork,' he says.

I leave a beat of silence and then ask, 'How do you feel about women?'

We trace Mike's inability to relate to women and how he casts them as commodities back to his formative years. He was scolded and neglected by a mother who he now describes as 'callous'. She would make him sit up at the table and finish his meal hours after it had gone cold, despite his tears and despair. In the morning, she would even re-present him with food that he had failed to consume the night before, once forcing him to drink a glass of cold gravy before he was allowed to leave for school, all the while asserting that he was selfish and pathetic. Mike is now enacting this type of toxic dynamic when facing criticism from his wife, which is re-traumatizing for him.

We work through a great deal of relational trauma and Mike says he is gaining insight into his beliefs about women and also into his own self-worth. He has found the therapeutic relationship with me difficult, he admits, as he can't take control. But he is finding my challenging of him, without criticism, reparative.

As we end the session, Mike says he feels empowered because he has managed to stay in the therapeutic relationship with me, 'a real-life woman'.

The last session

'You know what, Nat?' Mike says, as he looks up to the ceiling. 'Birds . . . they're people and that, aren't they?'

It's our last session and, as he leaves, he thanks me and throws some crumpled cash onto the desk.

This is the NHS, and I am providing a service which is free at the point of delivery and so I pick up the cash and hand it back to Mike.

You can't win them all.

The chase

I now have a very busy clinic at the hospital. I am treating children across three sites, literally running between them, with back-to-back clinics, no time for lunch. I am darting around, coming to rest only infrequently. My nightly cardio practice comes in handy, particularly on the day I frantically chase a child across town. Or, at least, that would be the *Daily Mail* headline.

Tyler is in his fourth foster placement in as many years. He has been dropped off by his foster carer at the hospital, left alone for the session with me, and told to find his own way to school afterwards. Tyler is ten. He has been sent to see me to talk about the trauma and neglect he suffered in the first few years of his life. I don't feel comfortable letting him go off to school alone after such explorative work. He is bright, but also vulnerable. I ask him if I can walk him to school and he reluctantly agrees, but says I have to keep my distance because I will make him look 'uncool'. We set off, two metres between us, but when he sees some boys lurking outside the corner shop, wearing the same school uniform as him, he takes off. I try to keep up, my lanyard swinging violently around my neck.

I have chased a child to school, I think, as I arrive at the gates and go into recovery mode, bending over with my hands resting on my knees, panting and red-faced, trying to regain my breath. I've done my civic duty here, he is safe. Then I notice a couple of teachers, who are welcoming the children into school at the gates, looking at me, perplexed and clearly concerned to have seen one of their pupils chased down the road by a stranger. I stand bolt upright, toss my lanyard over my shoulder as if it's a feather boa, and stride off as nonchalantly as possible.

My mistake

I make mistakes. They never sit well with me; my stomach drops through my pelvis when I realize or when they are pointed out by Dr Lane. She always tells me that mistakes are part of the job. Humans are messy and sometimes more mess is created as we unpack them. I focus on the word 'unpack' – such a therapist term. I imagine trying to sort out a jumbled toy box, unpacking it one toy at a time, until the floor is strewn with teddies and cars and building blocks. For a moment, things look a lot worse, but then I begin to put things back, more organized than before.

Dr Lane teaches me about the value of mistakes, even when they lead to ruptures. Ruptures in the real world can be painful, final, drenched in guilt and shame. In therapy, they are treated with respect and compassion and navigated within the safety of a sustained relationship. Mistakes are to be valued.

I have made a few mistakes in my short career already. When I was assisting Dr Macklin, I introduced water-snake toys as a sensory exercise to the inpatients of the all-male psychiatric ward. As I handed them out, I demonstrated the motion that can be created from moving the water inside the tubes of malleable plastic back and forth. Unwittingly, I had modelled and facilitated what looked like a widespread and frantic episode of group masturbation. Another mistake occurred when I welcomed a man and a woman into Kiwi, announcing, 'I see you've brought your mum along for moral support'. The lady informed me through gritted teeth that she was, in fact, 'the wife'.

Some mistakes are worse than others, and my mistake with Anna is one of the worst.

Anna's referral simply reads that she is a fourteen-year-old suffering with episodes of acute anxiety and panic. When she comes in, I try to build more of an initial picture and I am curious about any physical manifestations of her anxiety, asking where she holds tension in her body, and whether she has any associated pain. Anna tells me about terrible headaches and facial soreness. I wonder out loud whether this could be bruxism – teeth-grinding and jaw-clenching in the night, usually due to stress. Anna bangs her water bottle down onto the desk, making me jump. I can see the fury in her as her shoulders rise, and also the dread – of me personally – as she leans away from me. I ask her to name what she is feeling.

She says, 'All you professionals are the same! You just have your own ideas and you don't listen to anything else.'

I assure her that I will listen, and I apologize for suggesting something before hearing her out, acknowledging that her symptoms are clearly very distressing for her. Anna settles in the chair a little, her short and shallow breathing becomes deeper and her shoulders lower. As she moves from fight or flight into safe and socially engaged, she pauses, and then she begins to talk.

Anna has a very young mother whom she is very close to. The mother, who has always been something of a beauty, Anna is at pains to tell me, developed a terrible pain in her jaw. She visited the dentist, who gave her these 'silly little plastic trays' to stop her teeth grinding in the night. The pain was unrelenting, but, as a busy mother of three, Anna's mum did her best to ignore it. Eventually, she was seen in hospital, twice. A scan was taken at some point, but she was sent on her way with a diagnosis of stress. Ultimately, Anna's mum couldn't tolerate the pain any more and tried for a third time to get an answer from the hospital. At this point it transpired that she had a cancerous tumour. Most of her tongue had to be removed, along with half of her jaw on one side.

Anna's mum will never eat again and is now fed via a tube attached to her body. Speech is also very difficult, although Anna tells me it's astonishing how well she is able to communicate. She is one of the most resilient women, as I will discover when I eventually meet her, and still beautiful, despite her facial operations.

But today is Day One with Anna, a crucial day, and I have made a mistake. I have reaffirmed that professionals can let her down by making their own assumptions too fast. I do my best to repair things with Anna, and spend longer with her than I really have time for so that I can listen intently to her story.

As Anna finally leaves the room, I reach into my bag for my phone, a quick glance before the next patient. Five missed calls. Max. There is a knock at the door and I thrust my phone back into my bag – out of sight, out of mind.

When panic attacks

I am fully engaged with my next patient and forget all about my phone until they leave, at which point I allow myself to feel panic. Five missed calls must mean something is terribly wrong. I call Max back. He doesn't answer. Now I am really worried. Something awful must have happened and I have ignored it for fifty whole minutes. I go outside the hospital into the cold air, to the smoking area that is really an old bus stop a few steps away from the entrance. I take a deep breath of nicotine-filled air and call Max again. On the second attempt, he picks up. He sounds frantic. He is breathing heavily and telling me that he is panicking and I need to come and get him from work. I have seen him become a little breathless and anxious a few times recently, but nothing like this. Usually, he calms down if I hold him close to me and rub his back until his breathing slows.

I assume he is in shock and can't get the words out. Is it his mum? An accident? I rush back inside and explain to my boss that there has been an emergency and I need to take the afternoon off for personal reasons. This is a huge deal. There are people depending on me. And yet I do it. It feels like a dereliction of duty, but I remind myself that I am only human.

I speed off across London and brace myself for whatever is happening to Max. But, when I get to his workplace, he seems calm and quiet. He climbs into the car beside me and I drive him home. He is holding my hand tightly on top of the gear stick and his breathing still seems a little laboured. We don't speak – I decide that can wait until we are home. Once there, I make tea for us both and ready myself to listen and support.

Max says, 'I just panicked. I just felt sheer panic.'

I am confused, annoyed and concerned in equal measure.

I spend the rest of the afternoon and evening talking Max down from his residual anxiety and concern about what people at work might think, offering comfort and acceptance. But I can feel the flicker of annoyance in him. He seems irritated when I suggest he needs some support, that I can't leave work again like that. He disengages from me a little.

I consider what I have left to offer him, digging deep into my repertoire of strategies.

I have seen patients have panic attacks. The terror in their eyes, their very real belief that they might actually be dying, is awful to witness. When I was assisting Dr Macklin on the all-male psychiatric ward, one of the psychiatrists used to induce states of panic on purpose during sessions with patients who suffered from anxiety or panic disorder. This can be done by presenting a fear to them, having them visualize the situation they most dread and asking them to imagine being present in it. Once their body entered panic, he would then have the patient start to do push-ups or sing as loudly as they could to show them that panic creates the same physiological response in the body as high-intensity exercise or exertion, and that they wouldn't in fact die as a result. It was a risky little emotional game to play during a time of crisis, I always felt, but I have since heard other psychologists recognize this practice when teaching patients about fight or flight.

I rally. Panic is awful and Max has turned to me in his moment of distress. The very last thing he needs now it has passed is to feel shamed by me. I am conscious of this not just from my professional life, but from my own experience of how isolating anxiety can feel. To complicate my emotions further, I also feel satisfied that he can share all this with me and part of me hopes it will bring us closer.

I go back to work holding on to this narrative.

Three people in the relationship

Things settle and Max and I enjoy the longer summer evenings, taking every opportunity to stroll through parks or sit on friends' little rooftop terraces, talking intently until the early hours, or clinking wine glasses and drinking cocktails in beer gardens around town. We are going to more parties with friends and Max seems increasingly energized by the heat. Being with him is still physically and emotionally draining, but I can't help feeling almost blissful.

When, one evening, I take a break from partying and stay in, boiling pasta and grating cheese, Max appears, telling me he hasn't really been able to have fun at the party without me. In the kitchen light, I can see his face has changed, a look I have noticed before a few times, either in the depths of the night by a bedside light or cast in table candlelight. Now, in the bright overhead lights of the kitchen, I can see how his face is strained, almost contorted, and his eyes are like saucers. His pupils are enlarged and frighteningly deep and dark.

The pieces start knitting together in my mind.

I have mistaken the high energy levels, lack of need for sleep and the acute sensitivity to touch as passion, lust and excitement, and I have believed that our connection is in some way transcendent, that we feed off each other and energize each other. But it isn't real – it's cocaine. The panic, anxiety and hypervigilance are also explained by his habit. I feel embarrassed by my naivety and lack of insight, but also can't help feeling slightly impressed with myself for keeping up with him *without* a stimulant. No wonder I have started to feel burnout.

Max denies my theory. He says he has been known to 'dabble'. Then adds, 'Like everyone in London.' But he insists he hasn't been using cocaine when he is with me and he doesn't need to. I want to believe him, so I collude with his version of events, minimizing the drug use, pushing it to one side in my mind.

The truth is, my mental picture of Max and me is now

tarnished. Maybe this is mostly explained by my ego injury – the passion I thought was being created by me was actually being created synthetically. I try to rationalize it all, telling myself that it's normal to take drugs in your twenties and maybe it's just a social habit and our connection exacerbates his extremism. I throw myself back into things with him, but I feel myself pulling away again, little by little.

Partially withdrawing within a relationship has been described by psychoanalyst Margaret Crastnopol as 'the unkind cutting back'. This is because when one partner starts to withdraw a little, it has a micro-traumatic effect on the other partner, causing them to panic and either frantically pursue the withdrawing partner or reciprocate by withdrawing for self-protection.

In response to my pulling away, Max pursues me, continuing to recreate previous good dates and experiences we have had together, arranging the scenes like a set, but it isn't the same as before. It feels a little like he is method acting. In any case, Max's 'best behaviour' mode lasts only for a few weeks and then he starts to slip again – lots of little trips to the toilet on date nights, returning with a pressured need to tell me an impassioned story and a heightened sense of self-confidence.

Now I can see it.

There are three people in the relationship: me, Max and his friend, Charlie.

This makes me feel torn. Do I want to be part of this? Is this enough? Or is this heading somewhere more sinister? I have never seen Max as someone who needs rescuing, so what would my role be? Partying companion? Cheerleader? Or just always trying to keep up?

Under the guise of trying to save money, Max starts carrying around a hip flask full of whisky. This is introduced as 'just for expensive rooftop nights out', but soon becomes a constant fixture, just like the little bag of white powder in his top pocket. These items are always on him, like a worrying tool belt of consolation and stimulation. He hid it from me before, or maybe I didn't see it, but now he feels safe to show me or to let it slip.

Max's frantic need to devour also applies to me. One evening, I am exhausted when I arrive at his house after a long day and a gruelling commute home. He suggests we skip dinner. I am so tired and past hunger, I don't resist. He bundles me straight into bed and we eat crisps, drink wine and watch trash TV, managing to get to sleep entwined in each other's arms before 9.30 p.m. It is in fact just what I need, a warm and refreshing tonic. The next day, I feel lighter.

I can see that this is a success story, and that it has been logged by Max. I wait to see what happens next.

Kelli's analysis

The next time I see Kelli, I am violently hung-over. I could cancel, but I will still be charged and I don't want Kelli to read some deep meaning into it. Psychotherapists never see anything as happenstance. So, I arrive at her office, stuffed to the brim with salt-and-vinegar crisps that I have thrown down in the car outside. Hangovers always make me feel anxious – the increased heart rate, sweaty palms, dry mouth and disorientation all prime my brain to develop a story to match my state of arousal. There must be something to feel anxious about if I feel *this* anxious; there's no smoke without fire.

The session goes past in a blur of fragmented and chaotic panic. I latch on to things, trying to make them fit – is this the bad thing creating my sense of fear and dread, or is it something else? Kelli makes some deep interpretations: maybe I haven't had enough mirroring experiences as a child; maybe I am having a crisis of identity because I am balancing two incompatible selves: a self who drinks, stays up all night and is wildly spontaneous with Max, and the responsible, reliable self whose work entails containing children's mental-health needs.

While I appreciate Kelli's hard work excavating my subconscious, I can't help but laugh to myself on the way home. The money would probably have been better spent on paracetamol, Lucozade and a decent meal. Sometimes analysts might overanalyse things. I am just burning the candle at both ends and need a good night's sleep.

Survivor guilt

I realize that I have no *real* idea about tiredness or sleep deprivation when I talk to Tom. He works as a technician on the escalators in London Tube stations and comes in with suspected PTSD. He was present when a cleaner was working underneath one of the escalators and someone hadn't fully turned them off, leading to the man's decapitation. Tom informs me, in a very matter-of-fact way.

I am horrified, but hold a neutral expression as best I can and ask Tom how he is coping.

He has survivor guilt, intense guilt for being present and unharmed when another was killed, and he is distorting his memories to such an extent that he believes it was somehow his fault. When something awful happens at random, our brains try to find a logical explanation so that we don't experience the world as chaotic, since chaos is frightening. So, we take ownership of it, to help us feel in control. I have seen this with children in care whose thought process might be, *Maybe if I am very quiet today, I won't get abused.* Tom is looking for an explanation of the unexplainable and locating the blame in himself. Tom also can't sleep, with images of the tragedy playing and replaying in his mind, the trauma of the moment being recycled into the present, over and over again. He has started to believe that other people sleep in his bedroom with him at night and he stays up chatting to them (oddly without distress). He also has a compulsion to shout out the name of the Tube station, over and over, at random moments.

Severe sleep deprivation can lead to psychosis-like symptoms, such as hallucination and delusions. Thankfully, these symptoms can be remedied by restoring proper amounts of sleep. This is our most important goal. I signpost Tom to his GP for something that might help him sleep more than the over-the-counter remedies he has tried, and we get to work on rescripting the event and removing blame, pressing *stop* on the continuous replay.

Restless sleep

Exhausted from another long day at work, Max suggests we skip dinner and I nod along with it. I'm hungry, but I don't resist. He flings an arm around me and manoeuvres me straight into bed. He produces crisps and wine, and suggests we watch some nonsense or other on TV. Despite my new sense of unease with Max, I manage to get to sleep, his arms around me. It is early, and I get the sleep I crave. But, the next day, I don't feel lighter.

What's in a name?

Max, I realize, is in the throes of a repetition compulsion, another form of addiction: the unconscious desire to repeat experiences over and over, because there is a familiarity in them – even when those experiences are not good. We all do this to some extent; re-enacting past events and repeating our behavioural patterns because repetition is linked to our pleasure pathways. You see this in children, who love to repeat games. We've all engaged a toddler in peekaboo or hide the dolly and then regretted it as they shriek, 'Again! Again!' and grind us down with their unbridled energy. With each repetition, they become more and more in control of their responses and expectations, gaining mastery, which makes them feel good. I am starting to feel like Max's object – the ball he wants to throw again and again; and he is enjoying gaining mastery over me. Conversely, I am clearly losing mastery over myself. I am more like a rag doll.

What has been a flicker of a doubt lurking inside me ignites into a flame and I realize I feel trapped. Naming it feels good. 'I feel trapped,' I say out loud, in response to the tightening in my chest. 'I am not a toy to be played with, or a substance to be used up.'

It strikes me that I am becoming his next drug. I am standing still as I realize this but, in my mind, I am making huge steps.

Victoria train station may not appear to be the best place to have this conversation with myself, but the wonderful thing about London is that I could be snogging a parrot or juggling rats in full view, and everyone would just keep on walking by, ignoring me. I am standing outside a little coffee van dispensary at the centre of the station, absently watching all the people rushing by. Something about Victoria train station helps me to find the words, to access and identify what I have been feeling.

Gazing blankly up at the departures board, I start to think about terror attacks and disasters – never far from my mind when I'm in a major transport hub in central London. Experiences like terror attacks, in which people feel powerless with no prospect of rescue, often generate a trauma response that is triggered each time the victim feels inhibited or trapped. The feeling of being trapped and powerless is deeply distressing for any of us. I realize I am feeling trapped and powerless in my relationship with Max. I now recognize he is my emotional captor – he rescued me from pain and heartbreak when we met and now, even though I want to leave, I am worried about how I will cope without his distracting and intense input, and I feel as though I owe it to him to stay.

In this moment of realization, a steadying sense of calm washes over me. It comes from working out what's wrong, the *aha* moment of naming it and accepting it. Clarity. This sense of relief is bodily and chemical as well as cognitive. My neuroception is allowing me, at a primitive level, to acknowledge potential cues to a lack of safety, and a lack of self, with more certainty.

Saying the words aloud – 'I feel *trapped*' – brings me such relief.

Finally acknowledging what I've been feeling about Max releases emotions I have been hiding from and trying my best to ignore. As I say the words, the tension that has been built up by the suppression of these feelings leaves my body, producing a wave of elation.

So often, this *aha* moment is what patients look for in a therapy session and, when they find it, it's a profound experience.

'*Longing* – yes, that's it, it's the *longing*.'

'Absolutely, it is the feeling of *betrayal* . . .'

'That's the thing, she never did *advocate* for me.'

When something is sitting just outside our conscious awareness, it gives us a sense of the unknown, and our response to the unknown is usually fear. Then, when we can name that thing – in this case, an emotion – it gives us a sense of clarity. In naming my feeling, my sense of being trapped, I can separate the emotion from myself, I can stop feeling overwhelmed by vague dread and I can focus on the problem. I can zoom back a little from my internal world and see things more clearly: 'I *feel* trapped' is very different from 'I *am* trapped'.

Simply naming a feeling with patients often brings about a sense of relief. It brings about insight, a feeling of control and a reappraisal. Although I don't yet know what to do about my own *aha* moment, I know that I have a choice: I can take action to reduce this feeling, I can take some control to shift out of this state. This alone brings relief.

There is a little more complexity to what I am feeling with

Max, and I'm still trying to find a word for it. I have witnessed many patients struggle to find such descriptors for the sense that a relationship no longer feels *right*. Different terms resonate. For some, it's a discomfort. For others, a disconnect, or maybe an incongruence. It's not necessarily a painful feeling, but it is very apparent.

I comfort myself with the thought of my upcoming trip. At the end of the summer, I am going to America with Alex, for a wedding. I will be away for two weeks. I will have space and time to step away from my situation – and this is important, as we can't see something fully when we are immersed in it, I remind myself. I will know what to do once I'm in America. It is far away from London and just the thought of this distance between me and Max feels inherently comforting.

Surely this is a sign.

Kelli slips up

'Tell me the sense or the feeling that comes to mind when you think about this upcoming time away from Max,' Kelli says.

I circle around a few words in my mind, but nothing fits and I feel a little frustrated.

Kelli senses it. 'I'll tell you what word came up for me as you were talking: respite.'

It doesn't immediately resonate or chime with anything inside me, but I do feel an attraction to the word. Maybe I do feel as though I need a break.

Kelli wants to dig deeper into my internal world, my underlying anxiety and slight dread. 'I am sensing some existential groundlessness,' she offers.

Seeking distraction

I lie in silence staring at the painting of the shipwreck on her wall. I always wonder if it is a psychological test or tool. Is it meant to help me open up, jog my subconscious along? I have to admit, I see something new in the painting every session, or I see it from a slightly new perspective that I couldn't see last time, but now seems so obvious.

As I consider the possibility that Kelli is some sort of wizard, she interrupts my thoughts: 'Existential groundlessness can come about when our subconscious recognizes that it needs to take a new course of action. It knows our needs are being thwarted or frustrated, but at the same time it doesn't want to let go of the familiar, as this feels safe, even if it is suboptimal, and it feels anxious about trying something new.'

This seems to resonate; a deep sense of feeling torn is dragged up from the pit of my stomach.

'Let's look at some of the defence mechanisms that have been at play for you,' she says brightly. 'After all, your defence mechanisms have been developed and sustained for a reason and should be respected, looked at with curiosity, not contempt.'

I try to jot this quote down on an imaginary notepad in my mind, knowing I will use it with patients myself. But my subconscious remains quiet, not wanting to reveal itself.

Kelli steps in. 'Rationalization. Would it be fair to say that has been at play? You have rationalized all of Max's behaviours, given them reason, cause and context. This has given you motive to stay, to take care of him. But the fact is we can understand and explain any person's behaviour, given their context, even that of serial killers.' She falters a little. 'Not that I am comparing Max to a serial killer.'

Ah, maybe even Kelli makes little slip-ups. That's comforting.

'Anyway, you seem to have taken an enormous amount of responsibility for the feelings and actions of Max, and, in some ways, you have tried to emulate him while still trying to maintain a sense of self. You want to be a free spirit, a spontaneous, experimental person, but also someone who is taken seriously.'

There's a long pause. That's the torn feeling explained.

'Being taken seriously has been very important for you in the past, I seem to recall. Wasn't it important for people to take you and Steve seriously as a couple?'

We both know what she has done here, like a clever callback to the start of a set by a proficient stand-up comedian, when they bring the story full circle. The trainee therapist in me wants to applaud. And I hear what she is saying. There is a touch of co-dependency about my relationship with Max, and I am trying to become enmeshed with him, to deny parts of myself.

Kelli mirrors my internal monologue: 'If you let go of Max and "Max's chaos", you will have to acknowledge your own internal chaos, and I think that's what frightens you. But maybe it would make you feel liberated and give you that respite you crave more permanently.'

I think that's what we call a breakthrough.

Abandonment

It doesn't occur to me that my upcoming holiday will represent a problem for patients until I see Sophie, who was admitted to the hospital following an overdose. I look ahead in my diary to find a time for our next session, in three weeks. Sophie gasps. 'I *knew* you would do this to me. You don't care about anybody but yourself!' She continues to castigate me at speed, with plenty of profanities thrown in. She is very angry.

We end the session by addressing her separation anxiety and sense of abandonment, assessing whether the sense is real or perceived. We disempower the idea that my holiday means I simply don't care about her. She is comforted by the thought that I will be holding her in mind, and that at least I won't be 'cheating on her' with other patients, but I am still the perpetrator.

Sophie is my first experience of entering a relationship with someone with borderline personality disorder, characterized by intense fear of abandonment and rejection. And she won't be my last.

Black holes

When I meet with Dr Lane, her eyes widen as I begin to describe Sophie. When I come to the end of my description, we both say in unison, 'Borderline!'

I am comforted for a moment that my thinking is correct. Dr Lane and I discuss all the classic persecutory views held towards the borderline presentation. Patients are described as 'the black hole', 'the untreatable' and 'the difficult' by many in the profession, and borderline personality disorder as 'the dustbin diagnosis'. The media has glamourized certain aspects of the issue. Characters in films such as *Fatal Attraction* and *Girl, Interrupted* are portrayed as sinister, unstable and dangerous. But Dr Lane and I both share an excitement, an aliveness, when discussing such patients. We focus on the positives, and I write a list which I can look back to if I struggle with border-line patients in future.

The borderline patient is highly, highly responsive to what is going on between us in the room. They have great intu-ition. They read people in seconds. They are the Jason Bourne of the consulting room. They are also completely authentic; their emotions are so big and weigh so heavily that they are difficult to mask. The list helps. Dr Lane suggests I use the feedback Sophie gives me in the room. 'Work with the rage, observe it and respond to it,' she tells me. 'All she really needs is validation.'

I leave thinking about how all emotions are valid. They exist, and therefore they should be responded to, even if it's to challenge them. They should not be minimized or ignored.

Playing the role

Max's anticipatory anxiety has really started to grow. He is in the pre-contemplation stage of acute separation anxiety and keeps casually suggesting I shouldn't go to the wedding in America. I think of how I have managed Sophie and I hold on, playing out my role as Max's girlfriend until the leaving date finally rolls around.

The breath I let out as I sit down in the airport departure lounge feels as though it has been held inside me for months. I feel relief, but also apprehension. This is only a hiatus. I now need to figure out what to do.

The first night of the trip is a drinks reception for the happy couple. I feel lighter and lighter as I circle the room, flanked by Alex, sipping champagne, sometimes dancing and taking selfies with newfound friends. I sleep peacefully next to Alex, happy to be somewhere else, with someone else. Despite her warm little body, full of fizz and canapés, taking up more than half the bed, I feel alone, but in the best way possible.

Othello syndrome

We wake up late and chug down orange juice in bed as we review the events of the night before and swipe through filters on selected images for Instagram.

When I next pick up my phone, it springs to life with message after message and missed call after missed call. I feel my stomach sink and brace myself to call Max back. It is early in the morning for him, and he yelps through an explanation for his incessant calls. He has found the wedding hashtag (he has looked long and hard) and he has used this to track down a very grainy video of me on someone else's Instagram profile. It belongs to a man I have never met. In the video, I can be seen in the background at the back of the dance floor. Max splutters that it looks like I am dancing too close to another man. I am clearly 'cheating again'. Again? As I listen to the sheer panic in his pressured and chaotic speech, I hear a hint of rage. Is this feeling valid? My mind clicks into rational, assessment mode. Othello syndrome, I muse. We have entered the aptly named paranoid delusional state, whereby a partner holds the fixed and immovable belief that the other partner is cheating. I note that I am making sense of him as I would a patient – that is how detached I feel. I make my excuses and end the call.

The vice feeling in my chest returns and I have the

overwhelming desire to break out of my relationship with Max. I know I need support to do this, so I gasp out the whole story to Alex. She is meticulously applying lashings of mascara to one eye, mouth wide open in concentration. As she takes in the truth behind the smoke and mirrors concealing Max and me, she drops the mascara wand into the sink, stunned. She says she *knew* something wasn't right (best friends always know), but she felt she couldn't say a word as I would be defensive, protective of Max, and would distance myself from her. Her relief is palpable.

As we plan my escape, I am jubilant. I am liberated.

The little voice

My latest patient, Hugh, says being with his partner Rachel is 'like I have a stone in my shoe. Sometimes I can ignore it, put up with it, and that is easier when we are on a beautiful holiday beach and we've had a few cocktails. But other times, when we are on our own . . . when we sit in silence, when we are on a long car journey or when we are brushing our teeth at night in tandem, the stone digs deep into my heel and I want to scream.'

Alex and I have talked about such feelings, referring to this as 'the little voice'. It's a common phrase which we all understand. I imagine it as a stick figure that pops up in your peripheral vision when you least expect it, mentioning things you would rather ignore. You can be sitting on a train, watching the countryside whizz by, getting comfortable and feeling smug about catching the 4.55 exactly as planned, and the stick figure will pull up next to you: 'This isn't feeling right, is it?

You're not really yourself when you're with him,' it says. 'You're not really that happy, are you? You're not actually that into him, are you?'

We once chatted about the stick figure with our friend who had been seeing his girlfriend for ten years. 'Yes!' he exclaimed, in his very own *aha* moment. 'That's so true! My stick figure was on the bus yesterday. It said, "If you get home and find she's passed away, it will actually be fine."'

And yet they are still together.

Sometimes we are so encased in the fear of being alone that we relentlessly – maybe idiotically – maintain the status quo.

The break-up balm

Ending a partnership that gave you an uneasy sense of incongruence can feel liberating. You have answered your own calling, silenced the nagging little voice and thrown that stone out of your shoe. Initially, it feels thrilling. For me, it's almost euphoric.

Having now seen many patients in my little Kiwi consulting room, I have started to find my feet with relational issues such as betrayal, alienation, conflict and, most notably, heartbreak. The universal nature of this pain is comforting for me. Having witnessed heartbreak in several patients, I have come to know the stages of the process, especially for the person who initiates the separation, the one in control, and I know it can begin with euphoria. I start referring to this stage with patients as 'the break-up balm' and feel pleased with the phrase I've coined. But, while the relief and the adrenaline are exhilarating at first, sadly the balm does not last. It is followed by a crashing comedown or the anxiety of transition. Usually after a week or so.

In my balm phase, the pseudo-high wraps around me as I break the news of our parting ways to Max. He listens glassy-eyed, a slight smile fixed to his face. At first, he seems a bit numb, then he goes into full shutdown. An eerie silence hangs between us. In a split second, we have shifted from the deepest of intimacies into stranger territory.

Next, however, comes his protest. He doesn't verbalize it; he just stays close to me and tries to gather me up, pulling me towards him, as though literally holding us together will somehow re-bond us emotionally. If only it were that easy.

We hold each other for a few moments and I feel tears well up, but, simultaneously, I'm oddly detached. This is painful, but I am certain that it is right. I struggle to get him out of the house as he lingers and clings to me a little too long in our farewell hug. Once he has left, I wait anxiously for my own crushing heartbreak, remembering all too well what that feels like. I try to busy myself, making plans in my diary. The time usually filled by Max is now a void that I must fill with something else. I need to distract myself.

The break-up balm remains in place for a honeymoon period – a few days of ignorant bliss, you might say. But I find that, once the initial glow dissipates, the pain is more manageable, more endurable than I had anticipated. This time is different from my break-up with Steve. This is partly because I am in control this time. I have agency, so the loss is not compounded by shock and humiliation. And, crucially, I have been here before. This situation is known to me.

I'm fine

Many of my patients appear to follow the same pattern with their emotional journey. Hugh is a good example. When he finally takes the stone out of his shoe, he comes to see me.

'You know what, Natalie, I'm actually *fine*. I can't believe it, but I am *fine*. I am better than fine!' He beams at me.

This break-up balm is like the body flooding itself with adrenaline after a physical injury, to stave off the acute pain, panic and shock. It is commonly referred to by another name: denial. And so it is that, a few sessions on, the word 'fine' has receded from Hugh's vocabulary and his new descriptor for how he's feeling is 'hopeless'. He clings rigidly to the belief that he will never find a love that feels fully right for him; he is utterly convinced of that. So, it's time to consider the possible evolutionary basis of this belief.

Because the familiar is less risky, the brain drives us to stay with it and return to what we know. This is just human behaviour since time immemorial. As primitive humans, we were more likely to survive and procreate if we stayed with a mate. This is the adaptive function of self-doubt, the voice that says, 'Go back, you can't survive alone.' It kicks in to drive us back to the pair-bond, to keep us safe. To encourage this, the brain often serves us a rose-tinted version of what has been lost – a showreel of highlights, never the showreel of bloopers – to lure us back and to escape the discomfort we now face. But it's a quick fix that doesn't work in the long run. Still, the primitive brain gives it a good go because it craves short-term relief.

Rationalizing his feelings like this helps Hugh to make sense of his conflicted desires – his feeling torn. It helps him to see that the pull to return to Rachel is driven by *fear*. It's fear that makes him say that he feels lost, that his future is lost, that he feels untethered and panicked. I know this feeling too.

Hugh wants to name it, label it, but can't find the words. So, I offer 'existential groundlessness' – thank you, Kelli. This is a sense we all experience when seeking an anchor in a world that feels frightening and unknown to us. The unknown is what provokes anxiety. It arises when we try to make a change that is good for us, but scary and difficult. The subconscious pipes up: 'Don't change this. It has been keeping us safe for ages and we don't know what the alternative looks like. OK, so it might be better in the end, but what about all the hard work that's required to get there? Do you really need that right now?'

Hugh and I talk about how connecting with others might help disempower this distorted belief that he will *never* connect to another person again and is destined to die alone. Being open to developing real connections will likely help lessen his fear and hopelessness by reminding him that he has the capacity for love and that he will love again. At the end of our session, we joke that, as a scaffolding for love, he might try lust, which is one of the most powerful antidotes for a sense of disconnect.

Slut spiralling

At our next session, what becomes clear is that Hugh has read my scaffolding concept as a prescription for promiscuity. In the week since I last saw him, he has entered a self-proclaimed 'slut spiral'.

'Perhaps you just needed to hear that you had permission to do this, to feel it was OK to access something within the self? You needed to hear it was OK to explore the part of you that wants to connect to others more spontaneously,' I say to him.

And, with this prescription for exploratory sex in his back pocket, Hugh opens up that maybe he also likes men.

Aha, and so we reach enlightenment.

As I walk Hugh through his stages – incongruence, break-up balm, hopelessness, fear, exploration, enlightenment – I praise his resilience throughout the process. But, as I map out his journey, I notice, in the back of my mind, that it's me who's experiencing a profound sense of loss. I am yet to reach enlightenment or self-discovery. I haven't taken such brave steps. I remain enmeshed with Max.

Spending every waking hour with him led to us becoming interconnected and I'm now struggling to distinguish my own perceptions – my own purpose, my own feelings, my own opinions – from those we co-authored. Although I no longer feel smothered, and that is a very good thing indeed, there are still gaps in me that need to be filled. I feel a little empty. There is a void, but I don't feel the frantic pull to fill it with *someone* else – I want to be alone. I use some therapist-speak on myself: 'Sit with this discomfort and see what shifts in you.'

Enmeshment in a relationship is when boundaries become diffused or obsolete. You don't know where you end and they begin. You exist in the relationship to respond reactively to their emotions and meet their needs. You lose autonomy, identity and self as you become merged with the other, as if one doesn't exist without the other. And this can often lead to problems. One party can end up feeling smothered or controlled, with the other feeling the need to control. It encourages paranoia and surveillance-like behaviours. Any lived experience – jobs, hobbies, relationships and activities – outside the couple's 'shared world' starts to feel threatening, inciting jealousy and the type of rage that masks a fear of abandonment. Enmeshment is a couple at a party radiating a smug togetherness and chipping into conversations with '*We* like this' or '*We* do that'. Alarm bells about enmeshment should ring when 'we' is used consistently in place of 'I'.

I am still 'we', and I need to become 'I'.

THREE

Shame & secrets

Meeting Peggy

Peggy has a diagnosis of emergent borderline personality disorder. I have seen colleagues roll their eyes many times when faced with those four words, and, when Peggy's referral form comes in, she is no exception.

Once a week I sit around a cramped table with a host of colleagues, and we discuss all our cases, sipping bitter black coffees and scribbling notes. The purpose of these meetings is to decide who takes on each case, or whether it should be referred on to an external specialist service. This is billed as 'joined-up thinking', but feels more like squabbling about who has space in their bursting diary to take on another patient.

"'Congenital abscess on penis!" Why has this even come to psych? It can't be *that* distressing. For the love of God, who is triaging this? I do not have the time!' the outraged therapist seated to my right rants, until someone quietly points out that what it actually says on the form is 'congenital *absence* of penis' – aphallia is a very rare congenital anomaly – at which point our exasperated colleague turns white. I think I also see him briefly grab his own crotch, perhaps for reassurance. As he scrambles to recover his composure, everyone else avoids eye contact and someone else silently picks up the file as a signal for us to move on. I end up with the remaining few cases. This includes Peggy. The Post-it on the front of the file reads, *A prolific self-harmer.*

When I meet Peggy, I am struck by how tiny she is and how young she looks, despite being sixteen. She is wearing a huge, oversized, navy woollen jumper, and I wonder how small her frame is beneath it. Every few minutes, she pulls daintily at the sleeves and draws them low over her hands.

Concealment, I think to myself. Contrary to popular belief, those with self-harm scars usually work hard to hide them.

She is also wearing huge-rimmed glasses that make her eyes seem enormous on her little head, and she seems to be shaking uncontrollably. I think of her diagnostic label, borderline personality disorder, as a disorder of instability. She is physically unstable.

I want Peggy to feel safe with me in the room. I am conscious that, to get to this point, to be sitting here, she will have already been asked lots of questions and will have been passed around by various professionals, and I don't want to be just another faceless lanyard who gives up on her.

'Why don't you be in charge of the questions today?' I say, suggesting a role reversal and telling her she can ask me anything.

This seems to do the trick and she immediately appears more at ease. 'Really? I can ask you anything I like?' She scans her mind and lands on a few straightforward queries, including,

'What's your favourite animal?' and 'What did you have for breakfast?'

Then she looks at me and asks if I am married.

I ask why this is important for her to know, while knowing that she is assessing the competition when it comes to my priorities and relationships.

Peggy shifts very suddenly into intense anger. She glares at me, hard. 'This isn't real, though, is it? These aren't real answers. You're being paid to do this. It's just a front.'

Peggy's fury continues to rise and she begins hitting and kicking things, knocking over the tiny children's playbox that occupies the only free corner of the room, sending the balls rolling around the floor. I maintain my soft demeanour, not reacting. After a few minutes of this, with no response from me, she returns to her chair and exhales deeply. She resets and kicks away one of the stray balls as if to pretend the outburst never happened.

Once I feel she has settled, I try a new exercise, the one suggested by my dad.

'Imagine you are sitting at a round table, at your own birthday party,' I tell her. 'Can you imagine the room, the table, the lighting? As much detail as possible. As you scan around the table, you realize that every person there is a different version of you – a young you, you from your earliest memory, you when you're at school, you when you're with friends, you when you went through a hard time, happy you, angry you, and so on.' We talk through all the versions of Peggy, what they are wearing, their expressions, how they feel about each other and how they interact with one another. Do any of them take care of one another? Are any of them angry with each other? Do they like one another?

I learn that Peggy has a very different relationship with each version of herself, but all versions overwhelm her. Once she is aligned with one of the versions, she is completely engulfed by it and she steps right into its shoes. There is 'angry Peggy', who feels as though the world is against her. There is a childlike Peggy, who pleads for affection continually, rejected at home and unable to make friends at school. There is also Peggy the 'vixen'. Vixen Peggy knows how to get what she wants from others. Vixen Peggy has a way of being seductive, not in a sexual way, but in a way that draws you in and makes you want to care for her. There is certainly a very real Peggy who has been the victim of neglect, but there is also the Peggy who knows how to manipulate others emotionally. All the different versions struggle to relate to one another. They seem completely split, disparate, and yet I instinctively like them all, even vixen Peggy.

At the end of the task, I want Peggy to know that we all have different versions of the self, and we present these different versions in different contexts. I ask her if they are all true versions of the self and if they all have real feelings. Peggy seems to see where I am going with this. We agree that, just because I am sitting opposite her in this room, holding her file and wearing a lanyard, I am still an authentic version of myself and here to connect with her in the time we have together.

Peggy and I spend the rest of the session talking about the youngest version of her, the very frightened version. I watch her closely and, with desperately searching eyes, she starts to look around the imaginary table for someone who is clearly not at the party. I respond as if we are both at the party together, as though I am right there with her.

'What do you need right now, Peggy? What do you need to hear?' I ask her.

After a while, Peggy says, 'I just need you to hold my hand.'

And so I do.

Self-insufficiency

One of the key features of someone with borderline personality disorder is a poor or fragmented sense of a core self or identity. Peggy's self is fragmented into so many parts that she struggles to have them all work together or form a cohesive whole. Not so unlike Peggy, I am struggling to find and relate to my true self outside of Max. I feel as though I don't know myself fully; parts of me feel like a stranger and I am indecisive about what my needs are and what I like. I just don't know.

There is also the huge void of time that stands before me now that I am alone, and I have to fill it with just myself. Am I enough?

Trial and error

I make a conscious decision to shift into a work version of myself and be solution-focused about the problem. I will fill the gaps in me with new activities. Maybe I'll find some new interests. This will be grounding for me. I scroll through page after page of *Top 50 things to do in London* articles, but paintballing or axe-throwing on my own feels a little bleak and I don't think I am quite emotionally ready to withstand the Jack the Ripper walking tours or make-your-own-dildo classes.

Acting – I think that is something for which I might have transferable skills. Being able to enter into someone else's narrative and access empathy on a deep level feels familiar. The leftover break-up balm adrenaline and maybe a slight mania convinces me to believe this might actually be my calling. Forget Kiwi, I could be the next gritty-yet-relatable small-screen actress, transforming my real-life distress into art. How noble. I discover there are loads of award-winning schools in London to bear witness to my untapped talent. Ah – £11,400 per term . . . Maybe I'll stick with the day job.

Just as I am putting new activities onto the back burner, Alex convinces me that modelling is close enough to acting – it, too, is a performance – and, crucially, auditioning is free. After several lunchtime wines, she also convinces me that I should go along with her that afternoon to audition for a runway show. Alex is five foot eight and built like a traditional model; she has a great deal of self-confidence and solid, unrelenting self-esteem. I am five foot two and not built like a traditional model; I'm also wracked with internalized shame and paranoia and self-doubt. I try to envisage myself thrust onto a runway, a foot shorter than everyone around me and scuttling rather than strutting, likely apologizing at a rising volume with every off-beat step and with a bright red, blushing face. A sausage dog in a greyhound race. Alex reassures me it will be spontaneous and liberating, and all I'll have to do is stand and have my photo taken against a blank wall. Then we can go home and eat pad thai on the sofa.

When we get there, surrounded by towering, confident women, I am inevitably struck with an attack of chronic blushing and consider bolting for the door. We stand in a row against the back wall. It feels a bit like a police line-up: *Can you identify the woman who shouldn't be here?* They don't pan the camera, thank goodness. The photos are static. Otherwise, the footage would reveal a row of perfect pouts, then the very top of my head.

It's nearly over, I think.

The woman running the show then pulls out a little hand-held CD player. I don't really think anything of it, at first. Maybe she doesn't have any headphones but loves music? But, as she places it on a stool and looks at us eagerly, my throat begins to tighten and my heart begins to race. I can't quite decide what's coming, but I know it isn't going to be good.

'OK,' she tells us. 'We will play some music at random and then just come forward and freestyle dance.'

The ease with which she says this strikes me as absurd. As if everyone has this ability to pull off effortless dance moves. In front of a watching crowd. But I am the only one who seems fazed. This makes it worse. Like the sense of alarm you get when the plane starts shaking and you grab the arm rests of your seat and look frantically around to find that nobody else is doing anything, because it's 'only turbulence'.

The first woman is particularly stunning and her random song is by Destiny's Child. She saunters into a dance with extraordinary grace and effortless cool, moving almost with apathy. She strikes a few prominent angular poses to the beat, hips jutting, and sashays off.

I am second in the line-up.

I think I might be experiencing some sort of aura before a panic attack. I will copy two of her choppy moves – hips this way and then that – and then bolt, I quickly decide. But then a slow ballad – 'Mama' by the Spice Girls – pours out of the speakers. Perfect. At this point, I leave my body; the room becomes surreal, as if I'm looking at it through a tube. All I can hear is the music. I propel myself forward, spinning, into the middle of the room, looking around frantically and then scrambling for the door like a wild animal released from a trap. Outside, I sit down on the kerb, my head between my knees, and a little while later Alex pushes through the doors, greeting me with a relaxed smile, as if we have just been for ice cream.

Shame

This humiliation marks my second experience of dissociation and derealization; I had the same feeling the day of Steve's text. When we feel overwhelmed, the environment takes on a surreal quality. When we feel shame, stress and fear, the brain enters hypo-arousal. It is flooded with the stress hormone cortisol, and effectively shuts down. It is frozen and unresponsive, preventing us from being alert, directing attention and processing incoming information. This can be very confusing and discombobulating after the event, when we try to recall what happened. Furthermore, when we have gaps in memory, the 'shame feeling' that we are still carrying tends to fill those gaps with worst-case imaginary scenarios, creating anxiety. Patients often benefit from drawing a timeline of the event, based upon concrete facts, to organize it into a narrative that makes sense to them and to stop the torment of the imaginary versions.

When working with witnesses of traumatic events more significant than my social embarrassment and public ridicule, the police use a technique called 'the cognitive interview'. This includes strategies such as having the witness recall the event in reverse order, recalling it in a random order and then from the perspective of someone else present at the scene, to try to jog the fragmented and foggy memory. Our lack of memory function in times of stress is an instinctive response, the brain attempting to split off from our distress and rescue us from it.

On this occasion, my memory malfunction feels intentional, as though my mind *wanted* to abandon my body and leave it to embarrass itself. It's as if my hypo-focus is on steroids; my mind has blocked the moment out and washed its hands of the whole thing. I am aware even in the moment that this is not normal. I know that I am not processing the event properly, but I am grateful for how the brain protects us and I know I won't be practising the cognitive interview on myself for this life event.

The emails arrive the next day. Alex receives an invitation to take part in the show. Needless to say, I don't make the cut. I make a note to find a less embarrassing way of reclaiming my identity.

Horrors and villains

Identity, loss of identity and how to access your true identity become running themes with my patients, and I have started to take on all the borderline personality disorder cases. One such BPD case is Bella, who, after a relatively long period of emotional stability, is now struggling to regulate her emotions. She is having chaotic mood swings, flying into intense rages and then immediately breaking down into tears. She feels lost, overwhelmed and fearful that her emotions have taken over.

I take a sheet of A4 hospital-grey paper and draw a circle in the middle of it. At the centre of the circle, I write, *Me*. Then I draw other, smaller circles all over the page at varying distances from the central *Me* circle, before passing the pen to Bella and asking her to write the names of her relatives in the smaller circles. I usually find the proximity of each relative's circle to the *Me* circle indicates the closeness of each relationship. One patient fetched a second piece of paper, drew a tiny circle on it, wrote *Dad* inside the circle and walked away to put the paper down on the far side of the room – which wasn't, in Kiwi, very far away at all, but I got the gist clearly enough.

Bella begins by filling in the circles with the names of all her children. There are a lot, I think to myself. When I take a closer look, I see the children's names are not placed in the circles closest to her. Instead, the circles with her children's names are positioned in a border around the edge of the page. Red flag, I think to myself. As she reels off their names, I begin to see a pattern. Jason, Freddie, Damien, Carrie, Annie, Norman . . .

Bella responds to the flicker of recognition across my face. Clearly, she's seen it before. 'Yes, they are all named after the villains in horror films. I used to be obsessed with those films,' she tells me.

Bella goes on to explain her overwhelming compulsion to have another child.

There is a pause. We look at each other.

'I'm in my mid-fifties now though, so it's a bit trickier,' she's forced to conclude.

Baby addicts

I have worked with patients who feel almost addicted to having children. One had eighteen. For Bella, it is about 'being needed'. She thrives on the sense that the baby is completely dependent on her. She also craves the comfort of constant physical contact that being with a young baby offers. As her children grow older, even by the time they become toddlers, they seek less physical proximity to her and gain autonomy over their movements, wanting less holding and cuddling. Which leaves Bella feeling rejected and abandoned. This in turn impacts the children. As they move away from their mum to explore their environment, they are either met with anger and rage or smothered and detained. This hostile control leads to frustration and fury in the thwarted child and later de-velops into either disengaged passivity or fierce independence and shutdown. Both responses from her children leave Bella feeling disconnected and shunned, and she frantically looks around for her next source of love.

I also wonder how a sibling group who have murderers and rapists as namesakes might be impacted moving forward. The theory of the looping effect suggests that, once we iden-tify with a label, we react to conform to that label. Someone labelled as 'angry' is more likely to present as angry; they shirk responsibility as they feel it is predetermined that they will behave angrily. I wonder if Bella has created a predisposition for violence in the children and, if so, has she done this willingly?

As I ponder the impact of a name, I think of a friend of a friend named Nigel, so called because his dad is Niall and his mum Gill. A blend of each parent, he seems to be doing OK. But I wonder if his brother Craig feels left out.

Any port in a storm

I call my dad. I confess to him that I am thinking about dating, as I long for a partnership again. He is silent for a while and then says, 'If you look for that right now, it will mean it's any port in a storm, Natalie.'

Later, I have to google this expression, having never come across it before. The definition reads, *a person will use anyone or anything for comfort when in a bad situation.*

I think about it and decide to get off the dating apps and order a pizza.

Transforming

Peggy and I start building a detailed trauma history, to try to make sense of her and how she is coping and functioning in the world. When patients discuss a traumatic event, they present as they were in the exact moment the trauma occurred. It's as though the tape of their lives has been rewound and they play out the events, responding as they did at the time. If you observe them, you see that their mannerisms change, they adjust the way they hold themselves, even their voice and its cadence can change. Now, Peggy's form changes in front of me. As she opens up, she shifts into a more infantile state, just like she did when we tried the birthday-party visualization. She looks up at me with her huge eyes, imploring me to take away the distress and fear the little girl is feeling. I hold her gaze and share my compassion towards the young Peggy, and then she starts speaking.

'You didn't help me, though. It's all for show, it's all a pretence. You just say things and you don't do them. That's why I don't want to tell you what I did.'

Peggy is now transfixed. She is not speaking to me; she is speaking to her mum.

This is something which, in therapist-speak, we call 'transference'. The patient transfers onto the therapist their feelings and responses for someone else. At some point, Peggy's mum has clearly let her down in her life and she is currently transferring all the rage and despair this has generated onto me. My job is to contain it.

Peggy continues, 'When people let me down, it makes me feel worthless, so I hurt myself sometimes.'

I talk with Peggy on her level, as though she is a little younger than her chronological age, as that is how she appears. In a digestible way, I explain some of the complexities and complicated emotions children endure when they are let down and not protected from abuse by those who should protect them. I point out to her that, in order to combat the helplessness, and the sense of chaos and the unpredictability of their environment, children will try to take ownership. This means they locate the blame within themselves. It makes them feel they have some control in an out-of-control situation. I have heard many heartbreaking statements from children, such as, 'Maybe if I am very quiet and don't make a mess, it won't happen today.' This self-directed blame can lead to self-punishment and self-hatred, acted out as self-harm. When I explain this, Peggy seems relieved to think that her actions have a survival component, that they make sense and she isn't alone or 'weird'. She asks if she can show me her scars.

I have worked with self-harm in adolescents, typically with acts deemed 'superficial cutting', which is all that's usually included on the referral. Peggy's referral read, *multiple episodes of self-harm including superficial and more significant*. This is vague, but I like to find the patient's perspective on their self-harm. I ready myself to respond before Peggy lifts one of her sleeves. For a split second, as I look at her arm, I assume she has a sleeve of tattoos. Then I take in the intricacy of silver and red lines with jagged edges and coarse seams. Her arms are a patchwork of pain.

Peggy nonchalantly explains that she poured petrol onto her arm and set it alight, resulting in multiple skin grafts and painful operations.

I try to manage my response, but a lump rises up in my throat and I am fighting tears. The injuries on her tiny body are profound. The shock registers across my face and Peggy sees it; she reads every minute reaction. She holds my gaze as if to ask, *Can you handle this?* I compose myself and look straight back at her.

After a while, she appears satisfied with me, and now the look in her eyes says, *I am glad you can deal with this.*

Out of my depth

On my way home, unable to shake her injuries from my mind, I feel nervous for her safety. I am so struck by her and sense a connection between us, or at least an initial bond from me to her. I feel maternal and nurturing towards her, despite not actually being old enough to be her mum. My countertransference is a response to her transference. She has cast me in the role of mum and I so desperately want to fulfil it in a reparative way, but I can't help but feel anxious and out of my depth. I wonder what a more experienced professional would do to help Peggy. Maybe psychiatry would be better equipped? The inferiority complex kicks in again. I settle my nerves by reminding myself I can ask Dr Lane.

Out the window

Before I have the chance to call Dr Lane to talk about my inadequacies, and as though someone has heard my wish to watch a much better qualified psychiatrist in full flow, I am asked to go around to A & E to support with a 136. A 136 is part of the Mental Health Act and kicks in if the police are called out to an event in the community and they believe someone is a risk to themselves or others due to a mental-health difficulty. They have the power to take the person to the hospital for a mental-health assessment. A & E staff don't always enjoy having someone distressed, impulsive and potentially chaotic in a packed waiting room full of injured people and children. A lack of staffing usually means such individuals are left for long stretches of time, which distresses them further and can lead to agitation, a neighbour of anger and aggression. I am asked to stand in until the psychiatrist arrives.

I meet the 136, Delilah, in a side room in A & E. It's a stark, clinical room on the ground floor, just off the main waiting room, with a view of the small garden, which is designed to be calming. Delilah is fidgeting and clearly frightened. She has a panicked look in her eyes and is rambling nonsensically. I make her jump as the door snaps shut behind me and she instinctively lunges towards me, flailing her arms. I am startled by her, but can see she has no clear plan to harm me. I notice that she is staring at my hands, so I immediately show her they are empty, holding them out in front of me. I reassure her that I am not a doctor and that I am not here to do anything other than have a chat.

Hospitals scare a lot of people and, even when someone is confused or experiencing delirium, they fear that anyone entering the room might do something physical to them, most likely something painful. The word 'chat' usually calms people down. Delilah settles a little as I start to make comments about things around the room, my intention being to ground her in the here and now. I mention the breeze from the window, the yellow of the lights and the light blue paint on the walls. I ask her what colour she would choose for her mood right now.

She thinks for a minute and says, 'Red – all the voices are telling me different things—' But, before she can finish, a psychiatrist enters.

He crosses the room, revealing a clipboard in his hands. Delilah is alarmed, appears agitated, then enraged. She makes a shrill noise and leaps towards both of us. I stand stock still and try to gain eye contact with her, holding out my empty hands. *Look*, I'm saying, *I'm harmless.* I look for support from the psychiatrist, but he is silently slipping out of the window behind us, and Delilah and I watch as he jogs off into the garden.

The absurdity of this breaks the tension. Delilah either finds it ridiculous or feels less threatened, so she calms down. My inferiority complex and hero worship of psychiatrists is further shaken.

As I leave Delilah in the hands of a more senior and robust psychiatrist, I think about Peggy. I have seen the eye rolls of colleagues when self-harm comes up in our coffee meetings and the general idea of 'attention seeking' being passed around. I know busy and understaffed A & E workers often respond in the same way to self-harm, with frustration. I wonder if she has ever wilfully revealed her scars to anyone else before. I feel honoured to have her trust.

Trying to make sense of Peggy, I think about the self-harm feedback loop. Someone with unstable emotions feels compelled to seek connection with another person but lacks a strategy to do this. They soon learn that doing something disastrous to themselves can be a 'quick fix'. With a self-destructive act, they receive a short-lived or pseudo-connection with someone else: a loved one will have no choice but to show up for them when called and urged by an A & E nurse to attend. Failing this, an A & E nurse or some other caring professional represents a caring connection, albeit transiently. This gives the behaviour a function, makes it more likely to be repeated. It is not lost on me that I engaged in just such a cycle myself when I briefly became addicted to the sexual-health clinic. Maybe it was the genuine connection that kept me returning.

I wonder who Peggy hoped would show up for her when she lit the match that set her petrol-drenched arm alight. I wonder if, when they got there, they responded with eye rolls and wrote *Attention seeking?* on her notes. A supervising psychologist of mine, from my days on the psych ward, once said something I have carried with me ever since: 'If someone needs attention that badly, for God's sake give it to them.'

A desire to do harm

Richard has been struggling with a break-up. His beautiful girlfriend left him abruptly and blocked all contact. He muses about being in an accident. 'Nothing too serious,' he says, 'just a broken leg or something. Then she would *have* to respond. Maybe she would look after me and learn to love me again.'

I hear this sort of fantasy in the therapy room more than once. The difference between these inpatients and Peggy is that they don't act on it whereas Peggy does. Our fantasies are not our actions, and we are not our fantasies – something I say often to my patients, and it is usually met with an outbreath of relief.

I try to imagine the huge surge of adrenaline that would course through someone's body as they readied themselves to light a match that would set their skin aflame. The adrenaline and endorphin release associated with self-harm deflects a person's focus away from their psychological pain and reduces the tension. This positively reinforces the self-harm act, making it addictive, which is wildly unhelpful. In this dangerous loop, harm leads to distress and shame. Then harm is used to cope with and lessen this feeling, leading to more distress and shame, and so on. But here's the thing: this cycle is not so unlike social drinking.

Many of us, at some point in our lives, have drunk too much, lost control, lost our inhibitions, and have proceeded to do something out of character. In the morning, we feel shame and self-consciousness. Hangover symptoms often mimic anxiety and so we make up a story that fits with the sensations and feelings we are experiencing. The racing heart and internal shakiness (caused by dehydration) lead to an internal monologue that goes something like this: 'If I feel this anxious there *must* be something to be anxious about. Maybe I just don't remember it.' The paranoia makes us assume the fears are the absolute truth, and so we begin to rigidly believe the story we tell ourselves: 'They were all talking about me after I left . . . I never shut up. I was talking too much . . . I was flirting too obviously with his wife . . . Everyone thought I looked too old for that dress . . . She heard me gossiping about her at the bar.'

The brain creates a narrative that matches the feeling state. Sometimes an antidote to this shameful feeling is the 'hair of the dog', which can again lead to overindulgence, and again lead to loss of inhibition, thus creating the vicious cycle. Thought of this way, excessive social drinking could be framed as a form of harm to the self that applies to many of us.

I approach the end of my commute and blast my music to try to change my focus and shift my identity from psychologist mode back to self mode. It's an essential piece of self-care that I still practise diligently. With a little mindfulness, my thoughts become egocentric and I notice the speed with which

I'm able to shift identity and mood. I think of how Peggy switched so quickly from fragility to anger. I have certainly felt up and down in the last months. Would that be deemed instability? Peggy's fear of being abandoned again, just as her mum abandoned her . . . isn't that still my fear, after Steve's abandonment of me? I wonder how many of the BPD features needed to gain a diagnosis I can relate to – we can all relate to. Do two recent break-ups and one *almost* breakdown count as 'instability in interpersonal relationships'? Do I have an 'unstable sense of self'? Hmmm. I did lose my sense of self to Steve and then enmesh my identity and self-concept with Max . . .

Self-diagnosis

'I think I have borderline personality disorder!' I almost shout as soon as I set eyes on Dr Lane.

Usually, we start our sessions with a gentle check-in. How is your caseload? What is your internal weather like today – cloudy with sunny breaks?

Dr Lane looks at me, gently searching my face, and this pause is killing me. She reaches for a biscuit – I have shoved some Bourbons onto a plate in a nod to sophistication – takes a bite and chews thoughtfully.

'Hmmm,' she says. 'I think maybe sub-clinically.' Sub-clinically means something is present, but it is at a level that isn't cause for too much concern.

What?

Dr Lane says a lot of other things that afternoon about syncing our diaries, sharing essential documents and printing off relevant psychometric tests – yadda, yadda, yadda – but I hear little more than 'maybe sub-clinically'. That's not a *no*.

The rest of the day, I overanalyse everything I do with a heightened sense of self-consciousness in all of my encounters. Where do I usually put my hands when I speak? Am I shouting? How long is too long to hold eye contact with someone?

Kelli challenges my diagnosis

Kelli is my next target for a confirmation or otherwise. My head has hardly hit the back of the chaise longue when I splutter, 'Kelli, I am going to need help with *all* of my disorders.' By this point, I have also self-diagnosed adjustment disorder, which is a disproportionate or excessive response to a change in life or circumstance. 'I simply can't adjust to the fact that I have borderline personality disorder,' I tell her.

Kelli slows me right down.

Taking one thought at a time, she gently challenges me, citing evidence to the contrary: my long-standing friendships, my support network and my introspection. 'One very real abandonment and a temporary shake-up of your self-concept does not a disorder make,' she reminds me, and my self-diagnosis starts to seem less likely.

I'm surprised how much it hurts to be reminded that my abandonment by Steve was actually very real indeed, not a symptom. The shame still stings. With mixed emotions, I try to focus on the positive news that I probably don't have a disorder and I leave Kelli's room fifty minutes later, label free.

One of my favourite things about therapy with Kelli is the

mental processing that takes place between our meetings, especially after a particularly powerful session. Sometimes, I have vivid symbolic dreams and wake up in the middle of the night and scribble my revelations in the dream diary I keep by the side of my bed. I read it in the morning with mixed results. Sometimes my notes say things like, *Remember to forgive yourself for being bewitched by the concept of Steve.* But sometimes they say things like, *Hello sir, I would like to return this microwave.*

One night, my dream-diary insight reads, *How do people bond to me? I only focus on how I can bond to them. I need to stop focusing on the narrative I create around them or the status I associate with them and their potential.* I acknowledge that aspiring to be the 'doctor's wife' isn't genuine, fulfilling or safe. This is a major part of the loss process: *What do I hope to be now?*

When I share this insight with Kelli, she seems excited. 'Yes! Access your true instincts, stop intellectualizing and tell me how other people make you *feel*. Stay with the emotion and stay in the moment!' Then, in a monotone voice, she says, 'Ah, we have come to time.' And, just like that, the energizing moment of breakthrough is well and truly over.

The rescuer

A doctor at the hospital sends me a request to see a colleague of theirs, for some support. I agree because I feel obligated and don't want to burn my bridges at work, but, for numerous reasons, it's an appointment that makes me nervous. The colleague, Matthew, is a psychiatrist. He is about to have a career break as he feels overwhelmed in his personal life. He would like therapy alongside his antidepressants. He is my senior. This man is clearly more experienced and educated than I am. Why would he come to me?

My imposter syndrome is taking up space in the room as Matthew arrives for his first session. I feel like a Ryanair flight attendant teaching an RAF fighter pilot how to land a plane on the sea. I am straining under the pressure to be 'the strongest person in the room'. As he sits down, I blush, not only because of the imposter syndrome, but as a result of his powerful charm. His warm yet penetrating look feels somehow familiar.

As he begins to open up, we delve into his romantic life and arrive at the shared conclusion that he is trapped in a repetitive pattern of taking on a rescuer role. Matthew merges his work and private self, ending up prioritizing the emotional needs of his partner over his own, just as he would in his consulting room. With each partner, he has helped them navigate their struggles and ultimately flourish, but he feels resentment as the relationship progresses and the resentment morphs into rage. He ends up feeling unseen and unheard in his relationship and ultimately reaches exhaustion, so he retracts and ghosts his partner. He shares with me that he is seeking a space and therapeutic relationship where his needs can be expressed and met too. As I offer interpretations, Matthew and I keep drawing the same conclusions and sharing insights, and find we say many words at the same time, our eyes meeting as we do. This could simply be parallel processing due to similarities in training, but I can't help being enticed by it.

We follow up by texting each other under the thinly veiled

pretence of arranging 'peer supervision meetings' instead of meeting for therapy sessions. Then we simply start texting. Nothing untoward is said, but it feels illicit.

When I meet with Kelli and tell her all about Matthew, half expecting praise for connecting with someone who has the capacity and desire to bond, I hear a charge of fury in her voice. I try to picture her expression as I lie facing away from her on the chaise longue.

'Why do you put yourself in an inferior position in this interaction?' she asks.

We revisit my delusions about doctors, those feelings aroused by Steve and clearly still residing in my psyche.

As we delve further, Kelli explodes: 'He walked you down the garden path of his seduction techniques and how he manipulates women by presenting himself as the knight-in-shining-armour archetype. He told you he drops women when his needs "aren't met" and you still followed him, like a fucking moth to a flame.'

I have never heard Kelli swear like this before and it takes me a second to respond. We decide we have more work to do on my pathological accommodation of men to whom I feel inferior. But Kelli isn't blaming me. Her fury is directed at Matthew and his abuse of power. I feel deeply cared for by Kelli today, which assuages my shame a little. As I leave her office, she says, 'Bye, love.' I cling to this and feel its warmth.

I draw a boundary with Matthew, telling him I can no longer engage with him. I get no reply. I then see him in the canteen later on, using his strategies on one of the junior doctors.

Shame & secrets

The need to connect

I receive a call asking if I can come and see Peggy on the children's inpatient ward. I feel a rush of nervous adrenaline. When I arrive, a harried ward nurse raises her eyebrows at me over her pad of notes and nods curtly towards the door on the left.

Peggy is in a shared room with other patients, some very little and one just a baby. The room is hot and lit with a sickly yellow light. I pause in the doorway; it feels intrusive to enter. I ask the nurse if I can see Peggy somewhere private and, after a great deal of fuss, we are given the playroom. This time, I position myself well away from the colourful balls, drawing Peggy towards me. She sits down, devoid of emotion.

'So, I swallowed five razor blades, didn't I.'

She tells me the doctors have decided to 'let them pass'. I hide my flinch. Peggy gazes back with calm indifference as I sit looking at her, trying to maintain a neutral expression. It feels like waiting for a bomb to go off.

Animal instincts

Leaving the ward, a nurse grabs me, pleading with me to give some advice on another teen, Tracy, who is waiting to see the psychiatrist.

'We have never dealt with anything like this before,' the nurse says. 'We are trying to find a way to shut off the water in just her room.'

I stand in silent confusion as my mind begins to search for answers. It could be polydipsia, a condition that creates excessive thirst. I have seen a patient so affected by this that they drank water out of the toilet. Or it could be that Tracy attempted to flood the hospital, also something I have seen when a patient flooded the ward, tripping the electricity and causing chaos.

The nurse breaks my thought process. 'She thinks she's a dolphin . . .'

We stare at each other for a moment.

Zoanthropy is a rare psychiatric disorder involving a delusion that the impacted person has transformed into, or is indeed, an animal. In this case, a dolphin. As I speak with Tracy, it turns out she doesn't believe she *is* a dolphin, but during an episode of extreme dissociation she lost her sense of self, became confused and behaved *like* a dolphin. She turned on all the taps and thrashed around on the floor, resulting in a great deal of ridicule from the other young people on the ward.

I wonder aloud if there is any significance to the dolphin itself.

As we unpack Tracy's difficult childhood, characterized by neglect and abuse, she shares that her mum had worn a dolphin necklace which dangled near Tracy's face when she was scolded and smacked. I offer that the image of a dolphin might intrude when Tracy is feeling distressed and this might be why it is a dolphin her mind selects. I say, 'This makes perfect sense to me,' to try to dislodge her shame. Tracy seems to connect to this, and I'm encouraged.

We then challenge some of the names she was called by the other young people on the ward during the episode – such as 'freak' and 'weirdo' – and, as a counterbalance, I highlight her bravery and resilience during difficult times in her past. Before leaving the ward, I am clear with the nurses not to collude in any communications or questioning that Tracy might experience as shaming. As I stand with them, a psychiatrist arrives and I see the words *fish girl* scrawled on a Post-it note on his file.

Risk assessment

Peggy continues to have a huge impact on me. I feel an extreme obligation to help her, to make her stop using her body as a conduit for emotional pain. But she continues to swallow other items: glass, batteries, screws – anything that might harm her. I learn to carry out risk assessments on rooms before I take her into them, not realizing at first that even something as innocent as a rubber can be used to significantly burn the skin. I start to see things differently during my work with her, assessing everyday items for their potential risk – phone chargers, remote controls, bras, laces, any items she could tie around her throat to ligature or cut or damage herself. Outside of the therapy space, I pick things up and run through the possibilities of risk. I hold up a pint of milk in Tesco and ask Alex, 'Do you think you could feasibly drown yourself with this? Could you kill yourself by speedily engulfing something?' Another thought crosses my mind. 'Could you smother yourself with a cat, do you think?'

Raw emotions

I work with other patients who have personality disorders, but none strike me as much as Peggy. Maybe, in part, I like the borderline presentations because they are underdogs. They confuse and baffle with their behaviour, leading most people to shy away from them or avoid them altogether. The name of the condition doesn't help, often causing confusion. Lay people tend to interpret it as *almost but not quite* having a personality disorder. Theorists say it is so called because it straddles the border of neurosis (which we all have at some point) and psychosis (which is a more difficult kettle of fish and often includes hallucinations and delusions). It has recently become known as the rather more descriptive 'emotionally unstable personality disorder'. There's no hiding from that label. There's no confusion around the term 'unstable'.

The thing is, we all feel emotionally unstable at times, or find it difficult to regulate ourselves. I am struggling to regulate and calm down my fears, to quieten my systems which are geared towards responding to threat; they're now always on high alert. I am trying to re-enter the dating world post break-ups (now plural), and this is scary for me. The dating game arouses core attachment injuries, it brings up our earliest fears and insecurities, times we didn't feel loved or protected, times we lacked connection, and we fear being treated that way again by a romantic partner. Sometimes we try to seduce a romantic partner into treating us badly, in the same ways we were treated as a child, so we are in control, we know what we are dealing with. The emotions are raw and dating can tap painfully into our vulnerabilities, bringing up all of our earlier painful relational experiences, those which have informed how we now connect to others and protect ourselves from possible rejection. We can't escape the pain of it.

Usually, when we experience something painful or intolerable, we want a way out, a way to end it however we can. If we burn ourselves on a fire, our instinct is to move away; we learn to avoid its danger. But if we have a bad experience trying to bond with another person, or we have a painful break-up or loss, we have a harder time distancing ourselves. We are still attachment beings; we are biologically built to connect to other humans, so we can't simply avoid and deny this need. Instead, we are hardwired to walk constantly towards our most feared risk – of being rejected, of being abandoned, being left. Our first experience of being left can inform how we cope and make sense of loss and rejection later on, including our first interaction with grief. Someone dying can be experienced as an abandonment.

I witness eight-year-old Calvin's response to his first loss. I take an afternoon off to attend a memorial service for his father, a colleague of mine who has recently passed away. Following the memorial, we all sit down to have rainbow cake, to mark a celebration of life. I notice Calvin run over to the cake and begin fisting large handfuls of it and flinging it up into the air. As his mum tries to wrestle a fistful of sponge from him, he announces loudly, 'I want Dad to taste some up in heaven – we are celebrating him, after all!' Fair point.

I find myself spending more and more time thinking about how walking towards the chip-pan fire of dating with a shaken or broken heart and a shattered belief in trust in some ways mirrors elements of Peggy's story, and this helps me to get closer to understanding her experience. She pops into my mind, too, when I see other patients and friends having their own crisis moments in the relational world. For Peggy, her emotions are raw in all forms of relationship, and so acute and intense that she experiences the sort of pain associated with crushing heartbreak and betrayal in response to seemingly innocuous acts. Someone forgetting her name or not returning her high-five gesture, someone not replying to her text for a few minutes or not acknowledging that she is next in the coffee-shop queue – all these are experienced as brutal rejections. They cause an excruciating feeling of being ignored and abandoned. I wonder how she possibly copes with this emotional rampage every day. She is much stronger than me, that much I know.

But I see in patients and friends that we all jump to conclusions as we attempt to mind-read the other people in our lives, amplifying innocuous acts into painful ones, especially when it comes to dating and social media. Those double blue ticks on WhatsApp, in particular, are not helpful windows into the thoughts and actions of others. Haven't we all spent countless hours agonizing after sending a message to someone new, who doesn't then reply? Speculation runs rife, the imagination goes into overdrive. We predict and distort wildly. We can hear this mental anguish everywhere.

'How many ticks does the message have? Has she *seen* it?'

'They don't have their read receipt on . . . red flag! Who are they hiding from?'

'No reply – well, when were they last active on Instagram? Cross-reference with different social platforms . . .'

'How long does it take to have a shower, would you say? Because it's been seventeen minutes!'

'Maybe I should call, or just go round. *What if he's in danger?*'

The response is so extreme because the stakes feel so high

when we fear being rejected. We then attach meaning to this. What does it say about me if I can be rejected? What is wrong with me?

Secrets and lies

We like to listen in on stories of rejection and betrayal, but they also maintain and perpetuate the fear that it *could* happen to us. Maybe the purpose of sharing these stories is to keep us alert, vigilant and aware, to help us avoid being a victim of the same relational crimes. I am always asked by friends for patient stories of deception that have blindsided the other partner, and of course I have some eye-poppers to roll out.

There is the patient whose partner went missing in the middle of the night, later explaining that she had driven herself to A & E with chest pains, which also accounted for the loss of her bra. A series of lengthy heart appointments followed, escalating into overnight hospital stays, all of which she felt more comfortable attending alone. Needless to say, it was more of a crotch appointment that a heart appointment.

Then there's the patient who concealed an affair for years by always returning home in the early hours holding a kebab, the prop indicating that a boys' night had simply got a little out of hand. Again. In reality, he had left the boys after one pint, making sure he had secured photographic proof for social media, so that he could enjoy an evening with his mistress, alibi firmly in place.

There's the patient who deceived her partner by secretly moving in with him. He believed she still had her own flat, but she had in fact given the flat up months before, instead renting a storage space which she had to sleep in every now and then when they spent a night apart.

Several patients have managed to maintain double lives, the anxiety of which seems unfathomable to me; the admin alone must be overwhelming – two phones, two diaries, two identities. A footballer managed some of the admin quite cleverly by buying each of his mistresses the same gifts – clothes and lingerie in the same colour and size, so he wouldn't get caught out when he said, 'Why don't you put on that purple thing I bought you?'

Such lies require an unshakable self-confidence.

Unhappy endings

Endings are acutely difficult for Peggy, and this extends to the end of our sessions. Her strategy is to make a 'doorknob disclosure', a huge and distressing revelation as we approach fifty minutes, the point at which I'm ready to wrap things up. Peggy can't see the clock, but she has an acute awareness of when an ending is approaching.

Today, at minute forty-nine, she says, 'Have I ever told you I was raped?'

It is hard to pack that away with, 'We have come to the end of our time,' so instead I say, 'I know ending the session feels hard and I want to hear you and support you in full at the next session, next week.'

She also panics about me coming to an end, quite literally. She worries that something will happen to me between now and our next session, that I might die, which, while bad for me, would really only mean that I have abandoned her – even though it's clearly beyond being anyone's fault, let alone mine. Although I reassure her that I will consistently show up for her, the reality is that I don't know whether one day something will happen to me between our sessions and I won't be able to contact her. How could I know?

Endings are universally difficult; this challenge isn't exclusive to Peggy. Endings in relationships can shake our foundations, making us question who we are without our ex, who we are outside of the role we played in the relationship, or who we are in terms of our value. There's a real sense of loneliness in all the spare time we now have in which to relate to ourselves – some of the parts of the self can feel unfamiliar or unfinished, especially the parts that were formed in combination with the person who has now evaporated. I usually address this with patients by asking them how they feel in their own company, and I have them practise being alone, to develop this relationship with the self, by sitting with the initial discomfort this can bring.

For me, the loss of the self and the feeling of being transformed into a weak and lonely figure against my will is unfamiliar and still makes me shudder when I think about it. Unfamiliar, and yet it's a transformation that is captured in many familiar stories and fairy tales. Unfortunately, according to these stories, often the only way to feel fully alive again is to connect with someone new or to reconcile with the lost love. Princesses such as Sleeping Beauty and Snow White are literally transformed into a frozen or deadened state, only finding relief and returning to their true selves, completely revived, when kissed by or connected to another person, usually an impossibly handsome prince. In this way, we are filled from an early age with the belief that we must be saved from pain by finding another. The idea that we don't fully exist if we're alone is reinforced in so many of our stories, and it's a dangerous message by which to live.

Being kissed by a handsome prince or princess would be an easy shortcut (if we overlook the problems of consent). Shortcuts are incredibly desirable because they offer immediate relief. Peggy's shortcut is self-harming, but we all use shortcuts to connect when we are in pain, albeit in less pathological ways.

My patient Clara awoke the man she desired with a clanging of her keys against his front door at 2 a.m. When he opened it, she claimed she thought it was her own front door and that she had mistaken his for hers, despite him living on the other side of town and her only having visited his house once before. This was a shortcut to connect at all costs, despite its irrational nature. In that moment, Clara felt compelled to be close to him.

Jamie, after several whiskies on the rocks, arrived at the front door of the girl he had secretly been admiring in the office for months. He claimed he was locked out and had nowhere else to go. He had his sleeping bag tied around his waist; there was nothing spontaneous about his appearance. When I ask Jamie about it later, he says it was a drunken attempt to be chivalrous, a way of suggesting that he wanted to stay over, but without assuming he would sleep in the same bed.

So urgent are these attempts to connect, they defy rationality. They illustrate the frantic and overwhelming nature of needing contact. Peggy's acute fragility and longing to connect through extreme acts and her vigilance to perceive abandonment is how she instinctively knows when the end of the session is drawing near. She will try her very best to avert it.

Even without a diagnosis of BPD, we are all capable of visiting this place of hypervigilance to endings when we're feeling vulnerable in our relationships. We can all be acutely aware of the other person pulling away, or of micro-rejections if, perhaps, they don't hold our hand or if they avoid intimacy. Several of my patients have believed their partner to be pulling away from them based on what I think are pretty innocuous acts, and have jumped in to cut the tie first, rather than risk being broken up with. The need to stay in control and ultimately keep themselves safe from rejection is strong. But this can be self-sabotaging if our instincts are wrong. When our instincts are right, there is no ignoring them.

Kelli gets bored

Kelli exhales noisily through pursed lips as I am talking in today's session. 'Natalie, this is really boring,' she tells me.

I am winded. A heavy silence hangs in the air for a while. I'm almost tearful as I digest her words, so desperate am I to strengthen my bond with Kelli and for her to like me. The relationship has come to represent a safe place for me, and she so often gives me what I need – validation and reassurance.

She goes on, saying she can barely listen to me as her mind is wandering. She points out that my speech is staccato, matter of fact, and she can't connect. I am, she tells me, 'shutting down'.

Kelli explains that I have split off from my vulnerable, injured self and adopted a steely air of confidence and unflappability in order to protect myself. I am, apparently, constantly being my 'work self', a.k.a. 'the strongest person in the room' and the 'blank canvas' that can't be read or penetrated, and therefore, surely, can't be hurt. Not only is this 'acutely boring' for my therapist, but she says it will also cut me off from others.

Kelli tells me that my homework is to reconnect with other people and take the risk as my full, authentic self. She ends the session by reading me a quote from Anaïs Nin: 'And the day came when the risk to remain tight in a bud was more painful than the risk it took to blossom.'

It's a profound thought. But I am not keen on the word 'tight'.

The good patient

Kelli has asked me to seek connection. This must be some sort of remedy, I realize, a better way of coping than shutting myself away and closing myself off to avoid rejection, something Kelli would call neurotic isolation. In times of uncertainty, it's common for us to treat our therapist as some sort of omnipotent guru or wise leader, the manager of our emotional world. It allows us to feel protected as we regress to a more helpless childlike state, looking up to them like a parent, hence me seeking approval and praise from Kelli at every opportunity. To get this from her, I need to focus on my own needs and what I can gain from connections with others.

The dating app I choose is new on the market. It notifies me when potential suitors physically cross my path, and, I imagine, also serves as a useful tool for stalkers and murderers. I choose it to take some of the heavy lifting out of the selection process because, at the end of a long day spent asking people about their lives, I don't always feel like sitting across from a stranger and asking them about their life. But I want to push on with this because now I am highly motivated to re-enter the dating pool – motivated mostly, I have to admit to myself, by a strong desire to be the 'good patient' for Kelli and complete my therapy homework of reconnecting with others.

Some of my patients who are serial daters tell me they are sick of the introductory routines dating requires, but are particularly tired of the same opening questions: What do you do? How long have you lived in London? Where is your family from? A regular patient, Gina, in an effort to make dates more interesting, resorts to borrowing questions from our therapy session: What colour would you use to describe your mood today? Which attachment style would you say you are? How do you resolve conflict? She finds this line of questioning speeds things up a bit, but the results are mixed. Some dates simply flee. Others break down in tears. The ones who stick around show some promise.

In the nineties, the psychologist Arthur Aron published a set of thirty-six questions developed to accelerate intimacy between strangers. Handy if you're into intensity, but the approach can result in love whiplash. The questions include: Do you have a secret hunch about how you will die? What roles do love and affection play in your life? What, if anything, is too serious to be joked about? I share the thirty-six questions with Gina during one of our sessions and immediately regret it. As her eyes widen with intrigue, I see her with a clipboard and a clicky pen on future dates.

My first match on the app seems promising. Johnny's profile

suggests he owns at least one good shirt, enjoys a drink and has travelled to two countries. After a brief, stilted chat on the app, we agree to meet the following night. He chooses a bar in Shoreditch. Good choice. As I sip my first drink and my nerves begin to dissipate, he asks me what I do for work.

I have deleted my profession from my dating profile to stop people inviting me to read their minds and forcing me to explain that therapy is not quite the same as telepathy.

As I tell Johnny what I do, he splutters with excitement, 'Oh, thank God! I have this thing going on and I really need to speak to someone about it.'

I look down into my drink. Just three sips in and here we go.

'I have this hernia in my groin and I have to have a procedure,' he tells me. 'They said one of the risks is impotency and I . . .'

His speech starts racing and I immediately recognize the signs of anxiety. I slow him down, the way Kelli slows me down when I race through all my fears. With an internal sigh, I pick one thing at a time and ask Johnny to stay with it, to help me understand it better. I slow down my own speech, so he might mirror it, and take longer, deeper breaths. I talk him down from the precipice carefully and I see him doing as I'm doing: he takes some deeper breaths, and the short, sharp staccato of his speech shifts to slower, more thoughtful sentences. He regains composure and, despite the mood of our date being irreparably broken, I am glad to see him settled.

Watching someone panic can be panic-inducing in itself. Our brains scan the environment around four to five times a second for cues or risks of threat and danger. So, sitting in front of a panicked person can alert our own fear systems and make us feel unnerved. Having calmed my own nervous system with my slower breaths, I can focus in on Johnny's story. But he seems self-conscious now and, despite my best efforts to reassure him, we decide to call it quits. Outside the bar, he thanks me emphatically and strolls off into the evening, visibly lighter.

On the bus home, I feel deflated, partly because of my failed attempt at re-entering the dating world, not having fallen instantly in love, but also because I feel sorry for men who don't have someone to talk to about these things. Johnny must have been holding on to that anxiety and tension for so long. It was just bubbling under the surface and, given half a chance, he couldn't help but spill it all out to a stranger. I reach for my phone in my bag and call Alex to tell her all about Johnny and how flat I feel. Good old Alex.

Blushing

I am still pondering men's emotional support systems when I meet Harry, a new patient. Harry is seventeen and is crippled by social anxiety. He blushes every time he tries to answer one of my questions. I keep the first session light, and offer my email address, suggesting that writing his answers down might be easier for him. A few days later, I receive an email with the title, *Something*. It's from Harry. He says that he wants to share *something* with me but can't find the words. He has nobody else to talk to. He leaves it at that. I am on red alert.

My own battle with blushing is also chronic. It comes in waves – sometimes I blush all the time, I feel the tight hot redness creep up my neck and into my face, but other times the curse seems to lift and I can get by without worrying about turning beetroot. I mention my blushing to one of my colleagues, hoping she will give me the 'magic pill', the answer to stop my blushing forever.

'I think it's quite narcissistic,' she says.

Not what I was expecting.

'Why would you think people are paying so much attention to you that they hold you in mind long enough to judge you?'

This feels like a slap in the face. I reassure myself that maybe it's a strategy, a tough-love approach.

Later, I call my brother – who's training to be a doctor – to get his take. Some part of me hopes he'll say there is an actual magic pill. There isn't. I share the advice given to me by my colleague. He thinks about it for a minute and then says, 'It's like how hypochondria is said to be narcissistic, all that pathological self-focus, so maybe there is something in it.' A pause. 'Oh, but I do have a solution for you,' he adds.

Thank God.

'Anytime you feel like you're going to blush, just put a motorcycle helmet on.'

I guess this is what brothers are for.

The box

As soon as I see Harry in the waiting room, I feel pure relief that he is back. I've decided that for the next few sessions we will play cards. While Harry is engaged in the game and distracted by the process of shuffling cards, he is able to talk more easily, and I can see him relax a little in my company. For now, though, he remains resistant to talking about the 'something'.

After two sessions of cards, I bring in a small cardboard box and place it between us. I tell Harry that the 'something' is in the box. We don't have to open the box to look at it, but we can talk about the box itself – how it makes him feel, how carrying it feels, and what it means for it to exist.

Harry says he feels preoccupied with the box at all times, that it is taking over his life and makes him feel 'terrorized'. The sheer weight of carrying whatever the box holds feels distressing and isolating, and he tells me he has considered taking his own life at times because he feels so alone and hopeless. I feel connected to Harry and sense a pang of pain in my chest, the heartbreak of someone so young being in so much turmoil.

The physical response we feel to a patient as therapists is usually a good indicator of the authenticity of their emotion. I have seen many young people who come in and say, 'I am just going to kiiiiiiiillll myself,' or, 'I so want to be dead right now,' and I feel nothing. In such dramatized cases, after checking and assessing the validity of the statements, I often find out later that what they really want is a note to get out of PE or more screen time at home, but they have learned that saying something threatening like this sends their mum into meltdown and she hands over control of the entire house and all the electronic devices. My gut reaction is becoming a good barometer. A psychiatrist, Dr Tony Angelo, once said that it is crucial to tune into your response to a patient, as it can tell you a great deal. Your primal response to a patient can tell you who they are. He explained that, in his experience, by far the best test for identifying a psychopath, beyond all the measures, interviews and tools, is whether they make the hairs stand up on the back of your neck when they enter the room.

Harry and I are developing a close therapeutic bond, but I find the sessions heartbreaking, not only for him but for all the boys out there who feel they have to carry their box of suffering alone, battling with it by themselves, sometimes to breaking point. Men need safe spaces and permission to off-load without fear of judgement, they need the ear of a friend, and I decide to take this thinking forth into my dating, offering compassion, without becoming their therapist – a delicate balance.

Peggy makes me doubt myself

In stark contrast to those seeking to conceal and bottle up their emotions, Peggy returns with her unbridled energy. I haven't seen her for a few weeks as she has been going to a weekly group-therapy session. The group is a dialectical behavioural therapy group (DBT), which is the gold stand-ard for BPD patients. We have been waiting for this group for months and I hope it has delivered. Thankfully, she tells me it has helped – hearing the struggles of her peers makes her feel less alone. Peggy has been able to share her insights and has learned strategies in the group, people have listened and taken notice, she feels empowered and uplifted. Feeling seen and heard is so important for her and I am pleased she has found her place in this group. But I cautiously remind Peggy that the group is her space, not just a space for her to rescue others. I draw the 'drama triangle' developed by Stephen Karpman, with *perpetrator*, *victim* and *rescuer* written at the three corners.

Peggy is familiar with this triangle from previous sessions. I remind her not to over-identify with the rescuer role and warn how seductive this DBT group might be in making her want to save everyone else, while marginalizing her own needs.

As Peggy and I talk this through, she is gentle, thoughtful and calm. I feel a shift in her, like she has matured somehow. She becomes more excitable as she tells me about her self-care routines and her new dance classes. I enjoy listening and seeing her so animated, I notice she isn't questioning herself as much or looking to me to check whether anecdotes are funny or interesting. She has coped without the one-to-one support for several weeks and seems to have found her groove. I consider saying this to her and adding 'excuse the pun', but I am very sure she will say I am cringe.

On the drive home, my self-doubt kicks in. Was Peggy masking her emotions or was this elation a sign of hypomania, characterized by periods of overactive and high-energy behaviour? I have seen inpatients on wards have bursts of seemingly positive energy – dancing, singing karaoke, jumping around. All the staff relax, assuming this means the patient is happy, but this can also be a warning sign for dysregulation, leading to huge discharges of aggression.

I manage to grab Dr Lane for a quick call between official supervision sessions to talk this over. 'You know your patient,' Dr Lane says. 'What does your gut tell you? Was she masking extreme anger at you being gone for a while? Is she capable of that? Was her speech pressured? Florid? Was there a chaotic charge in the room?' Dr Lane settles the fear centres of my brain. Peggy is nothing but authentic. She is doing well.

Just About Coping

Between two loaves

I meet Liam at a pub in Hackney. On arrival, he is annoyed that his phone has died, unable to shake off his frustration. When we sit down, he places the blank, black screen of his phone face-up between us, looking thoroughly irritated. We make small talk. I can never suss out a date as well as I can a patient when they enter the room; my own nerves seem to take over. Then he, inevitably, asks me what I do. As I begin to explain, as briefly as I can, he takes a moment and then picks up his phone. 'My friend just texted saying a house party has got out of hand at the flat and I need to go back right now,' he says.

I stare at the black phone screen, then at him. He stares back.

I am about four sips into my tepid Chardonnay – a measure of progress on the last date, at least.

After leaving the pub, I nip into the nearest Sainsbury's to grab some wine to try to salvage something of the night, ringing Alex for a chat about the lunacy of the dead-phone lie. I stop mid-sentence as I turn into one of the aisles and see that Liam is standing there, choosing between two loaves of bread.

'I guess bread will really help with the house-party situation,' I say as playfully as I can muster. He scuttles away.

Loneliness has power

An old patient, Joey, comes back. I want to revisit what we discussed before and why he might have interpreted my advice to access his anger as me wanting him to start hitting people again. It seems things are still not going well for him.

Since our last meeting, he has been arrested for housing a small marijuana farm in his loft and is waiting to go to trial for possession with intent to supply. He has also gained several wobbly and poorly constructed tattoos on his face and neck; he explains he needs to 'look the part' if he is going to go to prison, so he had his mate Brian pop them onto his face last week. Joey has gained a great deal of weight and, standing at over six foot, he is now an intimidating figure.

I ask him what brings him back to see me and he explains he is back because of loneliness. His girlfriend and son moved out of the family home following his arrest and currently aren't speaking to him. He feels his friends only want him for his supply and so, now that's gone, they have abandoned him too. Joey feels he has become 'pointless'. We talk about loneliness and what it means.

Loneliness is different from depression, although they are often bedfellows. Depression is a void, an absence, it keeps us stuck, whereas loneliness contains longing – a longing for another. Loneliness knows that a connection to another is the cure and so it holds the hope and belief that we can recover and find relief from it. Depression is far more hopeless. Loneliness can be mobilizing, I offer to Joey; it is seeking and can drive us forward. This doesn't mean it's easy, I add; loneliness can distort our cognitions in just the same way that depression can. Depression puts a negative lens over what we see and how we interpret the world. Loneliness applies Vaseline to the lens, blurring our vision and telling us things like, *Maybe you are unworthy of connection*, or, *You are incapable of finding connection*. I check Joey's understanding to make sure he doesn't think I've asked him to smear his eyes with Vaseline.

Joey is tearful and says he truly is seeking someone and doesn't want to face this alone.

Together, we construct a text to his girlfriend, carefully including his needs so he doesn't feel he is being used. The relationship has to be a two-way street. We begin every sentence with, *What I would wish for us at this time is . . .* We go on to think about where Joey currently feels a sense of connection in any part of his life, to find anything at all we might be able to build upon, something that is achievable right now. Joey talks about his love for animals and how the effortlessness of an interaction with an animal and their unconditional love eases his anxieties. He seems a bit embarrassed by this admission, this evident softness, so I normalize his feelings and tell him about the research showing the merits of equine therapy, which involves spending time with horses. It has been shown to reduce anxiety and depression, and it also develops empathy skills. Joey seems pleased with this idea and leaves the session slightly brighter.

Later on, I sharpen my elbows and manage to get myself one of the fought-over hot desks, to read my emails. When I open my inbox, I find an email from 'kangaroo69'. There's no text, but attached is a picture of a large, tattooed man, his inked face beaming from ear to ear. He is surrounded by a dozen or so fluffy cats, some wearing pink body warmers, with a sign above them saying *Cat Café*. I never gave Joey my email address, but I overlook this boundary-crossing. His email has made my day.

Shame & secrets

Say what you see

Gina comes in for another session and, now that I am acutely aware of the terrors of the dating world, I feel a renewed bond with her. Gina is vivacious, successful and beautiful, and I am struck by this each time I meet her. She thinks I am lying when I tell her it's likely a lot of men find her intimidating, but I am sure they do – with or without the piercing questions and the clipboard. This week, however, her spark seems dampened. She appears troubled, self-conscious, unsure.

Sometimes, when I feel a bit stuck with a patient, I will examine how they look, how they are holding themselves, their appearance. This is what they are portraying to the world. It is telling some of their story. I find reflecting this back to them can be powerful.

'You look a little down today, Gina,' I say. 'Your shoulders are hunched and I can hear a wobble of uncertainty in your voice.'

She is immediately tearful.

I decide to delve a little deeper. Gina and I usually talk about the perils of dating, but I am sure this is a defence against examining her deeper, core pain. We have already discussed Gina's acute sense of being overlooked by her mum; as one of six children it was difficult to get a look-in and so her childhood was quite insular, sprinkled with the occasional bonding moment. Now, I ask Gina about her early experiences, her earliest memories and her formative years, and she tells me how her mum lacked maternal warmth when Gina was very young, possibly due to post-natal depression. She did her best, but, as her emotions were numb, she focused on the practical, meeting all of Gina's basic physical needs, making sure she dressed well, was always clean, and she made healthy meals from scratch.

Gina says, 'I know my mum loved me . . .' She trails off.

I reflect back to her, 'She loved you.'

After a silence, I ask, 'Did she enjoy you?'

After a further silence, I add, 'From what I have heard, I think she did.'

Gina retracts her body in the chair, moving away from me, a flash of anger passing across her face. It's a rupture in our relationship and I don't know where it has suddenly come from. I do my best to repair it, using all of my tools: sharing what I feel is happening between us, sharing my sadness at causing distress, asking her to check in with her bodily sensations to ground her.

Eventually, we get to the bottom of it. It turns out I should have been as careful with Gina as I have been with Joey when checking understanding. It seems the words 'enjoy' and 'endure' sound very much alike in my accent.

Once we find our feet again and share a laugh, Gina wants to discuss her relational torment in the dating pool. It's easy to empathize.

'Remember the guy who looked much older in real life than in his pictures, so we nicknamed him Fossil?' she asks me.

Gina always gives her dates nicknames, which usually amuses us both, but making them anonymous and poking a little fun at them may also be a defence against getting too close.

Gina explains that she and Fossil had been seeing each other for a few weeks and then he cancelled a couple of dates in succession. She began to feel angry, and the final straw came when he cancelled again only two hours before they had agreed to meet for dinner. Gina was ready to give Fossil a dressing-down when he phoned her, rather than texting. On the phone he sounded distraught, saying that his ex-girlfriend had taken her own life and he had only just found out and wasn't in any fit state to be able to make dinner. Gina felt teary herself, listening to him. She offered her emotional support and sent a takeaway over to his flat, to make sure he ate. She reached out to her friends on a group chat, all women around the same age as the young woman who had passed away. She shared the story with them and expressed her love for them – the emotion of the moment making her feel so grateful for the friendship in her life.

At this point, I am about to offer Gina some support around suicide and pain, but the story isn't over.

Hours later, Gina received a series of photographs taken by one of her friends. It was Fossil on a train, graphically kissing a woman who looked remarkably like the ex-girlfriend – who was clearly very much alive.

Gina laughed it off but was shocked and troubled that someone would lie about something so awful and, when she messaged Fossil to express this, he blocked her.

Gina and I think about deceit and the levels of malevolence some people will go to in order to avoid conflict and taking responsibility. My mind drifts to Steve, and also to Liam-of-the-dead-phone. We mirror each other in our sadness as we leave the session.

The strongest person in the room

I share my despondence with Dr Lane during a supervision session. I know discussion with her will cheer me up and that I'll gain some meaningful insight from our conversation. Dr Lane always offers a safe space for me. She is warm and always gentle, although sometimes she looks a little wistful and confused, as though she is processing things constantly as we talk.

Dr Lane empathizes with me – she says it is no wonder I feel flattened by Gina's last session; there are parallels between us. We are both at the same developmental stage, in our late twenties, seeking an authentic connection with another. She reminds me that we can be traumatized by our patients' experiences and we can mirror the fear they show us; it's sometimes called vicarious trauma. This is, in part, the fault of our mirror neurons – the neurons that fire when we see an action performed in front of us, in the same way that they fire if we complete the action ourselves. If we see someone in pain, our nervous system responds as if we are in similar pain. Gina is untrusting and fearful, she views the world as threatening, always thinking that others may take advantage of her or deceive her. I am also experiencing this fear.

Taking things back to a neurobiological level can be a comfort, as it removes blame and intention, and helps patients to understand their responses at a primitive level, which they cannot control.

'Take deception as an example,' Dr Lane says. 'It is innate, primate, inbuilt – even animals have it.'

Dr Lane tells me about trickster crows that have been

found to hide food by burying it in the ground, the hiding places known as caches. But if the crows are being watched by another crow, they will complete 'fake hides' to trick the other crow. Deception is a survival mechanism. It's complex and multifaceted. She's keen for me to reframe it. It's often a sign of vulnerability, she says, the concealment of a hidden part of the self, our shadow. We deceive ourselves when we enter denial. It's a primitive defence and we all do it from time to time.

We continue to explore brain functioning and to think about feelings and actions as survival strategies, and I thank Dr Lane for her thoughts, which are helpful to my understanding of deceit. 'But I am still feeling stuck with Gina's sense of hopelessness,' I say, 'which seems to have engulfed her.'

Dr Lane doesn't miss a beat. 'Hopelessness,' she tells me, 'is an important psychological concept. Those high in hopelessness tend to have a negative view of the self and their future, believing the future is bleak or uncertain and that they have little control over it. Feeling hopeless is highly correlated with suicidal thoughts and self-harm.'

I don't feel Gina is a risk for self-harm, but wonder aloud as to whether I should measure Gina's hopelessness using the Beck Hopelessness Scale at the next session. This measure looks at patients' beliefs about their future and gives an insight into their level or lack of hope. Patients are asked to answer *true* or *false* to a list of statements, including: 'All I can see ahead of me is unpleasantness rather than pleasantness'; 'I don't expect to get what I really want'; 'When I look ahead to the future, I expect I will be happier than I am now.'

It makes intuitive sense that hopelessness about the future

is linked to feeling numb, existing with a lack of meaning and imagination. It is clear why a loss of hope might make a way out seem seductive, a way to make the void end or stop. I'm still thinking aloud, but Dr Lane is deep in her own thoughts, staring down at her cup of hot tea and her bursting Filofax. I wait.

'You know, I sometimes wonder if thoughts about suicide are just a problem-solving exercise. After all, it is one of the options, if you were to write an exhaustive list of how to cope with suffering,' she says. 'It *is* an option. It is a way out.'

Shake up

I leave the session with Dr Lane feeling a strange disconnect between us; something about her last thoughts unsettles me, but I suppose thinking about suicidal ideation would always have that impact. Even so, there seemed to be a heaviness between us today, something unsaid – maybe that's why we couldn't connect.

I need some form of connection and I don't fancy the cat cafe, so, in a bid to shift strategies, I stop swiping on the apps and spend the night with Ashley, an old friend from Manchester. We have shared a mutual attraction that has bubbled on gently for many years. His company feels easy and familiar, and he has recently moved to a flat in south London.

In the morning, he slopes off to get a glass of water and, as I lie in bed, I start the classic post-coital consideration. He's a good guy, I reason, maybe it could be more than just a physical thing . . . This kind of thinking is the result of a spike in oxytocin, also known as the love hormone, released after physical intimacy. I'm flooded with it, and all the maybes and hopes and dreams that the hormone spreads. Then I walk into the kitchen, ready to embrace him, and find him aggressively trying to butter a slice of toast with a large wooden spoon – and, of course, butchering it.

'Soz, Nat,' he says. 'I don't have any stuff yet.'

He has lived here for over a month.

The oxytocin quickly drains away.

As I travel across London to get home, I am just about ready to throw in the towel on dating when my phone lights up with a message. It's Raff, an old dating match.

Sorry for the late reply, mad busy with work. Fancy a drink sometime?

I ignore it and go off in search of caffeine, but I find I can't ignore it for long. I click the message and have another look at his profile. Raff is handsome, works as a data analyst in the City and is Italian. The voice note confirming his sexy Italian accent convinces me to go on the date.

The reveal

Harry comes back to see me and, today, he asks if we can play cards again, because he thinks he might be able to open the box. As we begin to play, instead of asking him questions, I let him lead. He starts talking and I listen and carry on with the game.

He explains that, on Halloween, a few years ago, he went out dressed as a dinosaur. It was an intricate costume with individual sequins and a silk lining, which his mum had spent hours creating. Harry loved the feel of wearing the costume.

With it on, he didn't feel as socially anxious as he usually did. In fact, he loved the attention and the comments he received.

As I put a card down between us, I say with a gentle smile, 'I can really hear the thrill for you, and it must have been such a relief not to feel self-conscious.'

Encouraged, Harry continues: 'That's it: I got *more* attention, but I felt *less* self-conscious.'

Harry wanted to feel that way again. Initially, he thought it might have been a sensory response, the feel of the silk against his skin, so he began looking for items in his mum's and sister's wardrobes that were made of silk or had soft fabrics. But Harry soon realized that the thrill was more than the feeling of silk. Soon, he began dressing in his sister's clothes every night after school. Then he started to accompany her on shopping trips to try to encourage her to buy certain items he liked, but his sister was not as adventurous as him, and he felt censored.

I reflect that this must have felt extremely frustrating, which Harry affirms, saying he feels more himself wearing feminine items. I suggest this has become his sanctuary, where he feels congruent with the self and feels respite from anxiety, and Harry seems to respond well to this positive framing. He shares with me the fears he has had that I would think him 'odd or weird' for this behaviour, but I let him know that I actually feel very privileged that he is able to open the box with me.

'How do you feel about me now?' he asks.

'I feel exactly the same about you,' I say with a smile, 'only now I also think you are courageous for sharing, and I'm sad you felt you had to conceal this until now.'

My aim is to disempower Harry's feelings of shame, the 'soul-eating emotion', as Jung put it.

Jung's words are hanging in my mind as I leave the session. Shame sits next to guilt, but shame is cast upon us by another, or others, in a real or imagined sense. Harry has become pre-occupied with imagined shame: *What would my dad think of me if he knew I was doing this? Will I be disowned or rejected?* Many of us are tortured by imagined shame. We attempt to mind-read and predict the reactions of others. If this shame is not reality-tested, by bringing it out into the open in a safe rela-tionship, as Harry has done with me, it can lead to disastrous consequences. I dread to think what that might have been for Harry. Simply holding something as a secret inherently attaches shame to it. Shame can create a dangerous internal monologue: *I have done something bad . . . I am bad, I am not deserving, I am not worthwhile.* This can lead to a very dark internal place. It's why shame is highly associated with depres-sion, rage, eating disorders and suicide.

It's why those in my line of work are in such demand.

FOUR

Trying to connect

Dating high

Raff books a very swanky bar for our first meeting, which automatically makes me nervous.

I'm here, he texts.

The place is empty apart from one man standing at the bar, and he doesn't look much like Raff's profile picture. Still, he wouldn't be the first man to post a profile picture that bears little resemblance to the reality, so we start chatting and I notice he is extremely familiar with the barman, even knows his name. Then, after a few minutes, another man comes over to us.

'Not interrupting, am I?' he asks.

It is a man who looks a lot more like Raff.

'Oh my God, I thought you were my date,' I say to the man I've been chatting with, who I now see quite clearly works here.

I am flustered and red and I can't imagine what Raff has made of my mistake, but he puts me at ease. We chat all night, and our conversation is comfortable and full of energy

143

and variety. When I tell him what I do for a living, he doesn't flinch – far from it. He's relaxed and interested. He says he currently sees a therapist and finds it really helpful.

Eventually, the barman-who-isn't-my-date kicks us out.

This time, I leave the date on a high.

Crumbling

Not all people are as receptive to starting and receiving therapy as Raff, and I tend to find that those who are most resistant are the ones who need it most. Princess Diana once addressed patients outside a psychiatric clinic and told them that they were 'unlikely to find much help from some psychotherapist or someone just reading a book' – maybe this was an indication of the maladaptive and self-destructive methods she adopted in response to her mental anguish. God forbid she seek advice from someone educated on the subject. Things have improved since then; the general trend seems to be that more people are open to therapy. Gina tells me that, although some of her friends remain resistant, they now have a weekly ritual where they meet as a group in the pub, share wine and crisps, and devour the content of our sessions, affectionately called 'Natz Chatz'.

The problem, as with any profession, is that therapists sit on a continuum from fantastic to downright crap. My friend Roger was brave enough to go and see a therapist on Harley Street when facing the grief of losing his father. She fell asleep mid-session. He left the cash on her desk – which is more than I would have done – and snuck out, vowing never to open up again. My friend Caroline was beginning to build a rapport with her therapist when the therapist asked, 'Can we talk about your belief that relationships don't tend to work out?' When Caroline replied, 'That's not a belief, it's a fact,' and reeled off some statistics, her therapist began to stammer, was close to tears and couldn't compose herself, leaving Caroline in the role of rescuer. Which, incidentally, was the reason she had sought therapy – to stop saving people.

As therapists, we are taught a model known as the person-centred approach, developed by Carl Rogers, in which we learn to listen empathically and reflect back what the client is saying. This can be incredibly powerful when in the right hands, but in the wrong hands it can be maddeningly frustrating. Another of my friends, Belle, saw a therapist who worked in this way, and reported back that the session was more like sitting in an echo chamber or spending time with a patronizing parrot, as all the therapist did was reflect back, verbatim.

I understand how these experiences can make people feel resistant, especially when compounded by the fear that things might have to feel a lot worse before they feel better, and opening up that internal can of worms might be overwhelming.

I encounter one such resistant patient in clinic when Rosa arrives seeking support for her 'out of control brood'. I can hear a number of children causing chaos in the waiting room as she flings open the door to Kiwi, displaying an expression like a bulldog chewing a wasp, her mouth screwed up tightly into an angry twist.

When she takes me in, she is incandescent with rage. 'How old are you?!' she bellows, with the door still open.

I see one of the nurses stand up at the nursing station on

the other side of the room. She fixes her eyes on Kiwi and the back of Rosa's angry head. I am glad of this and feel immediately reassured. On a psych ward, if trouble's brewing, you pull an alarm – much like a rape alarm – attached to your belt, and a larger alarm is sounded throughout the ward and staff come running to your aid. Here, in the NHS hospital, I am left alone in a room the size of a store cupboard with patients who are unknown to me and could present any level of distress and pose considerable risk. I have to rely on the attention of the nurses at reception checking people in, weighing people, checking blood pressures, sending people off to different departments. They are so busy, they flit around all day. The problem is, some of the nurses don't have much time for me; they hold the view that my job is all mumbo jumbo, navel-gazing and ego-massaging. A waste of already stretched resources. It doesn't help that I am young, junior in my role and assumed to be fancy because I live in London. This opinion prevails despite my northern accent, the fact that I live above a chip shop and the untold number of biscuits I gift to the nurse station. Today, I am grateful that they are able to acknowledge when my physical safety might be at risk.

Rosa's rage grows. 'Do you even *have* children?' she shouts.

I answer gently that I don't, but that I don't need to be a parent to offer support. With this, she loses control completely, grabbing one of the plastic chairs from the edge of the waiting room and throwing it into Kiwi in my direction. Thankfully, as she does, a nurse appears behind her and says she is calling security. Rosa appears startled by her own action. I talk the nurse down, with genuine appreciation, quietly pick up the chair and offer Rosa a seat. We begin to talk.

I choose my words carefully. 'I see in your face that you are a bit shocked by your behaviour,' I say. 'I imagine you are under a great deal of stress. I want to try to help, not make things worse.'

Rosa apologizes and starts to reel off the stress she is under. She has five children, no help. One of the children is having chemotherapy and has a rigorous treatment schedule, while the others are so anxious and terrified about their sibling's illness, they don't sleep.

I feel overwhelmed listening to her; I can't even begin to imagine the level of pressure Rosa is under. I offer that she must feel completely overcome and sometimes it must feel an impossible task.

Rosa replies that some days she wishes she could walk out the door and not look back; she seems comforted when I don't recoil or judge her for this.

'Most people would crumble under this stress,' I say, and she breaks down into tears. I listen to her through the sobs and snot and offer her time and space. All the while, the children play on the floor outside Kiwi, the door untypically left open – partly to supervise them and partly for me to have an escape route should Rosa explode again.

When they leave, I thank the nurse for her help and nip to the shop to buy her a big box of Maltesers. I decide to tackle the safety-versus-dislike-of-me issue with the nurse who seems to have the most contempt for me.

'Listen,' I say. 'I know you really don't like me, and I don't like you very much, but let's just agree to always keep each other safe, OK?'

'I like you,' she says.

Hello again

On our second date, Raff and I go for dinner in a stunning French restaurant, all white tablecloths and highly polished silver, and then on to a dingy dive bar, where we do some uninhibited karaoke. Raff is at ease in both settings, making friends and cracking jokes with everyone. I like him. A lot.

And, just like that, we're dating. Each evening Raff and I spend together, he plans something thoughtful, fun and often indulgent. Each time, he insists on picking up the bill, always with cash. He is attentive and caring. He always recalls key things about my work and my week, sending supportive messages and fun ideas for future dates, even when he is shattered from working long hours. His work seems to be emotionally draining – though he is cagey about the details when I ask about what he's working on or what his colleagues are like. But some nights he meets me late and looks as though he has been hit with an emotional sledgehammer.

I decide to try the trick I use with patients, suggesting we play cards after dinner, and as we shuffle and deal, I ask him about the job. This time, with half an eye on the game, he reveals that the data analyst role is within intelligence, mainly terrorism. Recently, it has become traumatizing, and his employers have arranged for him to see a therapist – the one he mentioned on our first date. Raff tells me his therapist is a lovely older woman named Silvia, who has a cosy office and the personality to match. She sounds warm and nurturing. He tells me she always wears a brooch on her lapel, usually a bejewelled animal, and we hit on a new game – 'guess the brooch' – which we can play after each of his sessions. This feels like I am gaining some sort of access to his sessions and can ask about it in a light way, without irritating him.

I so admire Raff and those who can go to therapy without resistance, and I feel sorry for those who find it difficult to open up, even when they are really struggling. His chat is peppered with little snippets of 'therapist speak' that are familiar to me, and this makes me feel glad he is being supported.

Kelli is dubious

I go to see Kelli, like a child returning home from school eager to show a parent the picture they have made for them. After all, I have completed my homework, I have sought connection, I have stepped out of my shutdown state, my isolation, which was keeping me safe. I have consistently made bids for connection with Raff.

Kelli is cautious; she picks up on my need for her validation and my elation in my 'success'. I try to evidence my achievement with Raff further by pointing out that he has accessed therapy, so he must have self-awareness and insight; he has sat in a room like this and he has done his own work. As I begin to delve into my hypothesis as to why he might need such support and muse over his attachment style, Kelli reminds me to stay careful and curious about Raff, and asks me to stay focused on my own emotional needs. My homework is to check in with myself constantly: do I feel safe, seen, heard, soothed and secure and compassionately challenged?

The children

In order to help Rosa, we decide to take each child in turn for a therapy session, and each child is visibly excited to have the focus on them. This is common in sibling groups where there is a very sick child; the others feel overlooked. This is never the fault of the parent, but simply part of having to deal with every parent's greatest fear. And it's human nature for the child to want their parent's attention.

We give each child a designated slot to have one-on-one time with their mum, and give it a name: 'girlz time', 'Andrew's corner', 'superhero space'. This is just five minutes a week for them to be the focus for their mum; we have to balance the amount of time with what Rosa can practically achieve. But the concept of having their own special time is enough.

The little girl, Andrea, who is four, is scared of sleeping at night because she might have a bad dream. Andrea likes fairies, so I tell her I have some special fairy magic (glitter) in my bag and that, if she sprinkles this in a circle around her bed at night, with the help of her fairy godmother (mum), the bad dreams can't get in. The ritual and time spent with her mum will hopefully do the trick.

The little boy, Andrew, who is five, is struggling with sleep and also constipation. Little ones often hold themselves in a clenched state around the abdomen when they feel very anxious. We recruit Andrew's teddy bear, Barnie, to help. Andrew and I teach Barnie how to practise deep breathing. I make Andrew laugh by asking him to lie down on the floor and place Barnie on his tummy, making Barnie rise and fall with each of Andrew's inhales and exhales, Barnie saying, 'Whoooa! I am scared of heights!'

Rosa is grateful for these interventions and the children seem more content when they leave Kiwi – with a sticker, of course. I apologize to her that Henry the hoover might have a job with all the glitter, but she smiles warmly and says it's a small cost to pay for calmer children.

Unhinged

I meet Raff in central London at a restaurant overlooking the Thames. For some reason, I am still thinking about Harry and the concealment of his nightly ritual of dressing in his sister's clothes. As the starters arrive, I am deep in thought. Distractedly running the linen napkin between my fingers, I say out loud, 'Can you imagine having a secret you have to hide from everyone? Can you imagine what that would be like?'

Raff ignores me and fixates on the wine list.

I carry on, musing about guilt and how it feels.

'For me, it feels like a hot ball in my chest,' Raff says abruptly, snapping the menu shut. Rage flashes across his face and he waves his hand as if to brush off the conversation.

I oblige and instead ask him about his day – and, since it's Thursday, his therapy day, I play our game. 'What brooch was your therapist wearing today? Hmmm . . . a cheetah?' I attempt to use a playful energy and childlike innocence to bring up his therapy casually.

But Raff is shut down, disengaged, and changes the subject to food. We eat mostly in frosty silence, and I feel the hot sense of rejection mixed with embarrassment, a lump in my throat.

Thinking that my reaction might be a bit disproportionate – that not everything, after all, is about me – I try to ignore my gut and put some effort into repairing things with him.

As we leave the restaurant, I retrieve my phone from my bag to order an Uber; Raff always insists on paying for dinner, so I always pay for the cab home. But, as I peer down at my phone, I see the red low-battery warning. Then it dies. When I apologize and offer to pay him back for the cab fare later, the rage in his eyes turns to panic.

'I can't order one. I don't have my phone on me,' he says.

But he does – I've seen it. I look back at him, confused.

'I don't have the Uber app . . . Well, I do, but it's broken,' he says. He grips my hand and begins to walk. 'We'll have to walk down to the river and get a black cab.'

I hold still and firm. The lump rises again in my throat. And then I have a moment of clarity.

'You only pay in cash. You won't use Uber. We always stay at mine . . . You don't want a digital trace, do you? You're married.'

Raff is cross, but also frustrated, brimming with tears. We have a blazing row outside the restaurant. But he quickly deflates, the anger dissipates and he seems close to emotional collapse. Then, just as suddenly, he gets a second wind and begins his attack. I am 'paranoid', 'delusional', 'unhinged'. I feel something rise in me. I am gesticulating wildly outside the window of the restaurant, still holding a doggy bag of take-home food.

'I am *not* an idiot,' I shout. 'And I will *not* be the other woman. I *knew* this was too good to be true!'

There is no repair. Raff hails a black cab, we sit in angry and stunned silence, and he drops me at home, alone.

Lying in bed, I am not miserable or gloomy – I am apoplectic, catatonic with rage. I can't relax. I realize I have accessed something in me I knew was present the whole time we have been seeing each other but had been pushing down. Doubt.

Doubt

Raff messages and calls repeatedly in the morning. I don't return his calls or message back. The final message reads: *If you don't believe that I am not married, I will take you to Italy to meet my family, who I am sure would take issue with me having a mistress!*

I sit with the text for a day or so; I feel inner turmoil and I feel torn. I don't tell Alex; I feel like I need to sort out my own thoughts without her advocacy of me. On the one hand, I cannot simply erase the names he called me – paranoid, delusional, unhinged – but, on the other hand, he is offering practical concrete steps to show me who he is. Anger and rage are usually a defence against fear, I remind myself. Maybe he is anxious, unsure of himself. Maybe he isn't doing as well financially as he makes out. Maybe it's something that just doesn't matter. I do the back and forth in my mind, like two parts of the self having a quarrel: the pessimistic parent looking out for my well-being versus the innocent, pleasure-seeking child telling me to stop overanalysing.

During this ongoing squabble, tickets arrive at my front door. Flights to Italy. With the tickets is a letter, taking ownership of the name-calling, apologizing sincerely, acknowledging the impact his actions must have had on me and my self-esteem and gently requesting I consider letting him have another chance. At the end of the letter, a note in brackets that melts my heart: *(My therapist helped me gain insight and helped me to write this. I am so in awe of your profession).*

Italy

Raff's family live in a stunning house, set in beautiful grounds. He takes me to picturesque coastal restaurants and we drink cocktails on the beach. I fall back in love with him over sundowners; it is more powerful than the blissful fizziness and passion I felt for Max, and I allow myself to feel it; the mistrust is tuned out to inaudible. His parents are welcoming. They are older than my parents, gentle, low key, and warm towards me. However, they speak no English, so I crudely deliver Italian phrases that I have been practising on Duolingo, in preparation. They support my efforts with smiles and appreciative nods, despite my making no sense to them, and Raff steps in as interpreter. It's an arrangement that works surprisingly well.

After Italy

For a while, after Italy, it feels as though Raff and I are closer, and our relationship continues to develop. He meets my family in Manchester, eats his first pasty – falls in love with it, of course – and has Mum swooning with his charm and compliments about everything from our home to her lipstick.

On the return train to London, however, he seems drained

and wiped out. When he turns down a miniature bottle of wine, I know it must be bad.

The great pretender

Dr Lane has encouraged me to apply for further training, to embark on my PhD in psychology. This will involve a great many hours of my work with patients being scrutinized by more experienced psychologists. I will have to present to my university tutors and my peers to show my professional development, which feels daunting and exposing. I can get permission to use some of my NHS patients as anonymous case studies, but I will also need to recruit volunteers to have free therapy, using word of mouth and posters set up around university. I'll need a broad range of patients to present, so, in the department's weekly referrals meeting, I choose to take on cases that are less familiar to me, that I haven't tackled before, to test my skill set and push my boundaries. New challenges.

One of these new cases is Sam, who is seventeen, tall and very slight of build; his limbs look as though they have sharp edges. He has a long dark sweeping fringe that covers most of his face.

Sam's referral reads, *hypochondriac and possible malingering* – 'malingering' being a clinical way to describe a tendency to make out something is wrong with you when it is not. In the staff room, conversationally, Sam is referred to as 'The Great Pretender', a more fun way of describing factitious disorder.

When he arrives at Kiwi, he is carrying a list of notes, and my first question is to ask if he would like to work through what he has written. It quickly becomes apparent that it is a list of every possible side effect associated with every medication he has ever taken. He works through it meticulously, confirming to himself that he has each and every side effect – to an intense degree. Without a hint of embarrassment, he tells me he has priapism, an extremely rare side effect associated with an antidepressant, which involves a painful erection lasting over four hours. He adds that he has read about a man who sued his medical team after having an erection for thirty hours, and then declares that his own erection lasted for thirty-one.

I listen, keeping my expression soft, and ask him to tell me about who he is beyond this list of side effects and labels, but he does not engage. Instead, Sam reverts to reading from the list, moving on through the symptoms of serotonin syndrome – a very real thing for some people on antidepressants, occurring when there is too much serotonin available in the brain. It can happen when taking more than one drug that increases serotonin or when taking an antidepressant in combination with St John's wort. When he reaches a muscle-twitching side effect, Sam falls to the floor, shaking theatrically and intermittently glancing up at me with only one eye open.

His dependence on others for reassurance and comfort is clear. I suggest we book him another session next week, and at once he settles himself back into the chair and resumes calmly perusing his diary.

Paris

I find that I'm having to walk on eggshells around Raff, and he grows increasingly anxious about his work. He gets up later and later in the mornings, making himself late most days. I try to support, but he shuts me down with, 'I don't want to talk about it.'

Things worsen as several work-based trips are sprung on him last minute, including one to Paris on the day that terror threats there make the news headlines. When he phones me that evening, I am grateful to hear he is safe, and when he sends me a picture of the restaurant he is dining in, which takes in scenic Parisian life, I am glad to see he is managing to get some down time.

Back in London, he briefly seems less strung out, but his agitation and anxiety soon return. I try again to support him and to understand the reason for his withdrawal, but, when I check on him, he snaps, 'Stop doing the psychologist-speak on me.' Without this I have no tools. For someone who is gaining a skill set to respond to any presenting issue or emotion, I am completely at a loss when it comes to my own intimate relationships.

Munchausen's by proxy

Dr Lane and I discuss hypochondria. We think about whether it is possibly a way for people to mask emotional problems as concrete physical problems, as they tend to receive more input and response. Most of us struggle to fathom why someone would pretend to be ill or intentionally make themselves ill.

This fabricated and induced illness is better known as Munchausen's, and I bring up a complex case of the syndrome with Dr Lane. Brenda came into the hospital with her son, Rory. Rory was underweight and reportedly in constant, excruciating pain. Brenda was adamant the team should fit a feeding tube. The medics felt something was off and admitted Rory to the ward for a short hospital stay. In Brenda's absence, all of Rory's symptoms disappeared, which led to Brenda being diagnosed with Munchausen by proxy – inflicting intentional pain or illness on another.

As psychiatry assessed Brenda, the medical team and I tried to make sense of the whole picture. Brenda's history contained several risk factors for her diagnosis: her own mother had been a nurse, meaning she had medical knowledge; Rory had been a difficult labour and he had been kept in hospital for some time after his birth; Brenda has no social support and often reports low mood and depression. Taken together, these factors mean Brenda has learned to elicit care from the medical system by inventing illnesses in her son; medics are her only support network and access to empathic responding.

Dr Lane listens and agrees, picking up on the fact that Brenda's mother had been a nurse. She shares that the children of medics, doctors or psychiatrists, when asked what they want to be when they grow up, will often answer 'a patient'. Brenda may have felt overlooked in her childhood and learned to associate illness with love, Dr Lane says. She may, too, have over-identified with the label of 'mother of an ill child', as this comes with support, praise, encouragement and connection. This label is very seductive, Dr Lane says, for someone who maybe missed out on love, affection, praise and connection during their own childhood.

For Brenda, Dr Lane continues, this is a false self, and when she is identifying with this false self, she may become disconnected and detached from reality, making it easier for her to act in dangerous ways.

I am curious to learn how we recognize when a patient presents with a false self, when an inauthentic identity takes over.

Dr Lane explains that we all have multiple selves, and this serves a function; being able to identify with different representations of the self provides a buffer to difficult emotional states. Patients with multiple representations are less prone to depression, physical symptoms and illnesses following highly stressful events.

She gives me an example.

Stepping into the shoes of a hardened, stiff-upper-lip self when at work offers some respite and distance from the more vulnerable version of the self who may be struggling at home with rejection or anxiety. This latter version of the self may only be seen by loved ones. Dr Lane adds that we all have a different version of the self for every social encounter. 'You are encountering a version of my self, right now,' she tells me with a wry smile.

I leave thinking about false selves and their function. Dr Lane seems to suggest they are a mark of resilience. I have witnessed this at the hospital, with doctors and surgeons entering roles as they put on their uniform, becoming unflappable and engaging in the famous dark humour that inhabits all hospitals to help us survive. Glimpses of the true self wreck the illusion that everyone at work has it together. I have seen this in action when I was called to talk to a patient, Dean, who was about to go down for surgery. Dean's assigned surgeon came to see him before the procedure, to walk him through it. During the chat, the surgeon dropped his pen. When he tried to catch it, he just missed it, propelling it back into the air. He then tried to catch it again, beginning to look like a panicked juggler. When he explained, 'Sorry, I am all fingers and thumbs today,' Dean stared back at him, open-mouthed, and a panic attack ensued. Cue me.

We all need a false self, a role we step into, so that we can cope. Trouble arises when the lines get blurred and the work self bleeds into our personal lives, or vice versa, or when one version of the self is overwhelmed and the other versions become redundant.

A Christmas wreck

As Christmas approaches, Raff is fast becoming a wreck. He has bloodshot eyes from barely sleeping and has stopped working out, or going out, and avoids my friends and any opportunities to socialize. He says drinking and socializing make his anxiety worse. As those in my peer group approach their late twenties and early thirties, several have given up alcohol, recognizing the toll it is taking on them, so I try to rationalize this as a positive choice. Alex's dating life is the definition of chaos – she attempts to cling on to our youth, dating the lead singers of bands, drummers and men who claim the Arctic Monkeys stole their idea. This brings me some comfort; at least Raff is more stable than them. I can only hope that our next trip, which is to Italy at Christmas, brings him respite from this exhausted state.

A false self

We are preparing dinner in the kitchen of my flat while I practise my Italian. I have tried to introduce one evening a week when we only speak Italian, even when I stutter and stammer and struggle to reach for the words, though Raff always shuts this down, claiming it is too annoying. I have been having weekly lessons with an Italian tutor in a bustling Pret A Manger. As I am blaming the learning environment for my lack of progress, Raff's phone buzzes on the kitchen work surface and the word *Mamma* appears on the screen.

After a few minutes walking back and forth with the phone to his ear, the colour drains from Raff's face. 'What's up?' I ask. But he mutters something in Italian and waves me away. I have learned to read these cues and now know to leave it alone. I don't pursue it further, despite every bone in my body wanting to know what's going on. I wait, not wanting to act out of impulse, and I try to calm myself down as I collect my thoughts. I'll ask him later.

Kelli spots something

As I lie on Kelli's chaise longue, I stare at the painting of the shipwreck on the wall, but I can't see anything new, nothing is illuminated and I am finding it hard to conjure up any story or emotions in the image.

After letting me rest in the silence, Kelli interjects. She thinks it's very interesting that I can't quite access anything today and feel flat. 'It's what you're not bringing into the session that interests me,' she adds.

I stay quiet. We have been talking about Raff, and she points out that, as I speak about him, I wring my hands and scratch at my arms.

'Tell me about your arms,' she says gently, in the same tone I use when I ask to see self-harm injuries or scars.

I am confused. I think she is referring to the insect bites or allergic reaction that has erupted recently and I must have been scratching at, with no idea that I'm doing it or where it has come from.

Kelli is curious about conversion. Conversion occurs when psychological distress is suppressed and pushed down to a point that it manifests as physical or physiological symptoms. Typically, these symptoms show up as headaches, pain, muscle tension, spasms, twitches and tremors. But they can become even more serious, and I have seen this recently in a patient who ignored and suppressed her trauma for so long that she began experiencing pseudo-seizures. Such seizures are powerful and hard to distinguish from epileptic seizures when observed.

'I think your body might be trying to tell you something,' Kelli says.

I assume she is overreacting, but then notice I am scratching the mystery rash even as I think this.

'How are you coping at the moment?' she asks.

It's such a hard question to answer as the patient, I realize.

'Suppression of emotions is an emotional coping strategy,' Kelli says carefully, 'and usually co-occurs with the behavioural coping strategy of retreat. Don't isolate yourself. Keep talking to people in your circle.'

When I leave, I feel a particular warmth in our parting. 'Bye, love,' she says, and I feel deeply cared for.

On the drive home, I still feel a little confused about what Kelli meant about conversion and why she seemed particularly concerned for me today. I try to brush it off and decide to stop to buy insect-bite cream.

A Christmas goose

Sam tells me he has dissociative identity disorder, commonly known as multiple personality disorder. At the beginning of the session, for a few minutes, he speaks in a high-pitched tone, explaining that he is a little girl. He clears his throat, checking that I am paying attention, then speaks as a bullish man. Then he slips into an unidentifiable accent, which might be Scottish or Russian. Or neither.

I suggest that we all have multiple versions of the self in different contexts, and I ask what makes his experience so distressing or pathological.

Sam explains that none of the personalities can agree on anything. They all want different things. There is constant conflict and confusion. He doesn't know who he is any more or what he needs.

I remark on his resilience, then ask whether he will have goose on Christmas Day.

Sam is appalled. 'Of course I won't,' he almost shouts at me, and he then proceeds to list all the things he likes and doesn't like for Christmas dinner. As he reaches the desserts, about which he has some very strong opinions, I offer that he shows a great deal of certainty about the Christmas menu, and maybe we could work up from there.

Headhunted

It is the morning after the night before and Raff rings me, frantic, telling me he has been headhunted by a big tech firm and will need to attend a series of interviews, imminently, so we won't be going to Italy at Christmas. His florid language makes me think of the way Delilah spoke to me in that tiny A & E side room during her manic episode, just before the psychiatrist jumped out of the window. I congratulate Raff on the potential new job, make my excuses and end the call, then try to make sense of what he has said, the timespan and the dates.

In the evening, when he comes over, I ask, 'How can one of the interviews be on Boxing Day?'

'You're ridiculous if you think such important work stops for days off and holidays!' he says, then stalks away.

I immediately feel embarrassment, quickly followed by rage. How dare he speak to me like this? I turn to one of my trusted calming strategies: engaging my rational brain with a simple, repetitive, physical task. I start unpacking the suitcase I have packed for Italy, holding out, as I do so, for a rational explanation to come to me. But the discomfort of incongruence remains, and my little stick man is screaming, jumping up and down and waving a banner that says, *This doesn't add up!*

I've been aware of the stick man for some time, but he has stayed in the background. Until now. I have been successfully ignoring him, preferring the fairy-tale-romance interpretation of events. It's easily done. I realize that I have been engaging in psychic airbrushing, another beautiful concept coined by Margaret Crastnopol for when we deliberately omit to see something in ourselves or in someone else. We push it out of conscious awareness in order to stay in the relationship and maintain the illusion to ourselves. Quite simply, I don't want any disruption to the narrative I have created with Raff, and I am not brave enough to face the emotional discomfort of reality.

A bride to be?

Raff and I spend Christmas apart. I decide that my solo trip to Manchester is a good opportunity to reflect, a chance to see the wood for the trees, and also to have a frank conversation with my dad to gain some perspective. I often think Dad should be taking on clients, and I know that I am lucky to get his services for free.

He picks me up from the station and drives us home, but I decide this isn't the right time to bring it up – that word again: 'doubt'. There will be lots more opportunities over the coming days, I think. As we approach the house, my mum is waiting in the front doorway, and I can see that she is intoxicated with excitement, beaming. She ushers me inside.

'Oh, I can't hold it in any longer!' she exclaims.

'You nearly made it to twenty-five seconds. Not bad,' Dad says.

Mum reveals that Raff has texted her to say we should go jewellery shopping. He has sent champagne and asked Mum to find 'the sort of ring Natalie might like' – a kind of fact-finding mission. I feel myself shift, my thoughts and identity morphing back into who I was when I was with Steve, when becoming a bride was 'the win'.

When we return home to our family of origin, at any age, it is common to regress into old patterns of thinking, behaving and identifying. This helps explain why, when families get together for Christmas Day, it can become a stage for conflict and transgressions. The reunion reminds all members of the role each plays and the ways they interact with each other. It is easier to return to this status quo than to adapt to each other's changes, growth and development.

Reflecting on the role you play in your family can be an interesting exercise. Generally, there are four roles which I typically see play out in familial dynamics: the showman, the scapegoat, the ignored and the jester. The scapegoat tends to be a vessel for blame. Blame arises quickly when we feel threat and this person accepts it dutifully, rightly or wrongly. The ignored tends to be overlooked; they struggle to communicate their needs and they often feel unheard. The jester works hard to mediate between other members. They check in on the emotions of the others and try to keep them content in a quest to avoid conflict and the breakdown of bonds. But it's the showman who appears in me now. I am seduced by this return to the easy status quo of being celebrated for my success in finding a husband with whom to build a new family of my own.

If everyone stays in their lane, family time can turn out OK. Problems tend to arise between families and couples when one party goes to therapy and tries to make a change, or to shift their role. This has a knock-on effect for everyone

else, and they often don't like it. The scapegoat becoming
the jester? That's not right, they think. I have worked with
families who become very accustomed to one member being
mentally ill. That person becomes the scapegoat, which can
be handy for other members. I have also seen families become
reliant on a member being physically ill, even though they
never wanted the illness to invade their lives. They can over-
identify as the mother/father/brother of a sick child, and the
care this elicits from others. When the child is no longer sick,
they struggle with the change – the lack of focus, the loss of
their role as carer, supporter or hero.

Therapy in such cases is more successful when it includes
the whole family. Otherwise, the therapy can cause ruptures;
you can do the work with a patient, but you can't change the
context you send them back into. One of the hardest lessons
for me as a therapist working with children is that, in neglectful or harmful families, we can't just sever the damaging
bonds. If that dysfunctional bond is all the child has, we need
to try to preserve it and help them manage the pain it can
cause them. In my experience, all children removed from
troubled, neglectful or abusive families want to go home to
them, despite the physical and mental anguish of their world.
Such is the strength of the early attachment bonds, binding
them to even the cruellest and most callous of caregivers.

Standing there in the hallway, barely through the front
door of my parents' home, I feel the regression begin, the
need to perform and prove my worth in achieving the ultim-
ate goal of being the bride. The rest of me falls away – my
progression at work, my life in London, my growing resilience. It all becomes discredited in my mind as my heart soars

and I imagine the ring on my engagement finger – and, with this ring, the feeling of being secure and part of something bigger than myself.

This is, apparently, my big moment.

Ghosts in the nursery

The role that any child takes on in the family unit is the product of many complex elements, including the role each parent held in their own family of origin. If a parent had a detached mother themselves, they might enact some of this pattern when relating to their own son or daughter. An overbearing father might have taken on some of those qualities from his own father. There is also intergenerational trauma to consider. If a parent is traumatized by some lived experience, the child will have a stamp of that trauma within them, and there's a growing body of research to support this.

Equally, many parents disidentify with their own childhood experience and work tirelessly to not be like their mum or dad, or they simply want a better life for their own children than they had. We cannot fully escape our lived experience of being parented and our emotional responses to our own upbringing. This concept is beautifully described as 'the ghosts in the nursery' by Selma Fraiberg, who was a psychotherapist and pioneer in the field of infant psychiatry. When a new baby arrives, the ghosts or imprint of the parents' past experiences and relationships are present in the nursery with them. This doesn't mean they necessarily take over, but they are present and may visit from time to time, informing parenting and the way the parent gives and receives love.

As my mum makes the unexpected announcement about ring shopping, the ghosts in my nursery take hold. The ghosts come from both sides. Both of my parents are from meagre backgrounds, and Dad's childhood was also characterized by neglect. He is a prime example of ending the cycle of abuse, using insight and resilience in response to his own ghosts. Our household sits at the end of a long line of neglectful parenting and, with both parents from Irish Catholic families, there was the addition of shame. Catholicism often carries with it inherent shame, simply for being alive. Their families conformed to strict traditional gender roles. The men would work, the women child-reared, and every Sunday both my grandads would get 'three sheets to the wind' drunk in the pub, while my nana and grandma made Sunday dinner. Feelings were never discussed. With the chaos and the financial and emotional challenges of family life, there was little time for talk. They just 'got on with it', or perhaps went to confession at church, which terrified my mum and so many other Catholic children like her.

By the time I arrived, my parents' attitudes to family life and what it might look like had evolved, but the ghosts will always be here. As a little girl, I wore beautiful white dresses with huge pink bows and dainty patent shoes. Not much was expected of me in terms of a career. I was expected to get married. That is not to say that my parents weren't supportive. They were hugely supportive of me and my interests, but neither of them ever considered that I might want a real career and have a focus on my work. Things for my brother, however, were very different. He was expected to succeed and 'do well'. He was under a lot of pressure but he was also cherished and admired.

Even in families with strong love bonds, ghosts visit. We have to be prepared for them when they arrive.

Is it me?

On the ring-shopping trip, I regress fully into the little girl I used to be, the one who wanted so desperately to wear the white dress. I am excited and excitable, and everything I say seems to come out in a very high voice. Despite having every opportunity, the frank conversation with my dad never takes place and I return to London with a sense of unease. I am holding a secret. Deep down, I know this thing I have with Raff isn't right. But I push it down and ignore it. I'm good at that.

New Year

On New Year's Eve, Raff and I reunite at a bar in Soho. Perched on a stool at the bar, I smile.

'Have a drink today,' I say to him, 'for New Year. So that you can relax, or to celebrate something?'

I approach this gently; Raff has been ignoring my messages relating to the ring shopping and my excitement at what this might mean. My mum sent him a picture of a ring we liked, and he replied, *I think we can do a bit better than that*, but then he ignored follow-up questions and messages from her too, just sending kisses or Christmas memes. He has spent Christmas alone, working and preparing for his upcoming work opportunities, only seeing friends and family on Facetime. It all sounds so lonely and bleak, and I want to inject some fun tonight.

And, three mojitos later, Raff seems to be unwinding, or maybe it just appears that way through the rose-tinted glasses of my own three drinks. When he goes to the bathroom, I pay the bill. I know he will insist on paying, but, this time, I want to treat him. As I quickly check over the bill, I see that it includes three *virgin* mojitos.

Raff returns to the table and kisses me on the forehead. 'Thank you for the cocktails. I feel really tipsy and it has helped.'

'So, you feel tipsy?' I check.

'Yeah,' he confirms. 'Those mojitos really hit me.'

I brace myself and try to be as gentle as possible with my tone. 'Raff, I know you're lying.' I show him the bill. 'The problem is, I think you're lying about other things too, bigger things. If you tell me now, we can deal with it, together. But I can't deal with the lying.'

Raff is, of course, enraged. He rants about me having an alcohol problem and *therapizing* him all the time. 'You're paranoid,' he tells me. 'You overanalyse everything. It's pathological. It's psychotic.'

We go home separately.

I am shaken, unsure of what is the truth and flooded with self-doubt and shame. I haven't felt safe in a relationship for a long time. Maybe I *am* the problem; maybe *I* am sabotaging this one.

Maybe I *am* paranoid, I think, as my arms begin to fizz with the itchiness of those mystery insect bites again.

Just About Coping

Sleepless nights

I am working with a couple of paranoid patients at the moment. One, Carl, has intrusive thoughts about being hostile and aggressive towards others, shouting at people randomly and saying awful words to them. The thoughts begin with him imagining swearing at others and then they snowball into more and more offensive imagined acts that fill him with disgust and self-loathing. He never acts on the thoughts and doesn't align with them. On the contrary, he thinks they are abhorrent. But they continue to crowd in on him, and he is convinced he must be homophobic and racist and misogynist if these thoughts are able to form in his head. He will be talking to someone in a meeting at work or behind the counter at the petrol station, and *You're a wanker* will creep into his thoughts, followed by similar abusive expressions, which become increasingly offensive and eventually aggressive.

Carl is distressed and extremely sleep deprived. He spends hours at night saying to himself out loud, 'Don't do this, don't think this way,' and this keeps him awake most of the night. He has started to believe the public want to 'get back at him' or harm him in some way, to punish him for the thoughts, which he now can't separate from actions – it's as if he has actually shouted them in people's faces.

Sleep deprivation can lead to increased paranoid thinking and, at its worst, psychosis. Carl and I have been working together successfully to disempower his thoughts of self-punishment and to implement a helpful sleep schedule. He visibly relaxes when I share that we all have intrusive thoughts, that our thoughts are not our actions and, sometimes, the

more energy we use to push them out of conscious awareness, the more powerful they can become.

We talk through the 'white elephant' example.

I say, 'Carl, close your eyes and relax into the chair. Don't
think about a white elephant.'

Carl breaks into a small smile as he immediately starts to
think about the white elephant. We discuss how simply placing the word 'don't' in front of the request doesn't shift the
attentional field – it actually places more attention on the non-
desired act.

Most of us have fleeting intrusive thoughts. The most
common and distressing example is the thought of throwing
yourself off a tall building, known as high-place phenomenon,
or an impulse to hurl yourself into a well or a void, experiences described as *l'appel du vide* – the call of the void.

This term describes that little voice that tells you to stand
closer to the ledge or to drive straight into the wall, to drop a
baby to the ground when it is passed to you. It can feel almost
irresistible, like the call of the Siren song. These thoughts
generally pass by, as we are able to control them and not act
on them.

In my bid to decipher what is my paranoia and what isn't –
essentially meaning I am paranoid about my paranoia – I
think about my work with Carl. Somewhere in my paperwork
I have the measurement tools – the revised Green et al.
'Paranoid Thoughts Scale' – which I have used in our work
together. It's no doubt stuffed into a drawer or shoved into the
bulky old file Dr Lane has given me to hold psychological tests
and paperwork. I rummage around for a bit and pull out some

crumpled papers. I begin running through it to test myself. I pick up a pen.

In the last month . . .
I spent time thinking about friends gossiping about me.
  0 1 2 3 4
I often heard people referring to me. 0 1 2 3 4
I have been upset by friends and colleagues judging me
  critically. 0 1 2 3 4
People definitely laughed at me behind my back. 0 1 2 3 4
I have been thinking a lot about people avoiding me.
  0 1 2 3 4
People have been dropping hints for me. 0 1 2 3 4
I believed that certain people were not what they seemed.
  0 1 2 3 4
People talking about me behind my back upset me.
  0 1 2 3 4

In the last month . . .
Certain individuals have had it in for me. 0 1 2 3 4
People wanted me to feel threatened, so they stared at me.
  0 1 2 3 4
I was certain people did things in order to annoy me.
  0 1 2 3 4
I was convinced there was a conspiracy against me.
  0 1 2 3 4
I was sure someone wanted to hurt me. 0 1 2 3 4
I couldn't stop thinking about people wanting to confuse
  me. 0 1 2 3 4
I was distressed by being persecuted. 0 1 2 3 4

It was difficult to stop thinking about people wanting to
    make me feel bad. 0 1 2 3 4
People have been hostile towards me on purpose. 0 1 2 3 4
I was angry that someone wanted to hurt me. 0 1 2 3 4

Reading through the test, 'I believed that certain people were
not what they seemed' is the only statement I relate to. I am
even more sure that something isn't right with Raff. Something
just isn't what it seems.

I make a list of all the ways Raff has made me doubt my
beliefs and thoughts by saying things like, 'It's obvious big
tech firms wouldn't close over Christmas. Do hospitals close
over Christmas? Only an idiot would think that.'

It's gaslighting.

This term has become a bit overused, but it should not be
watered down as it occurs so frequently. True gaslighting is
when one person causes someone to doubt their perception
of reality, their knowledge and experiences, to the point where
they question their own functioning and abilities.

I barely sleep for the next couple of nights, but by day three
I feel rage. How dare he make me doubt myself like this?

The bluff

When I see Kelli, she angers me even more by using silence
during the session, which I know she does to get me to reach
an insight by myself, with minimal support from her. She
keeps reflecting back to me, 'I can hear you are very angry,'
which is infuriating. In this moment, I hate myself for ever

making this sort of statement to a patient, and I feel like saying back to her, 'I can hear that you are hearing I am angry,' but I don't.

She is quick to respond when I tell her about the text I sent Raff last night, which read: *How dare you make me contain myself like this.*

'*Contain* yourself. How interesting,' she repeats several times, and I can hear exasperation tinged with concern in her voice. It feels as though, behind the facade, she is desperate to scream out or jump up from the chair and respond more the way a friend would, like Alex would. She too is containing herself.

Afterwards, I think about Kelli and why the wording of my text about containing myself is significant to her. I think about containment. What have I been containing? I feel intense fury – and now, without analysing it, I act. I pick up my phone and message Raff.

Hi Raff, you remember my friend Caroline who works at the firm. She says there is a log of everyone that enters and leaves the building. I got her to check it and your name wasn't logged on the days you said you were there for the interviews??

My friend Caroline has worked there for some time. That much is true, and Raff knows this. But the rest of the text is made up. I see the three dots immediately, then nothing.

I am beside myself. I go for a walk and listen to a podcast. Hours later, I receive an email. When I see Raff's name in my inbox, I know this is it. He is finally ready to tell me the truth. I sit down and begin to read.

I am not who you think I am. Every day we have been together I have put on a suit to go to a job I don't have. I spend my days walking around central London. We always stay at yours because I rent out the flat my parents bought for me. I rent it for cash, so that's where all the cash comes from. I've had nowhere to live for years. The Italian lifelong friends you met were just some people I met at a local bar. I paid for their drinks all night so they would play along with it. We couldn't go to Italy at Christmas because my family invited others that speak English. My family believe I am a partner and manager at a nightclub, so I couldn't bring you in case you talked about my job. There was no interview and there were no work trips away. I hid at a friend's house and sent you pictures of France and French food from Google images. Then I just couldn't keep it up any more. I am exhausted. You will forever be in my heart. I do have an interview to do medicine at a London university, so maybe one day we will cross paths again in our work life. Forever yours, Raff.

I read it with my eyes wide and my heart racing. I am stunned.

This is pathological lying – it is persistent, pervasive and unnecessary. And I know that he has thrown in another lie at the end about doing medicine. He can't help himself. He is compelled to lie. But at least it isn't me. It's him. I knew it.

There was no reason for Raff to pretend to go to work in Paris and all those other countries. The point was simply the lie itself. I retrieve the official language: *pseudologia fantastica*, the fabrication of vivid and eloquent stories which sit on the edge of plausibility. It is typical that the stories serve to inflate

the storyteller to heroic proportions and positions of grand-
eur. In Raff's case, working in intelligence, protecting us from
terror.

My anger quickly turns to fear. Who is this person I have
shared a bed with, been intimate with, been alone with? Will
he turn up at my home in anger now he has been caught?
What is he capable of? I ring my dad – who, it seems, has been
waiting for this phone call.

'I always got the sense he watched a lot of CNN, that lad,
always saying he was working on intelligence for countries
just before I would see a terror event or some other disaster
on BBC news.'

I hear my mum shrieking in the background: 'Don't open
the door to *anyone*. He could be one of those acid throwers!'

When I come off the phone, I am left alone with my eerie
thoughts. Raff now feels like a stranger to me. I look back
through the pictures of us on my camera roll. The person
I spent time with has been replaced by someone who looks
the same but is someone else. This sensation makes me think
of Capgras syndrome, a delusion characterized by the belief
a loved one has been replaced by an imposter, a replica that
looks exactly the same but isn't them.

My head spins.

Compulsive lies

My innocence complex has led to me being duped before,
albeit less disastrously.

I once went to meet a new colleague on a psychiatric ward.
I nervously shook hands with him, and he then proceeded to

walk me down the long hallway of rooms, giving me details on each patient. They were a complex bunch, with extensive stories and medications, many of which I had not yet heard of. I was impressed by the psychiatrist's knowledge of each individual and their specific needs.

This continued for some time, until a voice came from behind me: 'Bill is leading the new psychologist around like he's the consultant again.'

The man standing next to me, who I had believed was in charge, began yodelling and wandered off, leaving me staring at his receding back.

'Bill compulsively lies, or maybe he believes he's the psychiatrist, who knows? He's been with us for six months. Never gets old,' my new colleague, the real ward psychiatrist, informed me.

Labelled

I feel like a fool, a gullible idiot. Yet I still can't help feeling worried about Raff. He is clearly unwell and I wonder about his mental state. I haven't replied to his email and I haven't heard more from him. I pluck up the courage to message his sister. She lives in London and speaks good English. Raff has kept us apart, mostly, which now makes sense.

Amelia messages straight back: *Let's meet for coffee.*

She orders us double espressos, and nervously stirs brown sugar into hers.

I take her silence as my cue. 'This isn't easy to say,' I begin, 'but he has lied about some quite serious things and I . . .'

Amelia holds her head in her hands. 'Not again,' she mumbles, her voice tinged with despair.

She reveals that Raff has done this before, which is why he left Italy. His parents gave him thousands of pounds to train as a lawyer, then, three years in, discovered he had spent the entire sum on a bar tab and not attended college even for a single day. She says, over the years, he has lied prolifically about everything and anything, and that it has all got too much for the family. He was under a psychiatrist in Italy, after a short stay in a private psychiatric hospital.

That must be where all the therapist-speak came from, I think to myself.

Amelia had assumed he was better because he had met me. I worked in psychology, which she thought would be helpful, and he appeared to be holding down the job at the nightclub.

We hug as we part ways, a mutual sadness between us.

On my way home, I text Kelli: *I need to come in. Do you have time for me tomorrow?*

Her response comes seconds later: *For you, yes.*

I feel the warmth of her and it is deeply reassuring.

Kelli annoys me

The next day, as I reel it all off to Kelli, she initially doesn't respond. I imagine her mouth hanging wide open, but I can't see her face from where I'm lying on the chaise longue.

Eventually, she shares that alarm bells had been going off for her, that I was behaving differently, as though there was something I couldn't own up to, something I was concealing. She tells me my body was telling me something. 'That's why you were covered in a rash,' she says. 'It was screaming out that my intuition was onto something. Trust your instincts.'

As we unpack the story, I see the host of red flags I missed along the way – or airbrushed out.

'You must be very angry. Are you very angry?' Kelli keeps saying.

I feel as though *she* is angry, but I realize I don't feel anger any more. I feel fear, hopelessness and isolation.

Do you ever really know anyone? Can you ever really trust anyone?

I stay silent as I remember how this all started with Kelli's homework task to connect to others. 'Trust connects us,' she had said. 'Distrust disconnects us.'

She started this. Which makes me think I don't trust Kelli now either. I don't trust anyone.

FIVE

Adventures in coping

Coping

Blaming is an instinctive way of coping, a way of not looking inward. Being angry with Kelli for pushing me back out into the world of dating and encouraging me to trust releases me from taking responsibility for the choices I made.

'Anger is all too often a mask for fear,' I say to Laura, on her first visit to Kiwi on a freezing cold winter's day. I am beginning to delve deeper into patients' worlds, to explore their histories, as I develop in my practical training – and I deliver this line with confidence.

Laura is in her early twenties and struggling to navigate her first real romantic relationship. She feels very anxious when she thinks that her girlfriend is pulling away from her, responding with anger and rage, sending angry texts and inundating her with frantic calls. During one particular night of arguing, Laura lost control and threw her girlfriend's phone at the wall, smashing it. This act had a final-straw energy to it and Laura was persuaded to book a therapy session, which she agreed to under the condition that it be for anger-management strategies only, nothing else.

'I don't want to talk about my childhood,' she tells me. 'I just need three or four strategies to control my anger, OK?'

Patients often try to section off or compartmentalize some part of themselves. They think they can bring just one thing into therapy, in isolation, with no context or explanation. This is usually because they are afraid of looking at the full self, the darker parts of the self, the shadows, the parts they hide from the world and even from themselves. Unfortunately, you can't just cover these parts with a dust sheet, encase them in a box or push them down deep, as we might push down the rubbish in a dustbin to make more space. When we ignore or deny parts of the self, they have a habit of manifesting in other ways. They might appear as physical symptoms, such as pain, tension, skin conditions or difficulty breathing. They can also appear as panic, dissociation, or sleep, appetite or libido disturbances. Anger, if ignored and suppressed, can manifest as low mood, depression or paranoia. Sometimes, in therapy, we have to go underneath the reported symptom to find out the root cause.

Laura is not suppressing her anger, it is coming out as uncontained and uncontrolled rage, so it's what she's not willing to talk about that is being suppressed. There is more to her than 'anger management'. I have a feeling this will be tricky.

Mind M.O.T.

The NHS and mental health services work by chopping our minds into sections. 'Depression as a response to chronic

PTSD . . . Well, you'll have to go to service A for the depression. They don't handle PTSD though, so you'll need to go to service B for the PTSD. The waiting list for service A is six months and service B's is twelve months. You'd better go to service A then, but *only* talk about the depression, not the PTSD. They don't do PTSD.' As if the patient is able to untangle which is which. Like cars, our different parts can only be examined piecemeal by different services. 'Faulty brakes – not me, I'm windscreens. You'll have to wait for Barry. He's on his lunch until March . . .' On the surface, this approach of looking at just one part of the person in isolation would suit Laura, because she wants a quick fix for her anger. However, people are not really like cars, and we need to look at the whole person and consider them in their entirety to understand what is causing their problems.

The angry child

As I do my best to delve deeper with Laura, I ask her when the anger became a problem, or when she first felt it as a deep discomfort. Laura seems confused by the question. She can't remember a time when it wasn't present. Rather than visiting anger, Laura embodies it. It is more than just resentment or frustration towards her partner, more likely a result of an early attachment injury, a difficulty in early bonding to key caregivers. In her early years, someone at home inadvertently taught Laura that anger was the only way of coping, or the best strategy. Maybe it was the only way of gaining input or attention and so she became an angry child.

This is sometimes known as the 'adaptive child', the result of a child adapting and evolving their behaviours and responses in line with the environment. The adaptive child is often triggered when we face distress, conflict and stress as adults; we revert to the responses of the adaptive child.

For Laura, in her childhood home, anger was permissible, anything else was not. Our early childhood experiences either represent modelling, so we copy what we see from our role models, or they represent a void, something that is missing, so we learn to overcompensate. For instance, an anxious child might be the product of an anxious parent, learning that the world is something to be feared. Or the anxious child could be a product of an impulsive, sensation-seeking parent without appropriate levels of anxiety. In this scenario, the child overcompensates to develop boundaries and a healthy fear of life's threats.

Laura's anger may have been the currency in her family home as a child, but it is no longer working for her. It is not a good coping mechanism in her current environment, in the relationship with her girlfriend. The brain struggles to let go of old habits that have become ingrained during childhood as a way of coping. The brain will say, 'Hang on, being angry has kept us safe this far – don't let go of it.' I decide to appeal to this part of Laura's brain and ask when anger is helpful and positive for her.

Laura is shocked by this question and says rather pointedly, 'I am here for you to fix the anger.' While she finds it hard to answer me, Laura eventually lands on how anger can be used to defend those you love and is related to the quality of loyalty.

I offer that we are often taught that we should regulate

anger, modulate it, especially as females. But – and perhaps this is the bit that makes her feel better – eradicating anger completely is not the answer.

Gender gaps

Right from the earliest stages of development, girls are taught to suppress anger and rage in favour of caring and bonding emotions. Boys, on the other hand, are encouraged to express more externalized emotions, such as anger and disgust, and to suppress their more tender emotions. Baby girls are talked to and cooed over more than baby boys, and, as toddlers, little girls are more often told to 'be careful'. Thankfully, this is becoming less binary, but it takes time to overcome behaviours and responses that are entrenched in our culture.

I have seen many females in therapy who have had to relearn that they can access anger and express it outwardly, rather than turning it inward, often as self-directed anger and self-criticism. We have to relearn how to express anger and sustain rage in response to certain acts against us, and that we *need* anger and fury.

Anger in a relationship can actually be a form of pursuit; the angry partner is seeking to engage with the other, seeking response and retaliation. It may not always be helpful, but it is far from indifference or shutdown; it's a sign of committed action. Anger is mobilizing and drives us forward. Its function is to overcome obstacles.

Unpacking this makes me realize just how angry I am. Polite, obedient, people-pleasing five-foot-two me is absolutely fuming.

The acceptance email

Somehow, I am successful. When I see the acceptance email, I am gobsmacked and ring Dr Lane straight away. She cheers down the phone and I thank her for her encouragement. I got a place to do a PhD on the counselling psychology course.

'It'll be hard, but you can do it,' she says.

I will be studying fourteen hours of my week, and it is suggested I read for a further twenty-two hours a week. *Twenty-two hours?!* The first thing I learn is that, every Friday afternoon, we will be studying statistics in a computer lab for three hours. The second thing I learn is that, for the rest of the time, we will sit in a room with a two-way mirror and practise our therapeutic techniques in front of our peers and tutors. As if this isn't excruciating enough, the rest of our patient sessions will be recorded and later played back, examined and pulled apart in front of our study groups.

We also have to stay in personal therapy throughout our training and keep a journal reflecting on every breakthrough, every break-up, every breakdown. This means I need to get back in touch with my therapist, Kelli, who I now haven't seen for several weeks.

Fucking Kelli

The first entry in my journal is titled 'Fucking Kelli', but I find it hard to fill anything in under this title, so I merely underline it three times. Really, I know that Kelli has just been a vessel for my rage. She has been somewhere to pour all of my anger, which is concealing my true feelings of fear – the horror and paranoia that maybe I have lost trust in her, and in others generally, since being duped and betrayed by Raff.

Since the 'Raff incident', I have behaved in very much the same way as I did when things ended with Steve. I have split off from my emotions, numbing out, blocking all contact with him, and this feels like a sort of win. We haven't spoken, but, instead of loss, I feel an eeriness, like I was dating a ghost. I feel as though my emotions aren't justified, as none of it was real. I can't grieve a story, can I?

Friends and family all say, 'I knew it!'

They are more focused on being right than checking in on me.

My toolbox

After three years of undergraduate psychology, I left university equipped with exactly zero practical therapy tools. When it came to actually dealing with people's complex emotions, I left with a qualification as useful as a plastering course. I was a dab hand in statistics, though – complex maths and mind-boggling equations that I had to learn to write out by hand, numbers that tell you if an experiment is significant or if the result is due to chance, catchily known as p 0.05. One of the most basic and fundamental principles is that 'A p-value of 0.05 does not mean that there is a 95 per cent chance that a given hypothesis is correct. It indicates that, if the null hypothesis is true, there is a 5 per cent chance of obtaining a result at least as extreme as the one observed.' Did you follow that? I never have. I think the undergraduate courses are still set up in this way to this day.

And it's not just me. Dr Lane has told me that she retained absolutely nothing about stats from her training, and, in the highly unlikely event that we need some stats worked out, we would hire a statistician, whose job it is to handle stats. This part of the core training takes up a lot of the space we could have used for learning about how to listen effectively, how to challenge gently and how to manage conflict.

Until now, outside of my weekly time with Dr Lane, I have attempted to skill up by reading, listening to podcasts and watching countless videos of psychologists and therapists on YouTube. There is a well-known video, commonly referred to as 'The Gloria Tapes', that is actually titled 'Three Approaches to Psychotherapy', which I watch on repeat. On the tapes, three of the biggest names in psychotherapy at the time are filmed delivering their own model of therapy to the same client, Gloria. It is essentially a competition to see who can initiate a breakthrough, in just fifteen minutes. Gloria then chooses who she wants to work with at the end – the 'winner' – but it is not very person-centred to rush someone across a painful and distressing finish line in the name of victory. I find the tapes quite helpful in terms of techniques employed, but also quite hard to watch, as the psychotherapists are pressured and sometimes hostile at points.

The seemingly harshest of these therapists, Fritz Perls, is more than challenging; he is sarcastic, condescending and antagonistic. But Perls 'wins'. In an attempt to make sense of this and justify his actions, I consider that the crushing pressure of being observed and filmed might have created tensions and made him behave in more extreme ways. On the one hand, I know being observed in my practices will be terrifying. On the other, it'll be nice to have more feedback and guidance. If I can be more certain that I'm doing the right things, the hope is that my imposter syndrome will finally go away.

Kelli's rule of thumb

When I do return to see Kelli, I know I must resemble a sullen teenager slinking back to a parent for some pocket money after breaking the rules. Either way, I am trying to stay in the relationship with her; now, with personal therapy a requirement of my PhD, I have to.

We talk about Raff, and I feel compelled to go through the time I spent with him, to see if Kelli can tell me what was real and what wasn't. I want to revisit each moment and ask her to give a thumbs up to signal real or a thumbs down for fiction.

Kelli won't engage in this, as she won't focus on the other person. This is about me, not Raff. 'Where does this leave *you?*' she asks.

I am frustrated with her; I am looking for answers, but she won't supply them.

Kelli is patient, eventually offering, 'I think what you are suffering from is pathological doubt.'

This resonates immediately, an *aha* moment. She goes on to frame my feelings as loss, saying that I have lost my reality; I have been betrayed by my conceived reality; I have lost trust in myself.

I still feel stuck in my role as the difficult child who wants to disagree with her. But I can't.

Blushing

Throwing myself into my work and my studies is my attempt to cope, to distract myself. I pick up a referral for idiopathic craniofacial erythema – in other words, chronic blushing. Paul is sixteen, a very tricky age to continually turn bright red in front of peers. He is crippled by the embarrassment of this; he freezes and is unable to speak when it happens. Worse, he feels it is out of his control. 'It just happens,' he says. 'I can't predict when, but I start to feel it creep up my neck and I know I am doomed.'

Before coming to see me, Paul had tried a few of his own coping strategies: growing his fringe long to try to hide the majority of his face, buying some blusher from Amazon to make it seem as though his face was naturally a redder hue. His efforts were met with more ridicule. I decide to work on the perceived lack of control first. We explore 'triggers and glimmers', working out which situations make it worse or trigger the blushing, and which situations are blush free or help to calm it down – the glimmers. We work out that Paul's blushing is not unpredictable and out of control, but is linked to social anxiety in specific contexts. Paul can stand up on stage and play guitar in his band blush free, but when in smaller groups or one on one with peers he takes on the hue of a tomato. Paul is terrified of the more focused, intimate social settings. He fears judgement when he has no guitar as a shield.

I empower Paul to feel in control by planning. There are three components in every situation: the place, the people present and the emotional response we have to it. We can usually take control of at least one element. For example, Paul could invite a peer to watch him play guitar in a place where he feels confident and less anxious. Paul could have an ally with him when entering scary social situations, either his best friend or his trusty guitar. Paul can also learn to have more understanding and control over his emotional response, thereby managing his physiology. We achieve this by having Paul take control of the story he tells himself when he blushes. I have him take perspective. I ask him, 'If you saw someone go red, what would you think?'

Paul would view the person with compassion, not ridicule, he tells me. He would will them to feel more at ease.

I ask him, 'If that person carried on competently doing a task or continuing to chat away, what would you think of their blushing?'

Paul says that eventually he would stop noticing it, and would assume it's not down to nerves.

Paul seems, by the end of the session, to understand that maybe blushing isn't 'social suicide', as he had believed at the start of the session. He leaves Kiwi with his head held a little higher and I am pleased to have been some help.

Dr Meredith Kennedy

Teaching sessions begin at university. I am in a small but diverse group of mature students, ranging in age from twenty-five to late sixties. Some of the group are international students, some are starting a new career – one has left acting, one has already completed another PhD elsewhere, one is a play therapist and has returned to studying after having a family. There are a few, closer to my age, who have worked for a few years to gain experience as support workers or trainees, like me. The group are all warm and welcoming; it feels supportive almost immediately. Sometimes we leave our small group of sixteen and join the master's students, bulking up the numbers to nothing short of a mob.

I travel across London, after a morning of seeing patients, for the afternoon session, which will be led by a revered and admired psychotherapist and visiting lecturer, Dr Meredith Kennedy. I am looking forward to the session and the speaker, with whose work I'm familiar, having watched many of her sessions on YouTube. Thanks to TfL, I arrive with only minutes to spare, but take my chances anyway and run to get a coffee.

While in the queue, I notice Dr Kennedy standing behind me, brandishing a Twix, and I gently offer her my place. She declines with a smile, so I add, 'I think it's a bit more important that you are on time rather than me.' She nods appreciatively as I express how much I am looking forward to the afternoon and we chat a little about how bad the coffee is in the university canteen.

The session is about chronic anger and resentment, how we can become trapped in anger. Anger can create a lens, Dr Kennedy tells us, distorting how we see the world, just as low mood can, informing our choices. For instance, if we are raised in an environment characterized and infused with rage and anger, we can find ourselves seeking the same in a partner. This is because we have learned that anger is the only strategy for relating. The brain seeks out familiar angry patterns, and also our physiology is skewed in such a way that we seek out and crave the high level of arousal we are used to. Ultimately, however, a consistently angry partner cannot meet our emotional needs, as anger is the one emotion that pushes people away. It means that the angry person's needs continue to be thwarted, causing them to have rageful and vengeful responses. This creates a vicious cycle, within which we are trapped, stuck in anger. That all makes sense to me.

As a group, we learn strategies to help patients safely release their anger and shift away from it. While I've encountered some of these techniques before, I'm eager to expand my knowledge in this area, but I have doubts about one particular strategy that Dr Kennedy recommends: encouraging patients to express their feelings by punching a pillow. Wouldn't that just reinforce in the brain that a sense of anger is connected to acting out physically, and hitting out? I wonder. I decide I am too nervous to challenge her – after all, she is the expert, and there are too many people in this room. As I decide to stay quiet, her eyes land on me. I haven't been listening, but realize, to my horror, that she has scanned the room looking for a volunteer to punch a pillow and, as I am a familiar face from the coffee exchange, she has chosen me. I am beckoned forwards.

Walking to the front of the room, I feel my face blush a bright tomato and I think I actually hear my brain say, 'You're on your own for this one.' My brain is once again flooded with cortisol and shuts down. Somehow, I engage with the task, feebly hitting the pillow on autopilot, face maroon. Mortified to be tasked with this in front of a large group, I return to my seat thinking of Paul. I think, This really is very hard to control. I take some deep breaths and try some of my own strategies to convince myself that nobody else will have really noticed or judged me.

All of my strategies appear to be shit.

I lean in to one of my peers and whisper, 'Did you see me go red?'

'Red?' Saima says. 'You were positively purple.'

Her Perls-esque brutal honesty suggests that she may need to work on her empathic responses to be a good therapist.

Kelli paces me

I tell Kelli about the blushing. She says that of course my body is responding to the heightened self-consciousness I feel around being duped by Raff. It's because I feel exposed and uncertain of others. I shouldn't be surprised.

Kelli explains, as though to an eight-year-old, that I have to feel this all the way through, as a process, in order to rebuild trust. We can't rush through this. Much as I'd like to.

Stages of grief

Several weeks after our last session, and as the days are finally getting lighter again, Gina comes back to see me in Kiwi. Her grandad has passed away. He was more of a father figure, being only twenty years older than her actual father, and was a key role model in her life growing up. His death has come as a shock. Gina gets out an A4 writing pad and I can see titles highlighted in different colours and double underlined. She wants to talk me through it.

Gina has written out the five stages of grief, the emotions

reported to be experienced by people who are grieving, based on the Kübler-Ross model. Gina has allowed herself to have two weeks at each stage, she tells me: first denial, then anger, bargaining, depression and acceptance. In ten weeks, she will be healed – unless I think a week is long enough and we can be done in five weeks.

I listen to Gina and offer that she must want to escape this pain as quickly as possible and to see a light at the end of the tunnel. I ask her, 'What happens if you are not ready to leave one state to move to the next?'

Gina seems stumped. 'But this is the right way to do it,' she says.

I ask Gina what she would like to do, outside of order and regime.

'I just want to speak to him, to tell him about my day and see what he thinks.'

'Let's do that, then,' I say.

Gina says this is lunacy, people will think she is mad.

Nonetheless, I ask her to ask her grandad what he thinks.

'He thinks it sounds stupid,' she tells me, 'but also that it might be quite nice.'

Gina says she will continue to try and speak to her grandad out loud, but wants to know what to do with the official five stages.

I know she feels safer in structure, so I don't invalidate her; I suggest she keeps the stages as a guide, but tries to make them more flexible. I share that she might move back and forth through them, that she may feel a combination of the stages at once. I let her know the theory was originally developed for people who are facing their own death, rather than facing grief, in the hope of disempowering the five stages a little for her. But Gina is seeking hard and fast answers.

'How should I grieve, then?' she asks.

'However the hell you want to!'

Gina sits with this in silence for a moment and I can see the inner turmoil play out on her face. After a while, I see a flicker of insight and relief, an *aha* moment. 'Oh, you're asking me to choose chaos,' she says.

I wonder if she has just had a conversation with her grandad.

Regression

Subconsciously, my relationship with chaos is changed following my session with Gina, and I embrace it, see it as resilient and powerful. Gina needs a dash more chaos, that's clear. But I do not, and I overcorrect. I seem to have no boundaries. At the weekend, I drink to excess with no fear of being messy or chaotic. As I spend time with the friends I studied with at university, before entering the working world and proper adulthood, I regress. I act as though I am a first-year student, sinking Jägerbombs in a competition with carefree abandon, mistakenly aligning chaos with power.

I end up on my own doorstep with an empty handbag. Keys, phone, purse – everything is missing, and I have only a very vague memory of how I got here. Banging on the front door proves futile. After a while, feeling hopeless and dejected, I go for a walk towards the local shops and see the lights on in the hairdresser's. Despite the late hour, they are open. Turns out they are having a boozy lock-in to see off a member of staff. With a newfound energy, I hurtle towards the shopfront.

As I get closer, I see an antique phone in the window, forming part of an elaborate display with false flowers, fruit and porcelain cherubs. Survival mode or desperation kicks in and I enter the shop, trying to grab the phone out of the window display until I hear, 'Madam, madam, that's not a real phone!' Thankfully, they sit me down and calm me down. They hand me a real phone, but the only number I know off by heart is my dad's.

There is no stronger infantilizing wake-up call than having to ring your dad, who lives 160 miles away, at 2 a.m., to ask him to call your flatmates to come and collect you.

Kelli tells me straight

In the morning, I enter a shame spiral as I consider with horror how I must have been behaving last night – shame and embarrassment that spins out of control. This means an urgent session with Kelli.

We talk about regressional behaviours, the psychological defence we reach for when feeling threatened or fragmented in who we are, which allows us to revert to an earlier stage of development, to retreat and withdraw psychologically to a time when we felt safer. Kelli also seems to think that it is no coincidence I drank to oblivion; Kelli doesn't think anything is just happenstance.

She urges me to set more emotional boundaries with patients. She says I borrowed my session with Gina and applied it to myself, to try to fix something in me. Choosing chaos was the right advice for Gina, but it wasn't the right advice for me;

it was like telling a binge eater to try hard to eat more sugar, or an agoraphobic to try staying in more.

Kelli ends the session with, 'Your patient work is strong, but you seem to be hobbling along, getting by.'

It inspires another entry for my therapy journal: *Kelli is being mean again.*

Abandoned in grief

When Gina comes back to see me, she announces, 'I chose chaos!'

I praise her for this, while making a mental note not to put chaos on a pedestal for myself again.

Gina has been let down by her friends in her grief; they have been unresponsive and unsupportive. In response to this, Gina felt she needed to be held, to have some basic physical intimacy, to feel cared for, so she messaged an old fling who was more than happy to oblige. This was outside of Gina's usual rule book, as she fears appearing vulnerable or needy to others, but she pushed through the natural barriers, her physical need was met and she felt empowered by the whole experience.

I have had several patients and friends experience social abandonment when in the throes of acute grief, with trusted loved ones and friends acting strangely or avoiding them at their greatest time of need. People once upheld as reliable and loving can act in odd and detached ways around grief. Seeing grief and loss in someone else brings up our own losses and triggers any unresolved hurt and pain from a lost bond that we've experienced. Grief has no ending, so bearing witness to someone else's grief can be re-traumatizing.

As a therapist, I feel shame if I experience a sense of dread when a grieving patient referral comes in. I always go to Dr Lane for guidance and for some sort of answer, and she always offers support and reassures me that, no matter how senior psychologists are, they often say grief work is daunting, that the unease of sitting with someone in their grief remains scary. Some colleagues avoid the grief referral altogether, a response which often mirrors the patient's functioning; many patients can feel resistant to grief – they simply do not want to grieve and will employ various defences as a way to cope, including denial, resistance, regression and refocusing.

Even if you choose to run towards someone's grief rather than away from it, it is sometimes hard to reach people who are grieving. In the shock stage, people can become very matter of fact, devoid of feeling. The facts are too big to process, so people dissociate and lose their ability to access emotion. I once received a phone call from a friend after her mum had been in a car crash, and while she was at the hospital we were waiting at her home for news. 'Hi, my mum is dead, so that's happened,' she told us on the phone. 'Do we need loo roll picking up on the way home?'

No strategy

For lots of other psychological injuries and emotional pain, you can offer education, strategies, treatment plans, behavioural practices and insight. With grief, there is nothing you can say for an *aha* moment, no little task or trick you can apply to offer some respite or symptom reduction. All you can do as a therapist, in the acute stage, is to be with the person suffering, walk with them through it, be available. The other thing I can offer is permission. Permission is crucial and allows the person to have and express thoughts that feel shameful or strange, thoughts and feelings they can't share with anyone else and also can't bear the weight of alone. I have witnessed those in grief disclose that they feel 'relief' or that they 'lost the wrong child'. We need to be given permission to express mixed feelings, not just sadness. The mind and body can also play tricks on us at times of loss.

James comes to see me after over a year of concealing agonizing shame and guilt due to his response to his wife's diagnosis of incurable cancer, and then, ultimately, her passing. James tells me that he felt a strange euphoria when the diagnosis was shared, as though he was *thrilled* when the doctors first broke the news. James breaks down into tears as he tells me this and I notice a huge exhale of breath, as if the word *thrilled* has been clenching his lungs shut for the past year.

'I don't know what's wrong with me,' he says. 'I'm not a good person.'

I ask him to help me understand how, on the one hand, he feels he identified with being thrilled, while on the other hand, he is feeling so much guilt and anguish about it. It's difficult to see how the two can coexist in a 'bad person'. I ask James for some other descriptors he might apply to his emotional response.

'Excited, exhilarated . . .' he says. 'But maybe urgent, frenzied . . .' he offers in despair.

I explain that, physiologically speaking, fear and excitement are the same thing; the only difference is the story we tell ourselves about the sensation. Excitement is marked by arousal, mobilizing us and shifting us into a state of alertness, vigilance, an awakened state. This is exactly the same as fear. I wonder aloud how being in this physiological state of arousal and readiness helped him to take care of his wife when she was struggling with her illness. James explains that it allowed him to care for her around the clock, that he didn't need a break, the adrenaline carried him forward, both physically and emotionally.

As we discuss this, the penny drops. He accepts that his physiological response served an important function, and that he may have just mislabelled it. James allows relief to wash over him as he says that maybe he can now look upon it with some sort of gratitude.

I ask James to tell himself a different story, one of rescue and survival.

Imposter syndrome

In our group supervision session, I share my struggles and the imposter syndrome I experience when working with grief. It helps to hear I am not alone in my sense of helplessness. We share stories about famous psychologists who have faced adversity and who have struggled with imposter syndrome. Steven Hayes, a well-known psychologist, developed acceptance and commitment therapy (ACT) because he suffered crippling panic disorder and endured frequent panic attacks. We discuss how those who work as therapists are sometimes called 'wounded healers', as we all have inner wounds. It is these wounds which allow us to empathize and connect with patients, but they also make the work tricky at times.

At the end of the session, my tutor says, 'Look for the wounds in your colleagues and mentors. If you look carefully, you will witness their struggles. Psychologists are humans too.'

Colleagues as patients

I am approached by a colleague seeking advice about the psychiatrist working in adult services at a nearby hospital, someone we often send referrals to. He has exhibited some odd behaviours in recent months, which have mostly been put down to eccentricity. Recently, however, concern arose when, during a meeting, he refused to take off his blue surgical gloves and it was noted that all the items in his briefcase were vacuum packed in plastic covering. Concerns escalated just before his holiday, when he revealed he was paying for extra luggage to ensure he could take a full suitcase of bottled water as he couldn't trust the water elsewhere. How can a psychiatrist suffer with contamination-based obsessions, I wonder? Is he overlooked in terms of people stepping in, as they assume he can cope or manage it himself?

Obsessive–compulsive disorder, or OCD, can take over people's lives. Part of it is a mistrust of confirmation, causing the sufferer to mistrust their own memory – 'Did I turn the oven off?' 'Did I shut the front door?' 'Did I clean the pan properly before I used it?' Part of the brain is activated in response to perceived threat, a worry that something could be contaminated. The area of the brain tasked with promotion of checking behaviours and grooming behaviours is activated. This involves checking things are safe from contagions and germs. Once the act of checking is complete, a signal goes to the frontal cortex that says, 'OK, we checked that we are safe,' and the checking system is turned off. Those with OCD either have a very weak version of this signal or no signal at all, so the checking system isn't switched off.

The disorder is clearly impacting the psychiatrist's functioning, meaning it is time to step in. I reach out to him several times with no response; OCD is usually accompanied by a great deal of shame. However, I know I have a duty of care to the patients he treats, so I have to pass this information on. My email to the hospital manager and to occupational health is carefully worded, suggesting we offer support and handle this delicately, with respect. Days later, the email to management remains unanswered and I send it several more times, highlighted as urgent. I also leave messages. Nothing.

As I search my emails, checking for a missed response, a *ping* signals an incoming email from Dr Lane: *Do you have that copy of that book,* Man's Search for Meaning *by Viktor Frankl, that I lent you?*

Yes, I reply. *I devoured it. The brutality and trauma of the Nazis and people's resilience in the face of it . . . I'll bring it to you.*

The next day, I am called into a meeting with two of the hospital managers, who preface the conversation with, 'This is about your email.'

Oh, thank God, I think. They are here to tell me that the support for the troubled psychiatrist has been arranged.

'The NHS system has flagged up that you have shared

terrorist content,' one of the managers says, a grim look on her face. 'It's about the Nazis.'

Betrayal

Back at university, my PhD group meets for another supervision session. I found last week's so grounding; my inferiority complex was shifted by the knowledge that even the most revered psychologists have their own mental-health struggles and demons. I enter the session looking forward to learning more, but am met by solemn faces. My tutor announces that the esteemed Dr Kennedy, the esteemed and married Dr Kennedy, mother of three, has been sleeping with several of the students and indeed some of the faculty. She has been outed by a student who caught her engaging in late-night activities in one of the lecture theatres. I am compelled to point out that my blushing in her presence was not the result of an attraction or tryst of any sort, but sheer stage fright. Once my name is cleared, I experience the news as a sort of betrayal.

The freeze response

Ten-year-old Tyler is back. Having being removed from his mum due to neglect, he has learned early in life to expect to be let down and is now approaching life with a mistrusting pessimism teamed with a fierce independence. Some children, when removed from abusive and neglectful homes by social services, can then become deeply distrusting of all adults. Including me. I am 'one of them'.

He meets my initial enthusiastic 'Hello!' with an eye roll,

still mortified by the fact that I chased him to school all those months ago. He is here, this time with his new foster carers, because they aren't happy with how he is 'lashing out when he is at home, but not doing this anywhere else – in fact, he is quiet as a mouse elsewhere.' This seems to be more about them than him, I think. The foster carers say they are keen for me to 'fix' him, and they say this in front of him. I usher them out of the room so Tyler doesn't have to listen to any more negativity about himself and his value.

I have been informed that, during supervised contact time with his mum, the staff present have become more and more concerned about Tyler's behaviour. He freezes, stays very still and barely speaks. A trauma response, I assume. Freezing tends to come into play when a threat is overwhelmingly large, such as a threat to life. It's one of four responses to a perceived threat, and in Tyler's case may be a fear of his mum or a triggered memory of abuse.

In response to the environment, we move up and down the ladder of our nervous system. If we feel safe, we stay at the top of the ladder. This is sometimes called the 'safe and social' state. Here we can engage with and connect to others freely. In response to a perceived threat, we move down the ladder. How far down the ladder we move depends on the severity of risk. If we feel we can fight the threat or outrun it, we drop down the ladder into 'fight or flight'. But if we perceive that we are no match for the threat, we drop further down into the 'freeze' or shutdown state, which is when we have lost all hope; we no longer seek to survive and instead enter a state of physical and emotional collapse. We disconnect from the present moment and dissociate. As we move down the ladder, we move down the brain stem, accessing more and more primitive parts of the brain. Upon reaching the lowest rung, the functioning of the rung above becomes redundant and we are reduced to our most basic and animalistic states.

I assume that Tyler enters 'freeze' and possibly 'fawn' based on a trauma bond with his mum, in response to her neglectful and abusive treatment. But I need to investigate.

Tyler and I draw a treasure map together. This is a way for me to get a picture of his world and the way he sees it. The different islands represent different parts of his life: home, school, football club and (supervised) time with his mum. I ask Tyler how he feels on each island, what it is like to be on each one, what buried treasure might be there and what we might have to fear on the island.

Tyler then adds a little island and begins to draw a picture of him and his mum standing on it. I praise his picture and ask for more detail. Tyler carries on drawing, and I encourage this in children when topics are difficult to talk about. The simultaneous motor task helps them to open up, as they aren't paying as much attention to what they're saying, so can be less considered and freer in their responses. I ask Tyler what I would see if I came onto the island with him and his mum. He says he is still and quiet when he is on his mum's island because, 'When you're bored and you're not doing anything, time goes really slow, doesn't it? I just want to be with Mum, so I make it last longer.'

That's very clever, I think. And we have all jumped to entirely the wrong conclusion.

Tyler's story is one I now share with patients as an example of how every behaviour serves a function, but what that function is may be far from obvious. Indeed, it may be subconscious. But, whatever the behaviour is, it is doing *something* for you.

The subconscious

The concept of the subconscious, the idea that there is part of the self we don't explicitly know, often makes patients uneasy. Our subconscious is always acting but we aren't fully aware of it and can't always access it. This raises questions about trusting the self. If there is a portion of us that is hidden from our own view and conscious awareness, how can we trust ourselves fully?

I haven't yet gained a formal skill set in working with the unconscious, but this will form part of my PhD studies, known as psychodynamic practice – unearthing impulses and drives in patients.

I have a few stereotypes in mind for what my psychodynamic tutors will be like: I envisage uptight, older, white middle-class men who look like Freud himself, relentlessly relating everything back to sex and our secret desire to seduce our own dads while brutally murdering our mums (or vice versa). I cast this out of my mind as absurd.

On my first day of psychodynamic practice, I meet my tutor, Dr Hubert, an older, white middle-class man with an ill-fitting stuffy suit. But he does not appear to be uptight and he is not without charm. He has a glimmer in his eye and a broad smile. We begin discussing my patients, and I eagerly await his take. I want to impress him, so I begin with a success story:

James and his shame in his grief after losing his wife, and how we transformed this together.

Dr Hubert listens attentively. 'Ah, he is trying to penetrate your psyche. Is he replacing his wife with you?'

I think he is trying to point out that I should have focused on the transference here, that James is subconsciously looking for a substitute for his wife, in me. I am disappointed that I missed this transference interpretation but, on the upside, I am starting to feel more confident in questioning my teachers and mentors. I don't have to agree with everything they say. It's an incredibly liberating thought.

Splitting

Dr Hubert's insights on how the unconscious shows itself are more helpful. Sometimes thoughts are too painful to be held in conscious awareness so we split them off, he says. They can turn up in intrusive thoughts, Freudian slips and dreams.

I realize 'splitting' is a coping mechanism I used with Raff – relegating all his inconsistencies and my gut feelings into the subconscious abyss, airbrushing out all of the clues. Watching someone else engage in this airbrushing, however, can be very frustrating, and it's something I am experiencing with a patient named Ella.

Ella is young and beautiful; she is training to be an architect, speaks four languages and has a wide social circle. Ella has recently discovered that Tim, her boyfriend of three years, has been having an emotional and sexual affair with a woman from work. Ella has asked Tim to choose and has come to me in pain, struggling with anticipated rejection and tormented by thoughts of the shared intimacy between Tim and his colleague.

Instead of choosing, Tim has managed to create two worlds. In the first world, he is at home with Ella, the two of them co-authors of a picture-perfect relationship with all the best bits: the intimacy, Netflix with pizza, cuddling and date nights. Every Thursday, Tim then goes off to the second world he has created – the world he shares with the woman from work – and he is gone until the following Monday. This happens week after week, like clockwork. When Tim leaves, Ella is thrown into panic, feeling abandoned and rejected, humiliated and alone, until Tim returns to his world with Ella, which brings her the respite she needs from her emotional pain. And so the cycle continues.

Tim always returns with a story, some unlikely explanation of why he was gone for so long. Ella accepts the narrative and takes Tim back. If challenged, Tim calls Ella 'paranoid', 'demanding', 'controlling', 'clingy' and 'needy'. She begins to internalize such messages, and to believe them, trying desperately to seem 'cool, aloof and independent' in order to counter them. Ella has lost her sense of self, her confidence, her boundaries and her self-esteem.

I try to bring Ella's awareness to the manipulation, but she is not ready to receive or accept it. She is frantically airbrushing and engulfed in self-doubt. As with the children who suffer abusive upbringings, adults in emotionally abusive relationships also seek to blame themselves. This gives them ownership and control; the narrative becomes, 'If the problem lies in me, I can fix it. There is hope, there is resolution.'

SIX

Seeing the red flags

Going private and going public

With a letter of recommendation from my university and proof of my supervised hours, I can now join a register of approved therapists, which means I can accept private patients. I join the British Association for Counselling and Psychotherapy database, which strikes me as not dissimilar from a dating site for therapists. Therapists add their photograph and a bio – a bit about themselves, their background, strengths and how they relate to others. Potential patients scroll through and find the therapist they feel they might click with the most. I add my details, attempting to seem as open and as warm as possible, and I use an existing picture of myself where I think my smile looks the most genuine, rather than a professional shot which might look less approachable.

Profile in place, I realize I don't have a clue about what to charge, since I have always worked in the NHS where the service is free at the point of access. So, I seek advice from Dr Hubert.

Dr Hubert hears the price I am considering and says, 'If you post that, people might think you're a charlatan.' He goes on to say that some people try to legitimize themselves by renting an office on Harley Street, the epitome of private and expensive medicine, and impose a price tag that matches, perhaps £350 an hour.

I leave knowing I need to strike a balance between looking like a Poundland-quality therapist and using extortionately priced swanky rooms to legitimize myself. In the end, I book a functional but spacious therapy room in an office building in east London – high end enough to have a coffee machine, but a far cry from Harley Street.

Missed red flags

My first private referral comes very quickly, giving me the same small hit of dopamine as from a notification on a dating app.

Viola sends a very matter-of-fact email requesting 'my services'. I wonder why she has chosen me out of all the therapists and know this might be a factor in her help-seeking. Has she chosen someone she feels is less experienced so she can seek to exert control, or does she simply want to save money? I leave the speculation to one side for now.

A couple of days later, she bursts into the room, wearing a tailored suit and carrying a leather document binder. She has a very powerful energy and, it turns out, a very high-powered job as the CEO of a huge international company. Which means Viola is tough to crack. I feel as though I am in a job interview. She dominates the first session and, while I try to ensure I bring the focus back to her, she is full of questions about me.

'Are you divorced? Married?' she asks.

'Why is that important for you to know? Would it change anything?' I reply.

'Just as long as you're not a hopeless romantic,' she replies, rolling her eyes as though in despair.

Despite the quick-fire round, Viola has something very likable about her. I can tell she is keeping a playful energy just about under wraps, but the power dynamic makes me feel like I should be rushing out to get her a double-shot extra-hot latte. I know that she is testing me, wanting to know if I am strong enough to contain her pain and if I have the resilience to stand up to her and to challenge her when necessary.

This crunch moment soon comes.

Viola recently found her wife in bed with one of the young PAs at the company they both work for, and solution-focused Viola closed the door on the marriage immediately. But she has been left with a deep wound of humiliation, and is terrorized by what people at work are thinking. She isn't ready to explore any emotional pain yet; it is all logistics and risk analysis. The only emotion Viola can tolerate is her fury towards herself, an intense shame for not knowing the affair was going on, for being 'a fucking cliché and a halfwit'.

I start to chip away, very slightly, at the self-persecution, the critical self-talk.

'Would you consider yourself to be a paranoid person?' I ask Viola, a question that allows us to explore why she is locating blame and anger in herself and not in her wife.

'No,' she says, after a pause. 'I make a judgement on some-one and stick with it, I usually trust my instincts.'

'If you are not paranoid and you were in a trusting relation-ship with this person, how would you instantly know about her transgression?'

'But I am an educated person. I manage and read people for a living. I am well established and I am fifty-two, for Christ's sake! How could I have not seen this coming?'

As we delve deeper, Viola shares that her ex-wife has recently been diagnosed with antisocial personality disorder. The diagnosis came about after she was involved in a brawl in a pub one night, leading her to seek medical and psychiatric advice. Viola launches a self-attack for not seeing this too. She gathers up all the red flags she has missed along the way and uses them to self-flagellate.

'There were books on personality disorders on our shared Kindle. She knew she had it long before they did. How did I not see this? It's my job to read and manage people.'

There's clearly work to be done.

My new inner turmoil, given that Viola is a private patient, is how much work to do and at what cost. I feel a pressure: to ensure she 'gets her money's worth' and not to take too long getting to breakthroughs.

Challenging the patient

Tim returns home with his neck covered in love bites, a detail that slips out when Ella is telling me the latest story to accom-pany Tim's absence. 'Tim did go out again this Thursday,' she says. 'He went for a massage with cupping and I know that's where he was because I saw the loving marks . . . cupping marks, I mean.'

It's a classic Freudian slip. And Tim's excuse is about as convincing as when my brother came down one Christmas morning wearing an oversized turtleneck jumper, claiming he just fancied going into the loft and rummaging around for said turtleneck at the crack of dawn. When my mum pulled the neck to one side, the sight of some huge and pretty offensive love bites cleared up the odd fashion choice.

I am a little firmer with Ella in this session than I have been previously, and she is a little less defensive, but she still clings on to her coping tools – splitting off the scary thoughts, employing denial and airbrushing away reality to stay in the relationship at all costs. Challenging patients can be really hard; it invites conflict, and it can damage the therapeutic relationship, but it is part of therapy and I have to withstand it. I have started to use the same phrase to make it as gentle as possible: 'Can I just check my understanding here? On the one hand X and on the other hand Y. Help me to understand how the two can coexist.'

I try this with Ella. 'On the one hand, Tim is committed to you and knows that going out on a Thursday night is very triggering for you, given the history . . . On the other hand, Tim committed to this Thursday plan and then came home with suspicious marks.'

Ella starts to slightly shift in her chair, and I sense she is also shifting in her mind. Her rigid defence of Tim is being dismantled.

Kelli joins the dots

I tell Kelli about my private work. She tells me she is proud of me, and I feel the warmth of her praise spread through my chest. I wonder about our transference; Kelli often represents a maternal figure for me, but today she doesn't make me look at this and unpack it.

She asks about my connections outside of my work. 'You seem to be working very hard to connect with your patients and this must be taxing on your own emotional resources. How are you taking care of yourself?'

I admit I haven't given it too much thought, but I have been using the tools university gave me, the reflective journal, to look at my patterns and try to gain some insight. So far, I have just been writing it all down as a narrative. Narrative structure can help our minds make sense of things and attach new meanings; a beginning, middle and an end can create a sense of comfort and containment.

'It's funny you should say that,' Kelli comments. 'I have been reflecting on you quite a lot in recent weeks and would like to offer you an interpretation.'

I try not to dwell on the fact that I am pleased Kelli has held me in mind outside of our sessions, wondering about me, caring about me. I encourage her to share her thoughts.

'It seems as though you are so immersed in and connected to those with emotional problems, difficulties or even pathologies, that they might have become the only people you feel safe to function around. They feel familiar to you, so maybe, subconsciously, in your personal life, you seek them out.'

This would explain Raff. Nothing Kelli has said to me during our time together has resonated with me as much as this. When something resonates so powerfully, it brings me a huge sense of peace – a sense of, 'Ah, that's what it is!'

Internal monsters

Daisy is a teenage girl with low self-esteem. When she comes to see me, we discuss self-talk, the negative internal narrator that so many of us have running all the time, but tap in and out of. I am yet to work with a patient who hasn't experienced a persecutory negative internal monologue, at least at some point in their life. When we personify Daisy's internal voice, so that we can separate it from Daisy herself, she decides she wants it to be a stuffy, boring, jobsworth-type woman named Dreary Deidre. I find this amusing – the description sums up the aura of the negative voice so well.

Daisy describes Dreary Deidre as being like the miserable slug-like receptionist in the Pixar film *Monsters, Inc.* She is able to report Dreary Deidre's put-downs and we challenge them together, disempowering her quite easily now that she is nothing more than a miserable slug. Daisy is now able to give her assertive messages that are blunt but do the job – like, 'Shut up!'

My own negative internal voice is also still rattling around in my mind, and it's saying, *How could you be so stupid as to be taken in by Raff? You are* trained *to read people.* The voice is loud and hard to shake. Telling it to shut up isn't working. Months have passed since Raff revealed himself. Time has moved on, but the self-doubt remains in me.

Counting the hours

I am racking up my practical hours, having already added a great number of the 400 therapy hours needed to fill the quota for my PhD training, many of which have been recorded, listened back to and critiqued by my tutors and peers. This week, I even receive some praise. I play a recording of me talking to the mother of a teenage girl who has been admitted to the ward after taking an overdose. She is talking very quickly and I slow her down and ask, 'How does it feel as a mother?' This seems to be what she needs to express herself and allow for her own emotions to have some space. My feedback is that I have good empathic responding. Armed with this and my continued desire to feel distracted, I resume my professional journey.

Dreams

Ella is back and is growing in her ability to trust me. We are close to a breakthrough when she starts talking about a dream she had.

'I was trying to get to your office,' she tells me. 'I really needed to see you, but when I got there, you were standing far away from me, kicking a ball at my stomach. You kept kicking it and asking me to grab it, but I wouldn't. Then there was a light explosion above us, but it was those little old-fashioned lights from the olden days . . . you know, the ones you would have to light with a match and use an oil or a fuel.'

'Gaslights?' I offer.

And, with that, we have a breakthrough.

Seeing the red flags

Gaslighting creates self-doubt, a mistrust of your own thoughts, which wears you down. It creates a lack of self-esteem and a deep questioning of self-value. The other person devalues you, makes you feel incapable, unreasonable, mad even. They create an environment of fear and anxious hyper-vigilance, which wears you down.

Just as Ella is struggling with internalized negative messages about herself, I am struggling with a great deal of persecutory 'self-talk' following my embarrassment over Raff. The negativity of the voice can be intense and cruel. We can be watering the plants one day, or folding the laundry, and receive a sudden flash of some cripplingly embarrassing moment from the past, whether that was holding a stranger's hand in a shop when you were seven, assuming they were your mum, accidentally reading a hand signal as an invitation to high five, or leaning in for a kiss that wasn't coming.

My newest patient is tortured by these moments, most memorably the time he was in a shopping centre with his nan at the age of eight, where he announced that he wanted to purchase a 'sexual jumper'. He had meant to say 'unisex'. We all sometimes have an internal voice which says, *Remember when you did that, you idiot?*

We seem to spontaneously revisit these places of humiliation; even more helpfully, our brains will sometimes paint a detailed picture of a future situation going disastrously wrong. Such struggles with shame and internal put-downs can flatten mood and create anxiety, bringing a sense of dread and impending doom. This manifests in different ways, including imposter syndrome, when we have a sudden jolt that we have been placed here – usually at work – by accident, and we have no clue what we are doing and feel totally out of place. I regularly experience a flash of imposter syndrome when I realize I am in charge of the mental health of the child sitting in front of me. Me? Someone who just willingly dated a maniac?

Self-sabotage is another manifestation of shame, most commonly procrastination – stalling and delaying tasks that might take seconds, compared to the hours of anguish we rack up while avoiding them.

Most of us can cope with the odd visit from the self-persecutory voice, but at times of high stress or emotionality the disempowering nature of the voice can be tough. It can lower our self-esteem so we can't cope with it, challenge it or push it away. It's a bit of a chicken-and-egg situation – when we are down, we attack ourselves, and when we attack ourselves, we feel down.

Feeling stuck

Viola is making me feel a bit stuck. It is very hard to watch the unrelenting self-directed anger and self-blame churning her up.

Dr Lane lets me rant on about it.

'I can hear the distress for you,' she says, and I know immediately where she is going with this.

We discuss the parallel processing between me and Viola, and how I am dealing with my emotions, which is mostly by distracting myself from them, and listening to Kelli tell me how angry I am every week.

'Why don't you use this?' Dr Lane suggests. 'I mean, it's like Viola was sent to you on purpose. You are trained to read people and even *you* feel you got it wrong – some self-disclosure here might help her.'

Make her feel less alone by telling her I made the same fuck-up – it's not a bad idea.

Let's laugh together

In my next session with Viola, she goes straight into self-attack mode again.

'It's my job not to get things wrong! What will people think?'

In response, I ask her, 'What would you think if I told you this had happened to me?'

This makes her pause, and I can hear the cogs whirring.

'You're trained to read people too . . . Do our emotions make us bypass our skills?' she wonders out loud.

Finally, some allowance for her emotions. I give away just enough of my own story for Viola to know I have been duped, despite it being my job to understand people, to risk-assess people and have insight into their psychological functioning.

I ask her if me sharing my story causes her to hold me in less esteem or to have any criticism of me, telling her not to answer out loud but to think about it.

Something shifts between us.

Viola says, 'If it can happen to a shrink, I guess nobody is immune. And, in a way, Nat, it makes you more human.'

Revelling in the story, she allows her playful side to be seen.

'He was just putting on a suit to go and feed the ducks,' she says in between gasps of laughter.

We both giggle for a really long time and I don't feel at all embarrassed.

Loss of hope

Dr Lane is late for our next meeting; I place digestives on a plate and make us coffee. When she arrives, her diary bursting at the seams, as always, she seems a bit frantic. She says she's sorry she didn't text. I notice she doesn't have her iPhone; instead, she is holding an old Nokia 3310 with a cracked screen. I wonder why but decide not to pry. There is a disconnect between us today and she is distracted, but I make sure to take my time to convey my thanks for helping me navigate self-disclosure with Viola.

She checks in on how I am coping, and says I seem more at ease and more peaceful. We delve into that a little.

'I think the difference this time,' I say, 'the reason the heart-break is less aggressive, is *acceptance*. There's no hope of reconcilement and no fantasy of rekindling anything because the Raff I knew is dead.'

Hope is often present after a break-up, even if only a small amount. Even if we think with 95 per cent confidence that the split is the right thing, 5 per cent of our brain hopes to bump into the ex at the shop or in the pub, or for fate to bring us back together somehow.

Dr Lane and I talk for a while about the disillusion of hope and how sad it can be, but also how clarifying. She then dashes off a little early, mumbling something about picking up her son from nursery.

She doesn't seem very peaceful, I reflect, and I wonder if she has a Kelli. This stays with me. Dr Lane holds so much in her mind and she is such a wonderful mentor, I hope she feels supported, as I do.

Coping

We all find our safe spaces and our coping tools. Mine has become to exaggerate the story with Raff. When it comes up socially, I am the first to deliver the headline: 'My boyfriend told me he was a spy for MI5, and I believed him.' I take the power out of it and borrow Viola's line: 'He was off feeding the ducks in an Armani suit!' I open myself up to ridicule and end up laughing along. My friends nickname him 'Pinocchio Syndrome' and send me the emoji with the nose that protrudes out of the little face. People ask me to retell the tale at parties and soon I have rehearsed it down to a T.

Self-deprecation is a social tool that disarms people, and often encourages more positive evaluation from others. But it only works when it's genuine. Self-deprecating public statements on social media have been found to generate negative social evaluations, in a similar way to virtue signalling.

In my case, self-deprecation is my new coping mechanism. I poke fun at myself before anyone else has the chance. This way, I regain control.

The body keeps score

Sam comes back to see me. I brace myself for another false epi-leptic seizure and, right on cue, he delivers a GCSE-standard performance in Kiwi's doorway, all the while clutching a crumpled list of symptoms. I do my best to distract, deflect and encourage him to bond with me over something other than an intricate constellation of symptoms gleaned from Wikipedia, but the compulsion is too strong and he trots out his list of ailments, assessing my face for shock and concern as they keep coming. I ask why he thinks it's important for me to know all of his physical sensations and then gently enquire if any of his sensations might be psychosomatic.

Sam is furious at the suggestion and, instead of hearing, 'Do you think it could be psychosomatic?' he hears, 'Is it all in your head and are you making it all up?'

A lot of people seem to have this response to the suggestion of psychosomatic presentations, which are caused, maintained or aggravated by a mental-health factor such as stress, distress, unresolved trauma or internal conflicts. They're not nothing. Far from it. Our bodies respond to and hold trauma. Our emotional response interacts with pain, immune-system func-tioning, hormonal functioning and much more. It is certainly not 'made up' or 'all in your head'. I try to de-escalate Sam and approach it a different way.

'How would you rate your pain, out of ten?' I ask him.

This is a common question asked by doctors and I know Sam is used to it.

'Erm, a nine out of ten, sometimes a ten, and sometimes maybe even off the scale,' he replies, without much thought.

'And, of that score, how much of it would you say is attributable to emotional pain? Maybe two out of the ten? Maybe three?'

Sam thinks about this for a while, deliberating, as though I am standing in front of him in a silk shirt and bow tie, a cheesy game-show host asking him which box to pick. He remains angry, though, and doesn't answer, so I try to remove the doubt, using concrete facts to show how mental-health states and struggles lead to and interact with physical illness.

'Did you know that, following a heart attack, one of the biggest risk factors for deterioration and suffering a second heart attack is depression?'

His ears prick up and he starts to listen.

This is not just about biochemistry. Someone who feels hopeless, has no motivation and doesn't value themselves very much is unlikely to take good care of themselves. The relationship between body and mind is complex, but it's also very simple.

My aim is to get Sam to access his emotional state. His current reliance on reporting physical symptoms is a coping mechanism, a mask for something he is struggling with. I just need to find out what that is. But he's determined not to let me in.

Multiple identities

To believe you can fool those around you without being caught requires great self-confidence and self-belief. Do those people who create and maintain more than one identity believe their own conflicting narratives? Multiple selves can be the result of mental instability or mental illness. In dissociative identity disorder (DID), previously known as multiple personality disorder, people can take on characteristics of other people, adopting their perceptions and mannerisms in order to protect the true self and dissociate from traumatic experiences. This is known as covert DID. This can become more pervasive and the person can be completely overwhelmed by different personalities and personas, known as alters. This is overt DID. The different selves can have their own distinct voices, likes, dislikes, views and feelings and engage in their own actions and behaviours.

We are all juggling different identities on some level. I am a university student, the lowest rung on the expertise ladder, the naive learner and a mere sponge for other people's knowledge. But the moment I step into the hospital I am the professional, the leader, the one holding the answers. And I have now added a new identity to my repertoire: the private therapist, sought out and paid to offer support.

People pay me!

This new identity still feels like an imposter.

The imposter in me

Renting rooms in fashionable east London doesn't come cheap and my lack of self-belief means I am charging such a modest rate that the rent for the therapy room renders the sessions financially pointless. In some cases, I even make a loss. I decide instead to rent a flat with a tiny second box room that will serve as my private therapy room – in theory, the additional income will enable me to afford the flat as my new home.

Leaving the safety of my flat-share and the familiarity of

my safe, symbiotic female relationships and best friend Alex feels a bit like being torn from the womb. I imagine the separation anxiety I will face when staring down at a lonely portion of beans on toast instead of sharing a chippy on the roof with the girls or making our weekly 'kids tea', where four adult women get excited over a plate of chicken dinosaurs, smiley faces and peas. But I know I need to move on. I throw myself out of the nest.

I talk this move through with Kelli, who is pleased I am taking this step. She says it suggests my emotional inner world is less frantic and less needy of others. Kelli also thinks this is a good chance to further develop my relationship with my 'inner companion', which simply means how I relate to myself, how I treat myself, how I talk to myself and how I self-soothe. Kelli makes me feel as though I can live alone, that I will cope.

The tiny, neutral-coloured room in my new cosy-but-lonely flat is reminiscent of Kiwi: a small space which I have come to find safe and containing, in the same way young children favour small spaces like understairs cupboards in order to feel secure. I am now under pressure to make my private practice work for me financially, so every time my imposter feeling rears its head, I step into the shoes of professional me and challenge it.

'Professional me is confident and can handle this,' I say out loud, gaslighting myself into being mad enough to pull this off.

This must be how compulsive and pathological liars like Raff lie to themselves, I realize. It's not so hard.

The corners of the mind

In small ways, we all lie to ourselves on a daily basis. Every time we call a memory to mind, we alter that memory. It is rewritten and grows less and less precise. We distort our lived experiences by integrating new information, knowledge and insights. The benefit of hindsight, if you like. Maybe this helps to explain what happens when pathological liars incorporate their lies over time and gradually come to believe a mix of truth and lies – and, eventually, just believe their lies. Repeating them may also cause what psychologists call the illusory truth effect: our tendency to believe something if we hear it enough times. It's a known method of propaganda, often associated with the Nazis and Joseph Goebbels, the most sinister example of how we process lies.

Remember that time you were lost in the supermarket when you were little, when you let go of your mum's hand for a split second and were filled with raging panic, thinking that you would never find her again? Well, that never happened. But, in an experiment conducted in the seventies by a psychologist, Elizabeth Loftus, telling people it happened to them caused 30 to 50 per cent of them to give a clear and detailed narrative of it and how they felt in that moment. Participants who signed up for the study were given four stories about their childhood, only three of which were true, with details of the true events gathered from the participants' older siblings. The false story detailed the participant being lost in the supermarket; it was made to seem legitimate with real details, such as using the supermarket frequented by the family. After all, a seriously savvy Aldi family would not be fooled by a story about being lost in Waitrose. The study illustrated that false memories can be readily generated, implanted and upheld.

The concept of repressed memories was popular for a time in the nineties. Some people experience repression as a subconscious psychological defence initiated in response to trauma, events so terrorizing that they cannot be held in conscious awareness, so they are pushed right down in the memory bank, into the abyss. It's a survival mode, a way of coping with events that, if dwelled upon, could cause total disintegration and breakdown.

However, the discussion of repressed memories in the media and social sphere meant that many people started to fear that something traumatic had happened to them in the past, which they had suppressed. This is a bit like when a hypochondriac learns about a new condition and immediately sees it everywhere and believes it must be happening to them. The fear was quite widespread within therapists' offices, with people believing that one day you could be walking around feeling fine, if a little stressed from work, perhaps, then one session with a therapist or some sort of trigger would lead you to recall a pervasive history of relentless childhood sexual abuse, an underworld you had simply erased from your brain or held out of conscious awareness – until now.

Our memories often grow extra details from a seed of truth, especially in the retelling. An anecdote about someone's boyfriend's grandad being a victim of Harold Shipman, the doctor-turned-serial-killer, might subconsciously morph into his boyfriend's grandad *being* Harold Shipman. A real incident in which a cousin died learning to fly a plane in 2011 might become the story of how their cousin died in the 9/11 disaster.

Imagination can be a very powerful thing as it can implant falsehoods and distortions in our memories. It's tragic events or those prompting negative emotions that are more susceptible to distortion.

Findings

Dr Lane and I can't meet face to face for our session, so we check in by phone. I talk about Sam and my sense of disconnect from him.

Dr Lane is quiet for a moment; I wait in the silence for a nugget of wisdom.

'I found a little boy,' she says.

This isn't what I expected. What? Where? How?

'A little boy was wandering the street near my home and I took him in,' she goes on. 'I just found him. He was so frightened . . . he was only about five. I wonder what he thought. Did he think he would ever be found? Did he have any idea of the danger he was in, or did he just feel sheer abandonment panic?' She's thinking aloud. 'He must have felt untethered, lost,' she says, tearfully.

We talk through what the boy was feeling moment to moment before the police arrived and safely returned him home.

Looking at the individual experience of the little boy helps me to feel less overwhelmed and more connected with how feeling alone – like Sam – can be scary.

Very clever, Dr Lane, I think, as I hang up.

But the thought lingers that she seemed very emotionally connected to the boy, his distress and the feeling of being untethered. Maybe her position of responsibility and leadership at the hospital makes her feel alone sometimes. Maybe she doesn't have time to focus on her own processing and upset. I imagine Dr Lane gives out so much to others that she has little space to focus on herself. I know very little about her personal life other than that she is married and has a son; this is a professional boundary and something I have upheld with her out of respect. I do know from conversations that she loves horses. We have talked many times about the benefits of equine therapy and the use of emotional support animals, which help with emotional regulation and empathy building. She seems to light up when talking about horses and I imagine this is how she unwinds.

Curiouser and curiouser

I have made a mistake with Sam. In our next session, he changes tack and reports a list of mental-health disorders longer than my arm. As he works his way down the list, the disorders become increasingly rare. It's clear he has taken a real interest in the subject matter, disappearing down a rabbit hole of journal articles to find ever more bizarre symptoms. He has every one of them. It's these that are causing his physical symptoms, he argues. I take some deep breaths and prepare for the long haul.

Alice in Wonderland

Now Sam claims one of his legs 'isn't in the room'.

Part of being a psychologist and a therapist is being a

detective. Therapists will often say things like, 'I am trying to unpick what is going on,' and 'I need to make observations of behaviours in different contexts and look at responses' – that is, look for clues. And so, assuming the role, like a Poundland Poirot, I stare off into space and consider my hypothesis as Sam describes his lack of leg and the confusion and terror around the odd sensation he's experiencing.

What is he trying to present with, I wonder? Is it body integrity dysphoria, maybe – the feeling a limb isn't meant to be a part of the body? I have seen this before, but surely he isn't seeking an amputation like my last patient. Maybe it's depersonalization – the feeling of being outside the body and observing yourself. But that's not usually leg-specific . . . Maybe a tactile hallucination, which is when someone hallucinates a physical sensation or a feeling of being touched? Most typically, however, this feels like bugs crawling under the skin.

Unsatisfied with my suppositions, I stay curious, asking about any other symptoms he might have. He tells me that his head feels much larger than the doorway and that's why he struggled to enter the room. He must have forgotten to act this part out. On seeing my brow furrow in a question, his eyes dart around the tiny room in a panic before eventually landing on the neat desk.

'My arms are as tiny as . . . as pencils!' he blurts out, trying to rectify his mistake.

Ah, Alice in Wonderland syndrome! A very rare condition where body parts and objects seem to have absurd dimensions. Sam seems proud of himself when I name the condition. A coy, almost contemptuous smile plays about his mouth. Have I been drawn into a game, I wonder? Either way, I win for getting the syndrome right. A little smile plays about my mouth too.

Simon says

At post-work cocktails with Alex, we are having a fierce discussion about mothers and their sons. I notice a man listening in and chuckling at times, like when I exclaim, 'It's a pandemic of narcissistic precious mummy's boys,' and Alex instantly responds with, 'This generation of men are corked.'

He sits nearby at the bar and listens intently to the conversation while stirring a whisky sour. 'Psychiatrist?' he asks.

'Psychologist,' I say.

'Oh, what's the difference?'

The short answer is, *prescribing*.

Psychiatrists prescribe medications, psychotropic drugs that impact and alter mood, thoughts and perception. Psychologists cannot prescribe. When we are fully qualified, we are called doctors, but not doctors who can write prescriptions. The weak ego in me often worries that, when I qualify, if I am ever in a restaurant where someone's choking or having a heart attack and someone shouts, 'Is there a doctor in the house?' I will feel an intense urge to announce, 'I am a doctor! But, sadly, I am of no use in this moment, unless someone wants to tell me how they feel about it.'

The difference between the two professions is something that still seems to mystify people. Psychologists try to make sense of *what* someone is experiencing – what started it, what the predisposing factors are, what triggered the problem to become intense or overwhelming, what things make it worse and what helps. We empower the person to take control and skill themselves up, bolstered by the supportive relationship. Therapy delivered in this way is successful. Brain-imaging studies show that, after a course of psychotherapy, the brain changes in the same ways it changes in response to medications. The changes found in specific regions deep inside the brain towards the thalamus mirror the changes achieved by an antidepressant, fluoxetine.

Some people seem to think there is a rivalry between psychology and psychiatry. I am not against psychiatry. As with any profession, psychiatrists sit on a continuum of good practice. On one end, some are pill pushers; a person is reduced to a label, a list of symptoms, which is in turn reduced to one or several tablets. Bish, bash, bosh. But, at the other end, some are incredible, applying psychological theory to assess, formulate and offer a range of therapies and treatments, which may include, but are not limited to, medication. Such psychiatrists have all the strings to their bow.

Psychologists and therapists also sit on a continuum, and I am becoming more aware of this as I progress in my career. I have seen my university professors fall from grace and I have seen professionals struggle with mental-health difficulties in much the same way anyone else would. For all my human flaws, I can see myself sitting on this continuum more clearly now.

After receiving the short answer to this extensive question, the man, who I'm by this time calling Simon, says, 'Impressive. I find you fascinating.'

Seeing the red flags

He peppers me with compliments over a second whisky sour and I decide that I find him extremely charming. I bathe in the light he casts upon me. We swap numbers and he leaves me to enjoy my evening with Alex, which I also like. I am left intrigued to learn more about him.

SEVEN

A string of *aha* moments

Kelli is silent

I often worry that Kelli thinks I am a crap therapist, so, still basking in Simon's words, I make myself comfortable on her chaise longue and let her know that I'm 'impressive' and 'fascinating'. Plus, I have recently received some feedback, emailed to me from Peggy's new mental-health worker. It's glowing and paints me in a positive light. I read it to Kelli.

Kelli sighs. 'First of all,' she says, 'whenever we get such positive feedback from a patient, as therapists, we need to be sceptical and curious about it – it often means they are idealizing you. You need to know why. Patients with BPD often idealize people, but they are quick to swing back to rage and hatred. It's nice, flattering and inflating to hear positives from patients, but you need to focus on their process, not on how it makes you feel reassured.'

Great. Kelli is calling me a narcissist.

'You represent a maternal figure to Peggy,' she adds. 'The relationship between mothers and their daughters is often fraught and full of fury.'

I sense her rolling her eyes.

Great. Peggy sees me as a maternal figure. I am not only a narcissist; I am an *old* narcissist.

'Second of all,' Kelli continues, bulldozing over my thoughts, 'why did you feel it was important to share this positive feedback with me?'

I pause, but then persevere. 'Because you think I'm a crap therapist. You once said I am just "hobbling along", or something like that, that I am just about coping with patient demands.'

I wait.

Kelli is silent.

I wait.

'Natalie, can you see what you are transferring onto me here? You are holding a fantasy that I think you are a crap therapist and have disregarded all the times I have praised your skills and your abilities with patients, and you have held on to this one statement.'

So, she admits she said it. But maybe I do need to work on how I respond to inflation and praise from patients. My turn to roll my eyes. I guess she's right. Why is she always right?

Back on the pedestal

I receive a flattering text from Simon, who now adds to 'impressive' and 'fascinating', telling me he thinks I am 'someone special'. He feels a connection and would love to talk more.

We meet at the same cocktail bar and compete with each other to tell funny stories, playfully talking over one another.

He insists on ordering me an Uber home at the end of the night, to make sure I get home safely. When a case of my favourite wine arrives the next evening, I realize the Uber was a ploy to gain my address.

Despite developing my analytical skills and the role of detective within my professional life, I remain a hopeless romantic in my personal life and so proceed to engage in behaviours aligned with this identity. My feelings ignite at speed; I spend a lot of time fantasizing about a future life mostly based on the imagined features and the potential of this man. I quickly begin to idealize Simon and put him on a pedestal.

Once more, I place the rose-tinted glasses firmly on the bridge of my nose.

Hopeless romantic

As I plunge into the fantasy world of the hopeless romantic, my brain does its best to pull me back from the brink. It is trying to avoid the trauma of my previous experience. To do this, it employs the primitive defence mechanism of imagining horrible potential scenarios of where the relationship might end up and playing these out in my head like a cruel film.

These intrusive thoughts about being abandoned occur at the most unexpected moments; in my morning referrals meeting or when I call a patient's name in the waiting room, a negative thought hits me, knocking the wind out of my sails. My brain then creates a way of coping with this. It chooses shutdown. In response to threat, it begins to create a numbness in me, a callous, superficial lack of caring, which takes over. I am starting to see what Kelli means when she says I employ a cold, steely persona. This is my tool as I enter this connection with Simon full throttle. With my shutdown strategy in my back pocket, I feel confident. When the hopeless romantic in me takes over and my mind is filled with obsessions about love and romance, I feel awakened by the excitement and risk of it all, but my physiological state is like someone about to square up to their most feared opponent in a boxing ring.

Holding two opposing parts of the self at any one time – in my case, hopeless romantic versus self-preservation – can create a feeling of being torn, a cognitive dissonance. It's an unsettling sense of uncertainty, even anxiety. This unease comes when we want to do something that is in opposition with our perceived values, when we have two identities we want to align with at the same time. This can occur in many ways: new mums trying to be the perfect mum while also upholding their status at work; a parent trying to be emotionally strong for their family while experiencing their own pain and fear; a perfectionist trying to live up to high standards while avoiding some tasks altogether for fear of failure.

We have all experienced the discomfort of this torn feeling. It is hard to sit with, and usually propels us into action, one way or the other.

No worries if not

My next private patient presents with a similar cognitive dissonance. Claire has been tentative in her email reaching out for support, very much a 'no worries if not' approach, and I sense that her opposing parts are *I need therapy* versus *I don't want to be told something I don't want to hear.* She sounds fragile and unsure of herself. I spend time on my reply to her, gently encouraging her to see me. Let's meet for one session, I say, to see if it's a good fit.

I have added a few touches to my therapy room and I am quite pleased with it: two small but comfy office chairs, a box of tissues – of course – and a painting on the wall that is abstract enough to seem psychoanalytic. Claire takes a seat and stares at the floor. The picture goes to waste. Her shoulders are rounded and hunched, like a visual apology for being present. She is defeated. She opens by saying she is probably wasting my time, that people have much bigger problems than boyfriends and it is weak to need to come and talk to someone about a relationship in order to cope.

I like Claire immediately. I have a sense there is a bigger personality hiding in there somewhere and I experience her as genuine. This isn't martyrdom or 'woe is me'. This is a real, palpable lack of self-value.

'All psychological problems and pain are relational,' I say.

When I offer this, she meets my gaze for the first time, so I carry on.

'All the way from the more severe mental-health disorders – psychosis, for example – to the day to day, some of our core pain is about being isolated from others, from society, being alone and frightened. The more day-to-day stuff, like the internal pressure to succeed, is about the need to gain praise, input and acknowledgement from others. It's all about connection and relationships. We are all attachment beings, so everyone who comes to see me is talking about a relationship in some form.'

Claire seems to relax as she takes in what I'm saying, and she begins to open up. Claire has been with Trevor for just over a year, they don't live together yet but they spend a lot of time together, unless he is called away for work. Things began wonderfully. He introduced her to new places, they learned new things together, they connected and talked and he said he worshipped her. He called her his queen. He was very charming and social. He was engaging and vibrant. Claire second-guesses herself for a moment and makes it clear that she doesn't want to spend the hour criticizing him, because he *is* a wonderful person. I explain that we are not here to demonize anyone; we want to work out where this relationship is leaving her emotionally and how we can make things more manageable.

Claire speaks of Trevor's qualities and attributes in the past tense. I point this out to her and wonder why this might be. I give her permission to explain the light and the dark in him, which exist in any person.

Things have changed recently, she tells me. Trevor is a very powerful man, she explains, and he has begun to put her down, which feels intimidating.

The comment about power makes it onto my notepad. It seems important. Claire has stated it as a fact.

'When you say he "puts you down", what do you mean?' I ask.

It started with very small things that she batted away in her mind. He asked her to stop wearing tights because he didn't like the indentation marks they left on her body. Then he cut up her credit card – 'For your own good,' he said – allowing her to buy clothes only when she lost the pounds she had put on due to work stress, telling her she really should quit that job anyway.

The word *allowing* also makes it to the notepad. Now I understand her perception of Trevor's power. It is from his exerted control.

To the rescue

Simon and I are having fun. He is effervescent on our dates and continues to be fascinated by my job. Like me, he enjoys wine, and we bond on a wine-tasting experience in east London where we are instructed to load up a 'wine credit card' with some cash and are then let loose on the custom selection of wines, like children at an ice-cream buffet. As the wine flows, Simon opens up about his past.

Simon has an extensive trauma history, with a great deal of loss, including his father taking his own life, suddenly and without a clear cause for Simon to cling to. Simon has seen a grief therapist, which he found comforting, although he says what resonated with him most was a sketch he saw online captioned, *When someone you love takes their own life, it is like there is an explosion in the room you are sitting in and you can't understand how you survived it.* I listen, but I am careful not to step into my therapist shoes in this moment, a lesson I learned with Max and Raff. They hated my 'therapy tone' or any attempt to step into the rescuer role.

There is an urgency that comes over me, however, to care, to rescue, which leads to physical intimacy. And it's immediately followed by a surge of emotional intimacy. A dangerous combination takes form within me – the rescuer part of me meets the hopeless romantic part of me – and it feels exhilarating, scary and unstoppable.

Spider-monkey self

The next day, as I explain to Alex the intense care and romantic love I felt towards Simon on our date, I defensively suggest that it was a case of in vino veritas rather than that I was pissed and triggered emotionally to save someone.

Alex looks at me sternly and suggests we go over some of our key findings from our collective experiences in the dating world, all of which are loosely informed by my knowledge of neuroscience and human behaviour. The most important thing to acknowledge, she reminds me, is the role of what Alex and I call the 'spider-monkey self'. Sexual and physical intimacy provide the most rapid and intense conditioning of our reward systems in the brain; put simply, we are flooded with hormones that demand we attach to the other. Like a little spider monkey clinging to its mother's chest as she climbs a tree, we instinctively feel the need to hold on, a key driver for cuddling after sex. The same hormonal systems – namely, oxytocin and opioid systems – make this attachment feel pleasurable while simultaneously reducing stress and distress, making us feel really good and less bad at the same time. Who could resist? The feeling is initially intense and hard to ignore.

Alex and I have relied upon the spider-monkey hypothesis on many occasions to regain rational thought, not least when I once exclaimed outside Clapham Junction station that a tall Tory I barely knew but had spent one night with, who had no discernible personality and zero charm, was in fact The One. This feeling quickly dissipated when his next post on Instagram read, *At the rugger, having bantz and beers.* Not even soft-focus rose-tinted glasses could distort this truth.

For the spider-monkey feeling, I use a technique I often use with patients when teaching skills of distress tolerance. If you stay with the feeling, access it fully and don't try to ignore it, it will reduce incrementally over time. The spider-monkey feeling usually takes around twenty-four hours, and so we wait.

After twenty-four hours, Simon remains on the pedestal. I get a raised eyebrow from Alex, but nothing more.

The coin task

Claire returns to see me, and I'm pleased that she has made it, that her courage hasn't seeped away in the interim. But she remains reluctant to give more specifics about what has been happening in her relationship as she clearly feels she's betraying Trevor. She keeps checking her phone, as if he can somehow hear us, or maybe in case he summons her.

I ask her how this power dynamic in her relationship is impacting her. She seems distracted, I say, and maybe even a little fearful. By constantly jumping to Trevor's defence, she creates a little tension between us. To change approach, I focus on the value she places on herself and try to bring her mind back to her own needs. I rummage around in my bag and find some coins – a pound, fifty pence, ten pence, two pence and a penny. I hold my A4 notepad as a flat surface between us and ask her to pick the coin she feels most represents her and to place it somewhere. She picks up the two-pence piece and

places it to one side of the pad. I then ask for coins to represent all the other important people in her life. She pauses, then
picks up the pound coin and places it in the centre of the pad.

'Trevor,' she says.

'Who else is important that we need to think about?' I ask.

Claire looks down at the other coins and picks up the fifty
pence, rolling it between her fingers for a while.

'I guess there's my mum, but she's not really speaking to
me at the moment.'

She holds on to the coin as she tells me through gentle
tears that there's no one else. She has drifted from everyone.
I don't need to say anything about intentional isolation. I see
the penny drop – pun intended. Instead, I ask Claire to think
before the next session about why she picked the two pence
for herself and how she is currently valuing herself in this
relationship.

I try to end with some hope. 'You didn't pick the penny,' I
say, 'so you still have some positive regard for the self. We can
build up from there.'

Missing

Claire misses the next session and, in my gut, I feel fear,
replaying in my mind how she anxiously checked her phone
throughout our time together. I text her. *I am sorry you missed
the session today; I hope you are safe and well. I will hold your slot
open for next week and I really hope to see you then.*

I wake up to a reply sent at 3 a.m.

See you next week, Nat.

I exhale with relief.

A string of *aha* moments

Sulky Simon

On our next date, Simon and I have breakfast. No wine or cock-tails this time. As we chat, it becomes clear that Simon has quite a small set of interests: rugby, Led Zeppelin and, not unlike a lot of middle-class men in their late twenties living in London, Alan Partridge. Simon quotes Alan Partridge at me through-out breakfast. Having shared with him my lack of familiarity with the show, this gets old quickly. I feel a little uncomfort-able, a little lost, so try to lighten the mood by poking fun at Led Zeppelin. Weren't they once accused of stealing a song by some US rockers? I ask. Aren't they alleged plagiarists?

Simon thrusts his plate away from him, as if having a sulk or making some sort of protest. I assume he's joking, so I mirror his strop, folding my arms and pouting. This doesn't shift anything at all, and in fact he seems more angry. I start to feel my shutdown response take the lead. I become silent, cold. I pay and leave. Retreat can be a subconscious way to take control. If I leave first, he can't physically leave me.

Later on, I have several missed calls from Simon.

Can you please take some responsibility for today? he says. *That band was my dad's favourite.*

Instantly, I feel guilt and shame. I reply with an apology and ask to move forward. The tension releases in my shoulders when he agrees to let it go.

Lingering malingering

Simon is on my mind, so, when I meet Dr Lane for a catch-up, I ask for her expertise on suicide, and the suicidal ideation people like Simon's dad must have experienced. The thoughts people have when feeling so hopeless that they desire to take their own lives are complex, difficult to understand. I ask her how we, as professionals, should respond. Do we have autonomy, are we able to choose our own fate, or should we preserve life at any cost?

Dr Lane says, 'It's a personal choice, but for me it's somewhere in the middle.'

She tells me about the young people she has worked with in the past in inpatient settings, the ones who self-harm, not as suicide attempts, but as their only coping strategy, like Peggy. Rather than try to stop the behaviour, professionals reduce the risks associated, making sure blades are clean to avoid infection and ensuring first-aid items are readily available. This doesn't sit well with me, as I feel the urge to try to reduce the behaviour, not just the risk of infection, but I can also see the limitations when it comes to the level of control mental-health professionals have over people's choices. We cannot fix, we cannot give reassurance, we can only offer it.

We move on to discussing Sam, who has a follow-up appointment with me this week. I can only imagine which obscure illness he will poorly act out this time. Dr Lane helps me to understand that I am not suggesting there is *nothing* wrong with Sam by saying he is false reporting or malingering. He clearly has some unmet emotional need which is compelling him to spend his time doing research, making his lists and coming into the hospital. His performances are clearly a coping mechanism, much like self-harm is a coping mechanism. It is maladaptive but, in some way, it is working for him, and so he keeps doing it.

We build a fuller picture of Sam. He is vulnerable. His parents threw him out at a young age for 'bad behaviour' – behaviours that seem to be typical of most adolescents. But his mum and dad have their own mental-health needs, and they couldn't cope. Sam has been provided with a flat from social housing, but he is ill-equipped to live independently. Frankly, this is something I can still struggle with, often resorting to ice cream for dinner or coming to work wearing bikini bottoms under my trousers because I haven't done my washing.

Armed with this insight from Dr Lane and a new approach to Sam, I have newfound feelings of compassion. I want to repair the damage from the last session.

Drunk-dial a therapist

After a busy week, I let off steam at a new bar in east London with Alex. Now that we live separately, we make a concerted effort to spend quality time together. As we reunite, we feel elated and the alcohol hits our systems quickly, excitement as the catalyst. We spend the night talking over each other at speed and laughing until we have forgotten the joke, and I wake up with a dry mouth, banging head, and the terrifying realization that my phone is still firmly clenched in my hand. This means I have done some sort of drunk-dialling. An ex? A new crush? God forbid a colleague.

As I inspect the phone screen, holding it away from my face, one eye closed, squinting, as if to make the news less impactful, nothing seems obvious. No calls, texts, Instagram messages. Maybe I have got off scot-free. Maybe, I dare to think, this is growth. But then I open Facebook. *Kelli Stevens* is typed into the search bar, a thumbnail picture of my therapist's face below it. I have drunk-searched my therapist; I am not sure if that's sadder than stalking an ex. I suspect it is.

I stare out of the window, clutching a mug of peppermint tea, tapping my ring on the side of the mug to make a distracting sound as my most anxious thoughts start to take over. I think about all of my patients, those who have told me they are desperate to know about the real me, who I am, if I am married, where I live, how I spend my time. Some of them have become very frustrated with the not knowing, but as a therapist it's my job to remain a relatively blank canvas, so that patients can project their thoughts and feelings onto me, without mine interfering.

This is a spectrum, however; I am not as cold and detached as some psychotherapists who sit in complete silence and offer little to no feedback during sessions, just a space for thoughts to unfold. One psychotherapist on my PhD course tried to convince me that sitting in silence and not responding to her patient for nine months' worth of sessions was the best way to help her to get over her miscarriage, because it equalled the gestational period. I remain sceptical. But I give little away about my personal life, unless it's helpful to the patient. I wonder how many of them have looked me up on social media because of this. And what they have seen.

And what is going on with me and Kelli that makes me want to look her up online? Am I in love with her? Am I experiencing my own erotic transference? I don't feel the deep longing, attraction and melancholy described by some patients when they fall in love with their therapist, but there is nevertheless clearly an interest. It seems this female connection has grown very important to me, as Kelli once pointed out during a session – an idea I rejected out of shame. I comfort myself that it's OK to have a profound connection with your therapist and to have a fascination with her life, as I scroll through my Facebook, deleting anything that makes me seem chaotic, messy, uncivilized, feral, outspoken or an alcoholic. This takes up most of the day.

Home visits

'How is it going, living independently?' I ask Sam, before he has a chance to open today's list.

Sam has recently moved into his council flat, known as 'semi-independent living' for teens who can't stay at home but aren't unwell enough to need inpatient care. Someone from social services pops in once a week to check in on him and to see how he is coping.

I see genuine fear, possibly even terror, flash across his face. Maybe, I think, the trips to see me are a reason not to be at home, alone, a teenager in a tiny flat.

'It's all right,' he says.

It's always better to listen to what the patient *isn't* saying. Sam can bang on about the pain in his little toe for fifty minutes but can't tell me about his homelife and how he copes alone.

'Sometimes I do home visits,' I tell him. 'Why don't I come out to you next time, save you the bus fare? We can talk there.'

Sam seems a little unsure. I can tell he's thinking about it, but then he seems to light up. 'Yes, let's do that,' he says.

Blood bath

I go to Sam's flat at 10 a.m. sharp, as agreed. His place is part of a small complex of dilipidated-looking flats. A battered sofa sits on the front lawn and the balconies are strewn with washing, push-bikes, children's toys and a fair amount of rubbish.

The main door is open and I push through it into the concrete stairwell. It's cold and damp. There is the inevitable smell of urine. Following the signs, I go up to flat four, where I find the front door is ajar. Calling out Sam's name and announcing myself, I walk in a little nervously. As I enter the kitchen, the scene that greets me initially overwhelms me. Sam is sitting on the floor, holding a penknife, a pool of blood next to him on the lino. His head is slumped forward, buried in his chest. I rush over instinctively and begin to reach for my phone to call an ambulance, but as I see his face I pause. He's checking my reaction, a contemptuous half-smile on his lips.

'Sam,' I say, 'can you tell me what's happened? Can you tell me what's happening for you right now?'

Sam is instantly animated, launching into a speech about having no friends and so he has hurt himself on the outside to show what it's like on the inside. I listen, validate and decide to join him on the floor, legs crossed. As I do, I look closer at the blood. It's a perfect circle, no droplets around it, nothing on the knife, and no sign of any injury on Sam's skin. The blood seems dried, as though it has been there for a while. I ask to see Sam's arm. He's reluctant at first, but eventually concedes. I see a small cut, professionally known as a 'superficial self-harm cut' – one of those cuts that bleed a lot and masquerade as a worse injury.

I check in with myself. Don't minimize this, I say in my head. It is still intentional harm to the self with a blade.

Sam begins to tell me that he is hopeless, and he reads out the definition of hopelessness verbatim, like a kind of human *DSM-5*, the psychologists' dictionary of diagnoses. I ask him about the social support he has around him and he says he has nobody, that he's totally alone and has no friends. To help gather my thoughts, and to see better how Sam lives, I take a look around the flat. It's tired and largely empty, which feels disheartening, but then I see a fully stocked, standalone bar in the corner of the living room, complete with optics spirit measurers attached to the wall. I notice some empty glasses on the coffee table, with remnants of beer, wine and spirits at the bottom. They might all be his, but I don't think so.

'Did you have a little party, a house-warming?' I ask.

Sam brushes me off. 'Oh, yeah, I had a few friends over to see the new bar.'

Friends. OK. The initial flash of annoyance that he has deceived me is challenged by the acknowledgement that he does have some social support and he isn't as isolated as I imagined. I can't help but be pleased by this.

I change tack. 'Sam, you knew I was coming at 10 a.m. Did you need me to see you in distress and pain? Every behaviour serves a function, even if that function is subconscious,' I say.

Sam looks puzzled and then annoyed that I have so easily worked out what's happening.

I told Sam I once had a patient who created an internal sense of boredom in an attempt to slow down the passage of time he spent with his mum, to make his time with her feel longer. I tell Sam that the patient did this subconsciously;

although it wasn't fun to feel bored, it served some deep-down function.

It's a penny-drop moment. He sees the function of his symptom creation and reporting.

'Nobody listens unless it gets really bad, unless people can see it,' Sam says, a sort of pleading in his voice.

'You feel unheard,' I offer. 'Ignored? Let down?'

Sam agrees and says he can't stop doing what he's doing because it works. If people can see physical pain, some sort of illness, blood, actual cuts, they have to respond, they have no choice, he says. 'Otherwise, I'm just the boy who cried wolf.'

He stops.

'If I get better,' he says, his voice smaller, 'you'll only see me for six sessions and then you'll leave.'

He has a point. Sam needs a therapeutic relationship, one deeper than the NHS is able to provide.

At one time, his behaviour was adaptive. This is how it was learned. The first time he accidentally hurt himself after falling off his bike was the first time his dad really paid attention to him, noticed him. Then the nurses at A & E were kind to him, listened to him, saw him and gave him a sticker for being brave. He learned that pain is rewarding, so it has become the strategy. His only strategy.

This learned behaviour is powerful, difficult to reverse and can escalate quickly. In inpatient psychiatric settings, the desire to 'not get better' for fear of being abandoned can morph and transform into a competition of who is the 'most ill'. Being unwell, staying unwell, is seen as valuable. It holds status. This can be seen in the trends that take hold of groups of young people – self-harm by cutting was an epidemic, then it was fainting and passing out, then headbanging. Young people who enter inpatient services will cut into their heads prior to headbanging to make the injury seem even more severe, more visually gory.

This also happens outside of psychiatric hospitals, and in school settings where some pupils have developed a mental-illness culture. Exposure via social media and TikTok and their toxic algorithms allows young people to over-identify and glamorize disorders and labels, with some misattributing their experiences to mental illness. This can be very scary. Sam is scared.

With his disclosure on the kitchen floor, Sam now has a window of opportunity to be released from this illness narrative. I stay with him for a few hours, and we talk about who he is outside of the labels. We talk about video games, making friends through online gaming, instant messaging and eating noodles with beans and cheese – his own delicious concoction.

The social prescription

Sam arrives at our next session with a crumpled piece of paper, the word *hallucinations* written on it. I see that we aren't out of the woods yet.

Hallucinations and 'hearing voices' seem to hold a huge fear factor for most people. Sam has probably chosen this problem as it causes alarm bells to ring with the professionals – with anyone, really. Hallucinations, or a lack thereof, are also notoriously difficult to prove. For the lay person, hallucinations seem to be firmly connected to psychotic illness and suggest a general 'madness', which might explain the stigma surrounding the reporting of them. They are actually more common than we might think. Visual hallucinations of loved ones who have recently passed away are relatively common, especially in older adults. The difference between 'I could have sworn I just saw them' and an actual visual hallucination is knowing that it's not real. But the feeling can still be really strong: 'I am so sure I saw them in a passing stranger.' People with OCD also sometimes experience hallucinations, as do those with visual impairments, like phantom vision – also known as Charles Bonnet syndrome – which is sometimes seen in older adults.

I suggest Sam puts the piece of paper to one side and that we will get to it at the end of the session, successfully guiding him away from symptom reporting so that we can talk about how he is coping and how he is taking care of himself.

At the end of what feels like a progressive session, Sam tells me he really enjoyed my visit to his flat, that it broke the monotony of the day, and he asks if I will do it again. I too enjoyed seeing him at home. It helped me get a better sense of him, who he is and his life outside of our sessions. Sam seemed more at ease in his own home, our interaction felt more natural, and I feel we have strengthened the therapeutic bond. Maybe this is because Sam has seen the commitment from me in coming out to see him. I am glad this seems to have made a real difference to him and he feels cared for, responded to, seen and heard. We decide on a home visit based on an agreement, and I draw up a contract for both of us to sign. I agree to uphold my end – which is to turn up on time, no matter what – and Sam agrees not to harm himself in any way prior to the visit, and to keep himself safe.

A string of *aha* moments

Behavioural contracting with patients can help them to achieve goals, as it holds them accountable. We still cling on to the medical model of care: going to the doctor, receiving a label and receiving a remedy. Otherwise, we feel we have achieved nothing. Patients tend to report more overall satisfaction if they leave an appointment with some sort of tangible prescription. Giving Sam a piece of paper with what we call a social prescription on it helps him to feel he has achieved something from his visit to me – and it also acts as a sort of placebo. When given a placebo, the highest functioning, executive part of the brain, the thinking part, assumes that a pain-management plan has been confidently implemented and it relays this message to the rest of the brain, releasing more opioid neurotransmitters, or pain relievers. The brilliant brain releases its own pain relief.

We give ourselves small placebos all the time by telling ourselves stories about our own behaviours. For instance, many of us overthink as a coping skill. It's something we find hard to let go of because we believe that, if we overthink a scenario, planning for every single eventuality, we will be more prepared for disaster if – or maybe that should be *when* – it strikes. In reality, overthinking will leave us depleted, anxious and ill-equipped to problem-solve and respond effectively, due to the sleepless nights and the energy we have wasted. In therapy, overthinking is often described as a rocking chair; you are constantly moving back and forth, exerting energy, while staying stuck in the same spot, achieving nothing. But we distort the function of overthinking, saying to ourselves things like, 'I have done a lot of work on solving my problem by thinking about it so much.' This mental placebo soothes us, gives us a pat on the back.

Sam leaves with his social prescription and I go off for my prescription Costa.

Not a real doctor

Simon and I go out for dinner. He is stressed from work, a start-up in east London, something to do with fintech that I don't fully understand – but, unbeknown to him, I looked him up on LinkedIn and on the company website, just to check the job is real this time.

Protecting Sam's identity, I share the theory about the social prescription and ask what he thinks. Simon shares for the first time that he has been prescribed antidepressants to cope with his grief and feelings of loss. I listen empathically, once again careful not to step into therapy mode. I feel the deep pang of pure compassion and I am drawn towards him; he is being open with a raw vulnerability.

Simon tells me he isn't keen on taking the medication for depression. I broach the topic of grief and the associated pain and melancholy versus depression.

'Well,' he says, 'you're not a real doctor, not like a psychiatrist, are you? You can't even prescribe.'

I recoil from the potency of it, the venom in the words. I remember our first conversation about the difference between what I do and psychiatry. This piece of information has now been weaponized as a criticism.

Simon remains sullen and sulky until the mains arrive. Despite the hurt, I busy myself making conversation and observations about the food and the decor until he thaws. He asks me about Alex, how she is and how her pursuit of a career as a stand-up comedian is going. She is very funny, he says.

I gush about Alex and then, feeling a little self-conscious, I joke about us having a bit of a 'co-dependent relationship'.

Simon sinks another whisky sour and then comments, 'Maybe your co-dependency with Alex is why you are a bit desperate, and so shit at romantic relationships.'

He laughs, but it feels sharp.

Love bites

The next morning, as I set out on my commute for a day of lectures, I still feel flat from Simon's comments. I try to make sense of where it has come from. We had just been talking about his antidepressants and grief. I can't imagine that kind of pain, the lack of safety he must feel in all relationships knowing his own father kept his struggles a secret. This helps me to put it to bed. I forget about it and get on with my day.

By lunchtime I'm feeling more positive, and I chat with my peer group over sandwiches and coffee. The conversation turns to romance and we share stories of bad dates and being treated as a cheap alternative to paying for a therapist by various suitors. Naomi tells me never to trust an actor, as they can shape-shift too easily, entering different characters and personas at will. She worked in TV 'in a previous life'.

Dylan tells us about a woman who deceived him. 'We dated for a year, then I found out she had a husband and a child. She told me the caesarean scar was the result of a lost appendix.'

I instantly feel better about being duped by Raff.

Jim chips in as we prepare to leave, saying, almost as a throwaway comment, 'The girl I've been dating is a lot to handle, a tad more than feisty, I'd say.' He blushes as he speaks. We are all poised, leaning in for more. 'Last night, we were at a bar and she sort of lost it with me. She got so frustrated she bit me.' He laughs and looks around the group for support.

Nobody laughs, nobody moves.

Jim follows up with, 'Oh, it was only a light bite. She struggles to find the language for emotions – she was brought up in a silent house.'

'Sometimes you can contextualize and justify people's behaviours too much, Jim,' Naomi says gently. 'Don't let the rescuer in you allow you to miss the red flags. She is an adult, Jim. Who bites as an adult?' She pauses. 'Anyway, who remembers what a t-value is? We have stats next.'

Red bunting

Red flags. I need to think about them in my sessions with Claire, give her the tools to see them, bypass Trevor's smoke and mirrors.

She comes back to my little home-made therapy room. Today, she is even more timid. It takes her a while to settle in the chair, as though she's procrastinating.

'Is there some advice you can give me to boost my sex drive?' she asks, tentatively.

'Is this a recent problem? Is this something that's bothering you? Has your relationship with intimacy changed?' I ask a series of questions in an attempt to get her talking.

Claire shares that she has struggled to have sex with Trevor as much as they used to, and he is finding this really difficult. I ask her again if *she* is finding this difficult, but she puts the focus back onto Trevor.

'He's had to resort to other things because of it,' she adds.

Claire tells me that, a few nights before, she decided to take control of the situation and try to seduce Trevor. They were going out with a group of mutual friends and Claire wore sexy lingerie under her black dress. During the aperitif, she placed Trevor's hand on her thigh so he could feel the buckles. They shared a knowing look and Claire felt pleased with herself.

Cut to later in the night and Trevor begins to put Claire down, becoming angry and frustrated with her, accusing her of looking at other men. Meanwhile, he strikes up a conversation with an older woman at the bar, whose lipstick has run across her face during the course of the evening. Claire nips to the toilet and, when she returns, she can't find Trevor. He has left with the older woman, leaving Claire standing alone in the bar, feeling the sting of utter humiliation. She returns home alone and her tears arrive as she undresses out of the lingerie and gets into bed, all the while frantically checking her phone.

'The feeling of humiliation must have been very painful,' I say, 'that sense of betrayal. What I notice is that you've opened the session by locating the blame in yourself, stating that this somehow occurred because of your sex drive. Do you think Trevor's behaviour is acceptable?'

Claire goes back and forth between feeling anger and defending Trevor. She continues to reference his power, saying, 'He's a very powerful man,' and 'He could have any woman he wants,' and 'He needs the cathartic release of sex due to his intense stress from work.'

I have to resist staring at her open-mouthed at this. It's reminiscent of the accusation of creating 'blue balls' – the line favoured by narcissistic teenage boys trying to coerce girls into sex.

My (suppressed) anger at this leads me to share with Claire the cycle of abuse.

'In some relationships,' I say, 'there is a cycle of relating that occurs. The first stage is the tension-building stage, or the walking-on-eggshells phase: one partner is stressed and is bubbling with irritation; the other partner may try to reduce this tension in any way they can. The next stage is the crisis point or the incident: something happens, whereby one partner is abusive – sexually, physically, emotionally, financially – or is in some way threatening. Following this is the seductive honeymoon phase. The abusive partner shows sorrow, remorse, guilt, and strives to rectify. What's crucial about this phase is that the abused partner gets their power back. The final stage is equilibrium. There is some peace, but over time the abuser's apologies and actions will become fewer and less sincere. We then re-enter the tension-building phase.'

This resonates with Claire. I have just described her life – and, she tells me, this isn't the first time the term *abuse* has come up. It has been skirted around by friends and family. But Claire still believes Trevor is powerful – he is a successful, proud and capable man. And she believes there is nothing that can be done to change the cycle.

Since the recent fallout, Claire has not spoken to Trevor. I ask her to continue with her silence, not to pursue a reconciliation.

Then together we can look at Trevor's reactionary behaviour through the lens of the abuse cycle.

I look forward to seeing her again and, this time, I have no worries that she won't come back.

Calling for backup

I am seeing a new private client referral, Frank. Frank, it turns out, is a very large man and he struggles to fit in the very small chair in my tiny consulting room. It's an undignified start to our relationship as he wedges himself in with care, but we laugh and get through it and press on.

I begin by taking a history. Frank goes through the various mental-health difficulties in his family; he then goes on to list his arrests. He tells me he has been arrested on multiple occasions for domestic violence.

I am suddenly and acutely aware that I am in a small room, in my own home, with a potentially violent man blocking the only way out. All of the risks and my lack of risk assessment hit me. I am still so naive.

After this session, my friend Jamie agrees to be present in the other room during Frank's future sessions, on one condition – that he can put 'bouncer for a therapist' on his CV.

True colours

Simon and I have arranged to take a train to Margate for a night at the seaside, to escape London and for a change of scene. We have a glass of wine at the station before leaving. The alcohol hits my system straight away, the way a large

Sauvignon will on an empty stomach after a long day. I need to nip to the loo. As a result, we arrive at the platform just as the doors are closing, and we miss the train.

Simon loses it, swearing and blaming me right there in the middle of the station. At one point, he attempts to kick a rubbish bin. This makes me extremely embarrassed and only seems to highlight the ridiculousness of the situation. He looks like a toddler having a fit. The general swearing and cursing morphs into a more personal attack, at which point I start to try to de-escalate him, calm him down. I apologize profusely and buy new tickets – there will, after all, be another train before too long.

Eventually, settled on the next train, I replay some of the things Simon shouted at me.

'You're a princess.'

'You're so selfish and you always get your own way.'

'You're high maintenance.'

All of this for nipping to the loo.

Before I can say anything, Simon says, 'I am so sorry, Nat. I was thinking about the last time I went to Margate with my dad. We walked down the pebbled beach.'

He is crying and so I hold his hand and tell him it's OK. I think the wine probably hit him too and made him act out of character. In Margate, we get on with the weekend, but – far from our plan of long walks by the sea – Simon doesn't want to do much other than eat and stay in the room. I go out alone for a morning stroll and, as the sea air clears my mind, I tell myself I'm having a nice time.

A string of *aha* moments

Rationalize it away

Back in London, I go to Simon's flat. It's not very late, but I am tired. Despite this, Simon suggests I go home. He has work to do, he says, and he needs his headspace. After a sharp pang of rejection, my shutdown mode kicks in. I pack up my things robotically and leave.

On my commute across town, I rationalize his behaviour. I will probably want alone time when I write my thesis for university, an all-consuming research project that looms in the near future. It's entirely reasonable to set aside time for work, I think.

Alex and our friend Paul meet me at the pub next to the overground and we have a drink to catch up. I tag us all in a silly picture on Instagram and go to the bar for more drinks. When I get back, I see lots of notifications. Instantly, I know. At a glance, in the preview box, I can see that Simon has bombarded me with messages. Some of his comments include name-calling: *Nice game playing*, reads one, and another, *With Paul, I see, you are pathetic and immature*. Seconds later, the messages are deleted so I can't access them, but more follow, as though he can't help himself.

Alex intuits that something is wrong with me, but I am too embarrassed to tell her. She watches my phone screen light up, go dark, light up again. I grab the phone off the table, away from her gaze.

I am too scared to block him, so I delete the whole of WhatsApp, just for tonight.

Falling off the pedestal

Claire is back. As she enters my little room, she is laughing. I see the energy I knew was there the whole time – a relaxed, carefree playfulness.

'You won't believe this,' she says before she even sits down. 'I did what you said. I didn't pursue, I waited. It was hard work. I thought for sure he would never contact me, that this would be the end of it and I would be stuck in this pity party of self-loathing forever, but . . .' She breaks off and starts laughing again.

She reaches into her bag for an apple and holds it in both hands. I'm confused, but stay with her, listening.

'He came crawling to me,' she goes on. 'It started with a few calls, which I was strong enough to ignore, then it became relentless: calls, begging texts, emails. One of the emails actually had *Moving on* in the subject box, but then the body of the email read, *I cannot.* I thought about what you said, tried to look at it through an abuse lens. I realized he was hoping I would only read the subject line, that I would panic and call him. But he wrote the next bit of the email just in case.'

We laugh together at this.

'That's not the funny bit!' she shrieks. 'I ignore, ignore, ignore, then I notice his car outside my flat, but he doesn't ring the bell. By the third night, I am a bit scared, actually, and I'm about to ring the police when an apple is thrown through the open window.'

She holds out the apple. Crudely sellotaped to it is a passport-sized picture of a man. Trevor.

'This . . . is his . . . tactic!' she says, and we both collapse in laughter as I take a closer look at the apple.

'How powerful does this man seem to you now, Claire?' I manage to say. 'This man who is too cowardly to face you and so resorts to fruit projectiles?'

Claire's last words in this session are that she has taken Trevor off the pedestal, and she is going to call her mum.

Procrastination

Noah comes to me for help with procrastination. We talk generally about procrastination being a self-sabotaging strategy. Putting things off only makes them more difficult to confront. I ask for specific examples of his procrastination. How much is this impacting his functioning?

Noah says he is really here to ask how to write a text message to break things off with his partner of four years. Patients wanting support with communication and writing text messages to end relationships or to respond in an argument is surprisingly common. He has been putting this off, or procrastinating. Abusive relationships are notoriously difficult to leave. Manipulation, brainwashing and fear thrive in the conditions set out by the abuser. Claire is one of the lucky ones, able to gain insight. But it seems non-abusive endings can also be so difficult for some people that they will avoid them at all costs; they can't take ownership of them.

'I can hear the fear in you, Noah,' I say. 'It can be frightening to take assertive action. But do you think a text is sufficient to show respect to this bond that has lasted four years?'

Noah is too anxious to face this head on and cannot entertain the idea of a more direct approach, even with my support. Role-playing the conversation and planning his escape from the discomfort of the situation, he eventually says he will have to 'find another way'.

The blind leading the blind

Noah finds his own solution. He pretends to go blind. He meets up with his partner wearing thick, dark glasses and tells her that he has suddenly lost his sight and wants to get through this alone.

I wonder whether his acting skills are better than Sam's and marvel at the lengths to which people will go to avoid conflict.

Still, it seems to have worked.

No holding back

I am trying to uphold the belief that Simon and I are doing well. I push down the abusive messages in my mind and air-brush them out of my awareness. As if nothing has happened, we go together to watch Alex do some stand-up. Nervous excitement overcomes me as we gather with other friends to watch her debut her longest set so far. Simon is also excited and seems supportive. We sit near the front and my focus is on the stage, but I see Simon notice Paul hurry through the back door of the gig, just in time. As the compère comes on to introduce Alex, Simon whispers, a little too loudly, 'I adore you.' I smile, but gesture for him to watch the show. My skin prickles as I sense the instant rage beside me. When I dare to turn back towards him, he mouths, 'You're a cunt.'

Later, in the bar, the congratulations and celebrations of Alex's performance are derailed by Simon's palpable anger towards me. Eventually, Alex asks him what is going on, as she can hear the insults being lobbed at me over the noisy chatter of the bar – as can a couple of my other friends, who look over, concerned and uncomfortable.

Simon doesn't hold back. 'She's putting me down,' he tells Alex. 'She's selfish and demanding. She's angry and hostile.'

Alex looks over at me, my shoulders hunched over, my head down. This is excruciating.

'But she's not doing anything,' she says, more assertively than I ever could.

This is the moment – the moment in the horror film when other people see the monster only one person has had to encounter so far. It's the *aha* moment of being seen and believed.

I am not being dramatic. He is unkind to me. Nasty, jealous. It's intolerable. It has to end.

Kelli gets it

I wake up flooded with self-doubt. Maybe I *am* being demanding. Maybe I have made Simon feel overlooked. Maybe I minimized him or made him feel inadequate. I should have supported him in front of so many of my friends, people he doesn't know.

But then I think about the word *cunt*. Surely that's too

much? But I'm still not sure. I need Kelli. I request an emergency session and she responds immediately.

'You haven't been to see me for a few weeks,' she says.

She knows. She always knows.

As I lie down on her chaise longue, I immediately feel safer.

'I am probably being dramatic . . .' I say. 'Maybe I'm applying my job too much to my own life and putting a lens on everything . . .'

Kelli ignores this tentative opening gambit and holds the silence until I fully open up.

I tell the most balanced account of Simon that I can. All the lovely times we have shared and all the difficult ones too. There are many of the latter, I realize, as I reel off the chronology.

As a therapist, I know Kelli will show compassion and understanding towards Simon due to his loss and his associated pain. But, when I finish, she very calmly leans over and puts a hand on my shoulder. The compassion and understanding are for me.

The tears come easily as I feel the warmth from her. In that split second before she speaks, I know what she is going to say.

'I want you to hear me when I say this, Natalie. This man is dangerous. I am concerned for your well-being. This is controlling and abusive.'

Kelli sets me some homework.

'Tomorrow, you will feel doubt,' she says. 'Self-doubt is one of the biggest consequences of emotional abuse. When you get home, write down a list of all the names he has called you. This is your evidence base to challenge your doubt. The only way to deal with a narcissist is to have no contact – and, trust me, he will contact you.'

The narcissist

I write the list. I see that all the names Simon has called me actually describe him: demanding, selfish, controlling, angry, nasty, cold, uncaring. This is classic narcissism. How did I not see this? Narcissists portray others as a mirror image of themselves, projecting their own character traits, behaviours, actions, fears, motives and distorted self-beliefs onto them. This creates intense frustration in those accused. The injustice of it. The hypocrisy. Narcissists avoid accountability at all costs and hold others responsible for their abusive behaviours – that's why many of those abused will say that they provoked their abuser, triggered them or upset them.

Yet my self-doubt creeps in, as Kelli predicted. Maybe I am overthinking this and maybe I gave Kelli a distorted story . . .

Then my phone starts up. Call after call, then message after message of name-calling and guilt-tripping. How dare I ignore him and not think about what this is doing to his mental health?

This is all self-referential classic narcissism. I can see it very clearly now. Everything is about him. The common pattern follows: abusive message, message deleted, abusive message, message deleted. The deletion means no accountability, no ownership. Denial.

This is abuse.

I text Kelli. *Thank you. I think you really saved me from something.*

EIGHT

The last patch in the quilt

Taking ownership

My new challenge back at the hospital is adolescents and young adults who are in denial about their chronic illnesses, including diabetes, and are resistant to taking care of themselves. I sometimes get moved around the hospital to different patient groups; I go where I am needed. When diabetic teens don't follow the self-care regime needed to manage their condition, it can lead to serious complications down the line: retinopathy, a form of sight loss; or neuropathy, which most commonly damages nerves in the legs and feet, and this lack of sensation can lead to unnoticed injuries. If not treated soon enough, the resulting wounds can lead to amputations.

But trying to discuss long-term health consequences, however catastrophic and severe, with someone who has an adolescent brain is like trying to catch moonbeams in a glass. This is not the teenagers' fault, of course. The prefrontal cortex, the rational part of the brain that processes long-term consequences, is still immature in adolescents. Teens tend to process information with their amygdala, the emotional part of the brain. Without the capacity to inhibit this amygdala activity with a fully developed prefrontal cortex, they struggle to regulate their emotions. This explains their impulsivity and risk-taking. With this in mind, however, I feel relatively encouraged so far by the success I'm seeing with some of the more 'out of the box' strategies I'm using to engage them.

'You know, the school system is not right for the young,' I begin, with each of my patients. 'The adolescent brain is going through so much change and specialization that you actually need more sleep, so getting you up at six thirty for school is like dragging me or your mum or dad out of bed at four thirty and expecting us to be able to function.'

They love this, and they buy in, often with, 'See, I told you so!' thrown in the direction of their mum or dad. I am good cop.

'This all-important sleep can be massively disrupted by the blue light and visual stimulation of our phones, iPads, video games,' I continue. 'Did you know, research shows we have worse sleep with the phone in the bedroom, even if it's under our pillow, on aeroplane mode?'

They hate this. I get a lot of eye-rolling in response. I am bad cop.

What they don't know is that I am very much employing a 'do as I say, not as I do' approach, since each night I have my phone blasting news and gossip directly into my face until the last few seconds before I eventually nod off from sheer exhaustion.

The last patch in the quilt

Next, I ask the older teens whether they are sexually active. I ask as casually as I would ask whether they ever eat sandwiches for lunch. Those that say yes feel understood. I have regained their eye contact and attention. I am good cop once again, so am able to continue.

'You know, poor diabetic care leads to neuropathy in your extremities. This is a lack of feeling due to nerve damage.' They nod, bored and tired of this warning, having heard it a million times before. Then I add, 'Damage to your blood vessels and nerves includes the ones that supply your penis, which means you would lose penile sensation and possibly function.' This tends to make the boys sit up and listen, and occasionally say, 'Oh, fuck!' And, all of a sudden, they can do their insulin at school, no problem.

In my current role, I am switching between working with young people reluctant to inject themselves with insulin and working with some of the children and families from the cancer ward. I am constantly struck by the resilience of both patient groups and notice that there are some parallels between them. Both are faced with chronic and gruelling treatment plans. But the key difference between the two is choice. The diabetics can (problematically) choose not to subject themselves to a needle, but the children facing chemo have no choice. While I barely have the resilience to face a root canal, these little ones face lumbar punctures, operations and the blasting of their bodies with chemical after chemical. They sometimes have to be held down while their bodies are prodded and pulled at.

This is why, following chemotherapy, I am often called in for the anger stage. These young people might smash up their bedroom, try to fling their sister off the top bunk or throw their pencil case at their teacher. Of course they are angry. If you had no autonomy over your body, no agency or control and you'd been pulled and pushed around for months, your energy depleted, if you couldn't run and keep up with your friends and you could barely eat for reasons you don't understand, wouldn't you want to smack Mrs Davies across the face with a ruler?

Resilience includes certain attributes and personal resources, such as hope, motivation, optimism, a strong sense that everything will be OK in the end, and also spirituality. Some of us have more of it than others – clinically speaking, I'm a complete wuss – but maybe we don't know how much we have until it is tested.

Mine

I notice a file with Peggy's name on it; it's bulkier than many of the others, so it is easy to spot. My heart sinks. I can't bear that she's back, after all the progress we made.

Then, a newer staff member, trained as a counsellor, picks up the file, raises her eyebrows and scans it, announcing that she will take this re-referral, the returning customer.

I instinctively reach for the file, almost snatching it from her. 'She's *my* patient!' I say, rather loudly. Then I try to smooth things over by explaining my history with Peggy, but the damage is done. After this, our new counsellor seems genuinely frightened of me, recoiling whenever she sees me, as if I might pull her hair at any moment, as though we're scrapping in the school playground.

The last patch in the quilt

What a wuss

I am sitting in the waiting room of the sexual-health clinic. Thankfully, my addiction to STI screens has waned and I am here for genuine reasons – a contraceptive coil fitting. The outcomes of my relationships with Max, Raff and Simon have left me wondering where I would be now if I had become pregnant, and I am taking measures – taking control – to avoid surprise pregnancies in future.

All three waved very large red flags in front of me, and I missed them. Given my job, you might think my radar for red flags would be extra sensitive, but while my skills and intuitions seem to be improving in my professional life, it's clear that, in my personal life, my intuition still needs rigorous training.

This weakness might be in my neuroception, the ability to subconsciously sense and identify cues of risk and safety. Our neuroception is informed by a combination of all our experiences and our level of emotional sensitivity. As with any psychological feature, like stress thresholds and pain thresholds, we each sit at different points on the emotional sensitivity and neuroception continuums. Some of us are overly vigilant, subconsciously reading all situations as unsafe, which can limit and paralyse us. Others lack the ability to assess risk, detecting no danger, which leads to risk-taking behaviours and red-flag blindness.

We all have our individual signature, which makes cues for safety and danger subjective, nuanced and bound up with our personal experience. Among my patients, Freddie has to say 'I love you' at the end of every phone call, since his friend died not long after what would turn out to be their last conversation, and the call ended tersely. Without this sign-off, Freddie's neuroception senses danger and he feels intense panic. Mike can't say the word *goodbye*. He has to say 'bye for now' because he is afraid the word *goodbye* is too final and signifies danger – tempting fate. Carly can't wear or see hair bands on people's wrists without feeling threat, since an ex-girlfriend once handcuffed her to the bed and left her there for hours, causing indentations in her wrists as she struggled to get free.

I wonder what it is in my experience that has made me blind to red flags, and makes me look past them and airbrush them out? What has put the block on my neuroception of danger in romantic endeavours? Do I simply override the warning system by intellectualizing, making excuses and hoping for the best?

As humans, we are able to override and counteract inbuilt survival instincts with thoughts and reasoning, something we see in cases of intentional self-harm. Alcohol can also blunt our survival instinct. While this has been tested unofficially by me many times, it has also been tested more formally with animals. The tests showed exaggerated aggression following alcohol ingestion in rhesus monkeys.

As my mind drifts to which brand of alcohol the monkeys were plied with, my thoughts are interrupted by the nurse brandishing a form for me to sign.

My deep thoughts about paying more explicit attention to danger cues have temporarily distracted me from the anticipatory fear of the coil insertion. I spot several danger cues as I enter the clinic room: the cold metal speculum laid out on a tray with other instruments of torture; the cold and clinical appearance of the room itself; the robust rubber gloves. I reassure myself. Lots of the medics with whom I've become friendly have had this procedure and, although it's uncomfortable, they come out unscathed and feeling more in control. This is my final thought before I black out in the stirrups, much to the horror of my female nurse.

She straps a blood-pressure cuff to my arm and voices concern over how much my pressure has dropped, as I slip in and out of consciousness. The staff bring me round and offer me tea, but I remain grey and limp. After a lot of bleeping and chatter, a very tall doctor crashes into the room. He assumes my consultant is my mum and shoos her out of the way as he gets to work, muttering, 'Move aside, Mum,' and doing nothing that she hasn't already done. I am almost jolted back into consciousness as I hear my consultant explode, 'She is *my* patient. *I* am the doctor and I am managing this.' The tall man backs away sheepishly and, as my consultant elevates my legs, I feel the blood rush to my head and I come back around fully.

After a cup of sugary tea in the waiting room, I think about my coil doctor. She claimed me as her own, as her patient, and took responsibility for me, just as I have done with Peggy. Bolstered by this, I set up an appointment to see Peggy again and find myself looking forward to it.

Modelling

Modelling a behaviour to help others take it on as their own is a strategy often used in behavioural psychology. But, after my coil experience, I am more acutely aware than ever that I have little in terms of resilience factors. Who am I to be a role model for those facing adversity? Who am I to model how to cope? In modelling, the learning of the desired behaviour occurs vicariously, purely through observing it. The leaner imitates without any obvious reward or reinforcement. It can also be used to normalize behaviours, removing shame from them.

With all this – including lots of self-doubt – in mind, I agree to teach modelling to the junior staff and care workers who are working with a teenage girl, Emma, who has some complex mental-health difficulties and has been struggling emotionally, especially at night. I feel woefully unqualified, but here we are.

I reply brightly to the email, trying to sound as breezy as possible to take the pressure off and make me seem like a friend dropping in for a chat, rather than any form of expert: *I would be happy to help and offer advice to the team*, I write. *It'll be a very informal session with coffee and cake.* The cake will be my bribe.

I need to find something in Emma's behaviour for her team to model, so I begin by spending some time with her. I have learned that this is crucial, as reading someone's clinical notes can paint a picture that is not really a fair overall view. Clinical notes are generally written by a person's social worker and often make an attempt at opening with some positivity, but usually end up reading something like, *Shannon is a bright young girl who enjoys arts and crafts. She loves to sing and has a pet cat called Annie. In 2009, Shannon took two nurses hostage, tying them up and assaulting a police officer. Shannon's favourite food is pizza and she also likes cooking.*

The thing is, patients know that, when you come to see them for the first time, you have just read their file and their list of worst moments. It's not exactly a clean slate. Emma greets me with this knowledge: 'I guess you think I am some sort of demon,' she says.

I share with her that a snapshot taken of anyone's life during their moments of pain would make for difficult reading, but that I want to know her full story from her. In the silence that ensues, I add, 'I have never heard of a demon with such a pristine balayage.'

This breaks the tension and she laughs, her hand instinctively going to her hair. But she continues to scan me up and down, confused now. Her therapist knows what a balayage is!

We eat some cake and, as she relaxes a little, she confides in me that sometimes she likes to suck on things at night – the soft labels on clothes or the ear of her teddy bear – to calm herself down. Emma is worried that this is 'babyish' and that people might laugh if they find out.

Afterwards, when completing my advice session with the staff, I tell them never to shame Emma or make fun of this calming habit, and I suggest they try some modelling with her. I ask them to show Emma that we all do things to comfort ourselves and to self-soothe: we twiddle our hair, we play with our rings or fingernails. I suggest doing such things openly in front of Emma and talking about them positively. I feel satisfied with the session and the responsive heads nodding. It seems I can do this.

Vanishing disease

When Peggy arrives at Kiwi, I see the new diagnosis as soon as she walks through the door. Her body, ever a conduit of emotional pain, is underweight. Her clavicle protrudes and her jaw is razor sharp. We begin to explore this development and I know that it will take several sessions to fully unpack the problem, but it very quickly becomes clear that Peggy wants to be small, unnoticed. She believes her reduced physical state will mean she is less likely to be targeted for abuse. Her body reflects her inner world of fragility and emptiness.

Then there's the physiology: the intense feelings of reward and adrenaline when she goes to bed hungry and the sensation of being empty, which is addictive. Peggy feels in control of something for once, and she is now totally dissociated from her own hunger. Dissociation is a safe place for her. She has dissociated from a lot of psychological pain and anguish in the past, so it feels like a familiar and effective coping strategy.

Eating disorders and restrictive eating can baffle people who don't share the problem. Why can't they just eat? Why can't they just take in some calories to make themselves feel better? I sometimes use the analogy that, when an eating disorder takes over, asking that person to engage in therapy or a treatment plan is like asking the average person to engage in something that will systematically disfigure their face, making it grotesque and filling them with self-loathing, and also make them a target for abuse. Would you sign up to that?

I try something controversial with Peggy. She cannot see what I see; the impression she has of her appearance is distorted. I ask her to bring in photographs of herself over the years so that we can make a visual timeline of her life, and I ask her to take some photographs of how she looks now, so we can add these to the timeline at the end. She looks at me as though I'm the patient and she's the doctor, but she decides to oblige me.

Whiplash

I have a constant and searing pain in my neck, which I can't seem to shake. It began a few days ago, after I felt myself getting crushed at a party where someone was messing about, fuelled by too much booze and joie de vivre. But I was reassured by a doctor I saw socially at a barbecue the next day that it's just whiplash and will go away in a few weeks.

Pain makes you tired, teary and irritable, which I know in theory and from my work with patients, but what I know now, in practice, is that the overwhelming feeling with pain is vulnerability. I feel fragile and frightened. I am tempted to give in to the pain and go to A & E, but the thought that I am being ridiculous, that my patients face much worse than this daily, that I am being overdramatic and a wimp means I do nothing. I wait for it to pass.

Topaz ward

Several days after seeing Emma and the team working with her, when I am still walking on air thinking about how well my first attempt at teaching my peers went, the lead psychiatrist on Emma's ward approaches me in the canteen. 'Why the fuck are all of the staff on Topaz ward sucking their thumbs all day?' he asks.

Disgust

In our next session, as Peggy and I look closely at the series of photographs she has brought in, I want to assess whether in each one she feels different, safer, less anxious, more herself. Each photo elicits a different response from her, and we seem to have a moment, maybe just for a second, where the distortion lifts and, in the most recent images, she sees what I see, which is her at her weakest and most vulnerable. In the final pictures along the timeline, she sees that the colour has drained from her face, that she looks angular, almost lifeless.

Peggy currently feels disgust towards food, a strong and physical sense of aversion and revulsion to anything perceived as high-calorie. Disgust is a very powerful emotion, which has evolved and been sustained because it prevents us from ingesting life-threatening foods, helping us to survive. The word itself, *disgust*, means 'bad taste', and there is a universally recognized facial expression which accompanies it, which I now see flash across Peggy's face as we unpack her feelings about eating, her sense of self and her needs.

Peggy holds a sense of self-disgust and shame, and she wears the latter like a chainmail coat she can't shake off. She feels that, if she eats, she is indulging, and views herself as grotesque, greedy, gluttonous and weak. Peggy can no longer associate eating in a carefree way with being in control, balanced and together. Knowing Peggy sometimes looks up to me, idealizes me in some ways as a replacement mother, I decide to use this as a tool. I start bringing snacks to our sessions, once again packing Quavers into my bag, and I eat them casually, without making any reference to them, hoping she will mirror me.

Snapshots

The next time I see Peggy, we continue our conversation about how she is beginning to make narrative sense of her life through the photographs of her at different ages. After a while, she starts to pick at the snacks I've brought along as she talks and gesticulates. Mid-flow, she stops in her tracks, scanning me. 'What's wrong?' she says. 'Have I done something to upset you?' Her mind seems to be racing. 'Do you hate me?'

Looking quizzically back at her, I say, 'What have I done to make you think that?'

'Well, you're crying,' Peggy says.

I return my focus to myself and away from Peggy. I am sitting awkwardly in the chair, my body twisted slightly to one side as I try to gain some relief from the pain in my neck and side. I hadn't realized that my eyes had started to brim with tears.

Straightening myself, I apologize to Peggy and she resets, getting back into her flow and her story.

It will pass, it will pass, I say to myself in my head as I focus on Peggy and stay with her as she guides me through her inner world. When, mid-story, she picks up and begins to eat a muffin, I try not to bring too much attention to it, but my eyes start to well with tears again.

This time, she rolls her eyes and pokes fun at me: 'Did you ever think in your lifetime you would be crying over a muffin? Ridiculous.'

Just About Coping

Promises

As Peggy starts to eat again, we are able to move back into our relationship. She has moments of anger and frustration with me, but she is moving forward and gaining weight. What remains unchanged is Peggy's continued fear of abandonment; she keeps dreaming that I will die before our next session, and her worry is that she won't be able to cope without me. I promise Peggy that I won't die and that I will always show up.

And this is why you learn early on in your training never to promise a patient anything.

The breaking of bonds

At our next session, when I should be with Peggy in Kiwi, I don't show. I haven't called ahead or emailed, I just haven't turned up. For the last ten days, I have been battling on with the excruciating neck pain. I have been brought to tears many times, and have been trying to self-medicate with scalding hot baths and neat whisky. Any excuse. But today, when it all gets a bit too much, I finally take myself round to A & E to ask for some strong painkillers to get me through the day. A quick in and out, I think.

It turns out to be a 'bad news meeting'. After some X-rays, which I wasn't expecting, the doctor holds my hand and explains to me that I need to be blue-lighted to King's Hospital. I have broken my neck in two places and they need a neurosurgeon to operate. I would say I am paralysed with fear . . . I am, however, flooded with panic. Upon hearing the word *neurosurgeon*, I, for some reason, assume brain damage as well as fracture.

'Is my brain OK?' I blurt out.

The doctor's response is, 'Well, you tell me.'

I don't feel this is a concrete answer. It's certainly not the answer I'm looking for. But I obligingly test my mental capacity by trying to name, in my head, all the mental-health conditions I can, to check that my knowledge is still there. The exercise acts as a trigger, and I remember Peggy. I have missed our session. But there is nobody around to tell and, as I have my own problems to deal with, she slips from my mind.

Instead of being with Peggy, I am fixed to a stretcher in the A & E department of the same hospital in which she is waiting for me, two floors above, and am left in a corridor until it becomes increasingly clear that the staff have forgotten about me. To add insult to injury, literally, they have positioned my stretcher directly under a clock, its hands slowly but noisily ticking. My head is fixed in position on the gurney and I can't move; the clock is all I can see. After fifty minutes, I think enough is enough and I start to shout: 'Help, help, help!'

A doctor rushes over. 'What the hell are you doing in strokes?' he yells, as he pushes me into a curtained room. I lie staring at the new, yet not dissimilar, view of yellowing ceiling tiles, and, for the first time in many days, I feel sleepy.

The ambulance finally comes at around 3 a.m. and whisks me off to King's, where I have my own room, a significant upgrade from a corridor. They place me in a neck brace until the surgeon can meet with me and make a plan. I am given morphine, which is deliciously numbing and blurring.

The ghosts of boyfriends past

Alex is first to arrive at the hospital. She is trying to maintain her usual demeanour of 'Everything is OK, everything is fine,' but her smile isn't quite reaching her eyes. She busies herself, texting our whole social network and desperately trying to make me laugh. My dad is next. He is almost mute with shock, wild panic in his eyes. He has left my mum at home, as she's too nervous to receive news and updates until there's a medical plan in place. Third up is my brother. The medic in him suspected that something wasn't quite right with the pain I had told him about, and so, when Alex's name popped up on his phone screen, before she'd even spoken, he was already making his way to the train station.

Then, several ex-boyfriends and ex-flings arrive, one by one, like the Ghosts of Christmas Past. With each arrival, I try to deduce their motive. Is this one the Ghost of Christmas Past, coming to show support and care now it's all water under the bridge? Or the Ghost of Christmas Present, bringing hope and good will? Or perhaps the Ghost of Christmas Yet to Come, representing fear and hopelessness, which is how, in my pain and misery, I currently see life unfolding.

One of them is Max. He arrives as both Past and Present, showing me warmth and care, and offering to help in any way he can. He looks sharp and handsome. Clearly things have worked out well for him. Then my old friend Ashley arrives, I assume summoned by Alex or maybe he made the decision to come in blind panic. As he walks towards me, I am struck by the trousers he is wearing; the fabric is a sort of patchwork, all different shades of denim. They're bell-bottoms, much too short, swinging well above his ankles.

'What on earth have you got on?' I ask.

He blushes. 'Oh, I was overcome with worry, adrenaline and many, many cans of Red Bull last night. I had a little accident, ruined my jeans and had to pick these up from the charity shop next door. Honestly, worst day of my life . . .' He catches himself. 'Oh, sorry – probably not an ideal day for you either.'

The surgeons come to talk to me about the risks of surgery and the risk I have been facing since the break happened. They tell me that, had the broken disc moved a fraction of a milli-metre, it would have impacted a major artery, which would have led to stroke, paralysis, brain damage . . . I sort of zone out in shock as the list goes on. They go away to discuss the best strategy and I remain suspended in my morphine cloud, and in the capable hands of a junior doctor. He reads out a list of risks for me to sign; for the most horrifying ones, he uses a monotone voice, but as he nears the end he says, 'Oh no, it says here you might have a hoarse voice forever. How would you feel about that?'

I reassure him that, if the alternative is death or paralysis, I will learn to cope with it.

I think back to my many patients who have had their lives altered or drastically changed by a diagnosis or an injury, those who have felt betrayed by their own bodies, or whose bodies have felt unfamiliar to them or no longer their own. When working with people who have weeping wounds, open sores, oozing pustules, bladder and soiling issues, I often take note of the response and resilience of the parents, carers, partners and family. More often than not, they take it in their stride, learning how to change dressings and apply ointments and creams, offering praise and support. These experiences have bolstered my belief in one of my favourite facts: disgust is inversely correlated with intimacy. The more we care for someone, feel linked and connected to them through love and a bond, the less likely we are to feel disgust towards them. This must be a further evolutionary function of disgust: it helps us to avoid the unsafe, but it fades away when we need it to, when we move towards those we love who are struggling with things that might ordinarily evoke a sense of distaste.

Without a deep emotional bond to their patients, nurses, doctors and surgeons must have ways to distort, reframe or lessen the feeling of disgust in order to do their jobs. I take note of how my medical professionals are caring for me and am flooded with gratitude – and, yes, something that feels a bit like love.

God is a woman

My surgeon is a woman. Her credentials and her manner instantly make me feel calmer; I feel safer the second she starts speaking. I am in good hands and, for once, I thank my God delusion. It's a delusion I have been fighting and challenging as my own training has progressed, but it's now helping me to cope.

Alex is coping less well. She looks frantic and panicked as the surgeon talks to me about trying to go through the back of my neck for the op, rather than the front, to avoid an obvious scar.

The last patch in the quilt

For some light relief, Alex wheels me down to Costa with my dad and brother in tow. Several surgeons from my team are in the queue, grabbing a quick latte. As if in response to this sighting of the people in whose hands my life lies, I lose all feeling in my right arm, which has been tingling for hours, but now hangs limp. I describe this new sensation in a whisper to my dad, not wanting to make a fuss, but he shrieks and the surgeons' heads all whip around to face me. My brother then relays the news in a more medical way – calm, factual, clinical. The surgery is scheduled for 'immediately'.

Despite the drama and the acute fear and tension, I feel surprisingly lucid, calm and peaceful, helped along by the morphine. I think about the information I have so often shared with many patients, about the nervous system being stacked in the body like a ladder. When we feel threat, we respond with fight or flight, a sort of 'I can' response. However, if we feel a threat is too great to fight or run from, we drop down the ladder into shutdown – the 'I cannot' state. The body begins to release its natural painkiller, endogenous opiates, which brings about a sense of calm in preparation for possible death. And this is the state I am in as I go into surgery.

Stealing the limelight

As I come around from the anaesthetic in record time, the surgeon asks if I want to know what they've done. I'm not sure I do, but she tells me anyway.

'We are sorry,' she says, 'but in the end we had to go in through the front of your neck.'

I waft this comment away, uncaring, as I attempt to move

my arm to see if it still works. It flinches in response to my hopeful commands, and relief washes through me. As they tell me about the titanium cage they have inserted to hold my spine in place, referring to my discs as being 'like roof tiles', Alex's eyes, welling with tears of relief, meet mine, before darting down to the vial of blood dangling from my neck. She doubles over with a low groan and collapses on the floor. Both doctors rush over to her. I push myself up on the big white cushions and manage a husky, 'You OK, Al?'

After a sugary tea, Alex is fine. I enjoy accusing her of stealing the limelight.

Deny, detach, blame

For legal reasons, mainly fear of being sued, I can't tell people how my neck was broken in two places by someone else. In any case, what actually happened sounds completely dubious, like a far-fetched cover for a strange and graphic sex accident. But, while I'm obliged to keep the facts to myself, I feel the need to share the trauma of the event and its aftermath. This includes the physical and emotional trauma, of course, but also the relational trauma I experience from those close to the accident, which almost pushes me to breaking point.

Denial is a powerful response that often comes from a place of shame and guilt. The typical pattern is deny, detach, minimize and direct blame, and I am now exposed to all of this.

As I cannot share my side of the story, I will share the story from the point of view of 'the other side'. Those closest to me settle on minimizing the accident, acting as though I broke a leg, whilst others completely deny an accident took place. They say I somehow inflicted major physical trauma on myself some other way – maybe in a car accident with no other damages or witnesses, maybe in a fall from a roof, maybe by visiting a dodgy chiropractor – then I just carried on with my life until it occurred to me that I could pin this injury on them. I pinpointed an event that I had attended, falsely reporting what had happened to me there with the clear motivation of suing the hosts, staff or companies involved. That's a story that might make some sense, but the intention becomes less clear when I take no legal action and gain no financial compensation whatsoever. Back to the drawing board, then. *Aha*, they think, maybe the motive is sheer malice. And the response to this is to treat me as the villain. As the villain, I am held responsible for distressing events that go on to happen in their lives – their losses, traumas, pain – all reported to be directly caused by stress I inflicted by maliciously breaking my own neck. Experience teaches me that, if someone portrays you as the 'baddie' in their narrative, you have to leave it alone. The more you try to fight the injustice of it, the more insistent people will become.

This reminds me of the experiment, 'On Being Sane in Insane Places', in which patients were told to report hearing voices, but, as soon as they were admitted to hospital, were instructed to stop the reports and act normally. Many patients, despite being completely fine, were held in psychiatric institutions for weeks. And the more they tried to prove their sanity, the more unhinged they were perceived to be.

This is where I am trapped. To move out of this place of feeling stuck requires the recognition that some ruptures cannot be repaired. I need to practise 'radical acceptance', something I have trained many patients to do. Radical acceptance encourages you to stop fighting, stop responding, to recognize that it isn't getting you anywhere and to let go of any bitterness that is making you feel stuck. 'Let go of bitterness' feels a bit like telling someone who is incandescent with rage to 'chill out', but, after a while, there is a spontaneous shift in me. I stop fighting, and stop caring. Distancing myself from all those supporting the denial and exceptional minimizing helps a lot; sometimes the breaking of certain bonds can ultimately be liberating. It takes me a long time, and it feels remarkably like going through heartbreak, but I manage to let go, of all of them.

A return to chaos

I have been convalescing at my family home in Manchester and there have been some positives. It has definitely brought my mum and me closer together; she takes care of me when I feel tired and fatigued, washes my hair for me when I'm in a wheelchair and talks me down when I feel too anxious to leave the house. The scar is healing and my mobility is now back to normal. I haven't been given any physio or anything, but my surgeon does ring to check in on how I am doing. I always find these calls emotional and I brim with tears as she asks about my pain and my movement. I have been struggling with sleep and feeling anxious and fragile, but also so grateful and lucky to be alive, and walking.

Back in London, I start to get cabin fever. I am desperate to return to work, and to get back to university. But the university has sanctioned me with a six-month break 'for my own good', and I am supposed to down tools and stop working on my research project, the focus of which is self-harm in women. Furious at this imposed break, I go to see the powers that be for a meeting. I realize this is a mistake seconds after taking a seat in my professor's office. Beside me is a miniature statue of a monkey holding a skull – a 'Thinker Monkey', common in therapist settings, as a symbol for examining the psyche and primal aspects of human nature. On the other side of me is a tall, overgrown leafy plant and as I peer through its leaves and look at the three observers gazing back at me from the other side of the desk, I feel like one of the monkeys at the zoo.

They peer at me over spectacles and say things like, 'We want to make sense of what happened,' and 'Is everything OK at home?' I actually welcome the concern. Despite it feeling a little critical, they are enquiring about and trying to make sense of what is happening for me, on the inside. They end by asking, 'Have you thought about using the scar?'

'How does one . . . *use* a scar?' I stutter, dumbfounded.

They ask me how people have responded to the prominent scar across my throat, which has had less than two months of healing.

Now that I think about it, when it was still heavily dressed in gauze and a big white square plaster, a man in a pub moved to rip it off, shouting, 'What's under here, then?' I also heard a mum whisper to her little girl, 'Oh, the lady must have done something to her neck; don't be frightened.' And everyone I have come across socially, even the people I hardly know, can't help but ask what I have done, as though it's any of their bloody business.

Suddenly I see what the university staff are getting at, and how this experience relates to my research. It has given me a small insight into what those with self-harm scars face every day. People look. They can't help it. And, each time the scars are seen, in a split second that person creates a story. My work has taught me that those who harm themselves are met with disdain, a lack of care, even anger – and that's just when they're in hospital. It is exposing and intrusive. I know that now.

I'm frustrated by the meeting, but, as I leave, I walk through the grounds of the university. It is so peaceful here and I feel like I'm soaking up learning, just by being present.

I make an effort every day, now, to notice how I walk, and I feel grateful that I *can* actually walk and move freely – I am hyper-aware that a fraction of a millimetre move in my spine would have changed my life forever.

Welcome back

I meet with the NHS team to talk about getting back to work. In typical fashion, they don't sit me down and try to examine or make sense of what has happened to me, or attempt to reflect on the meaning of life – they just want me back to work. My return-to-work interview goes like this:

'Are you OK? Can you walk? Do you need, like, a special chair thingy or anything? No? OK, fine. Let us know about your follow-up appointments at King's and you can have that time off. Welcome back! The staff microwave is broken.'

The last patch in the quilt

Don't cry, don't cry

I left several patients in the lurch, including Peggy. They were informed that I was off work 'due to medical reasons', keeping it vague, and a colleague was put in place to meet patients who could not be contacted. I learn that Peggy greeted them with a hostile indifference and a list of probing questions, an aggressive Poirot. A few patients complained about 'a lack of continuity' and communicated their sense of annoyance and frustration to the hospital management. But, for the most part, patients who knew me were concerned and wished me well. A few sent their best wishes through the nurses. Many are now shocked that I have returned so quickly and, when I see them, they check in on my emotions with compassion and curiosity, which I find touching. But I keep my guard up, I don't cry, not wanting any role reversal in the therapy room. It is always about them, not me.

Although I try to keep my own emotions at bay and out of focus, I think back to sessions with Kelli about my inner companion and my relationship with myself. I feel privileged to have had the love and support from family and friends, but I got through it alone, without a partner, and I took good care of myself. I didn't push myself, I ate what I wanted, I acknowledged the anxiety and didn't beat myself up for it. I coped.

The lesser of two evils

When I return to work, I find that I have been assigned to a new service alongside my usual patients. I will now also be working with adult diabetics with complications, many of whom are attending the hospital to have amputations. My first task on my first day back is to meet with the team. I meet the surgeon, Mr Raptis, first. Upon seeing my scar, he wants the full medical rundown.

I explain that I still have nerve pain, quite badly at times, and that my doctors have offered me medication. But I know the possible plentiful side effects of gabapentin, a drug that is also sometimes used as an antidepressant. It reminds me of those American infomercials where a happy woman spins around in a gorgeous meadow, carefree and cured after taking a certain medication. Then, at the end of the ad, a man's voice reels off an enormous list of side effects: 'May cause heart attack, explosive diarrhoea, projectile vomiting, your family to leave you, a wish to end it all.'

While I appreciate the value of antidepressant medication for some people, for whom it can be literally lifesaving, I am not sure it is worth me taking it for my pain. Anyway, having gone to work and walked about with a broken spine for ten days because I decided to just 'get on with it', it turns out my pain threshold is quite high.

Mr Raptis ponders my predicament, then challenges me. 'Why don't you have the second surgery, to open up the space for the nerve? Then the pain will stop.'

He knows the risks, so I don't teach him to suck eggs. Instead, I try to appeal to his human side and tell him how frightened I was when I lost movement in my arm. If I have the second op, paralysis would be a real fear.

'Ah, I see,' he says warmly – he has known me for some time. 'Well, it wouldn't be so bad if you had one limp arm.

You're pretty cute; you'll do OK.' He's making fun of what he knows would have been my first worry when I was more neurotic and blinded by heartbreak. 'You've come a long way; you'll make the right call.'

After this, he checks in on my progress and pain regularly and continues to use dark humour, as all doctors do, to lighten the mood.

Hard work

My new service with diabetic adults is very different from my more typical work in paediatrics and children's cancer. With a cancer diagnosis, everything is about speed. Even with long stretches of chemotherapy and prolonged treatment, it is like a rollercoaster for the families. Treatment regimens are cyclical – three weeks on, one week off, then scan, repeat. It is rapid and unrelenting, and there is a real sense of fighting, of pushing through and standing against the illness.

In my new patients, there is a chronic sense of denial, passivity and hopelessness, of giving in to the illness. The average person underestimates diabetes and the gruelling treatment regime of type-1. Most people misunderstand the disease and assume it is self-inflicted – one too many dough-nuts at lunchtime. However, type-1 is caused by a failure of the pancreas, resulting in the need for daily treatment. For some, that's injecting themselves three times a day. Most of us experience injections as an unpleasant event that we have to endure occasionally, usually for a vaccine. Imagine this multiple times a day, every day – and this is in addition to the finger pricks to test the blood. Injection sites get lumpy and have to be rotated. The body becomes a pincushion. And then there are things that affect insulin which are beyond the bounds of treatment control. Insulin is a hormone, so it is impacted by heat, stress, other medications, a person's growth, other hormones . . . the list goes on.

Dealing with the patients' denial is a core part of the therapy work I'm here to do. Many have denied their illness for years. Lots of patients feel hopeless and helpless and, having not wanted to carry on with their health-management regimes, now face life-changing amputations. I can't make their day-to-day any easier. There's no reframing or new meaning we can attach to the illness. The work is heavy and hard.

The consultant on my team leans in to me as she heats up her tomato soup in the unreliable microwave, and says, 'You know, I'd rather have HIV than be diagnosed with diabetes.'

I don't think I'll lead with that in my next consultation.

Deathbed

I am working alongside Mr Raptis today. He explains that we have an additional patient on today's list and that he is on his way down from A & E. As he starts to read the patient's notes, his eyes widen.

'What is it?' I ask.

'Let the patient tell you. Better still, ask his wife.'

Mr Leary is wheeled in by Mrs Leary. She forces the chair over the threshold of the clinic-room door with an eye roll, nearly tipping Mr Leary out onto the floor. She is past caring about little things like that. Both look severely unkempt and are missing several teeth, but nonetheless appear to be something of a team, both a little dismissive and uninterested in this medical appointment.

'Mr Leary has a recent amputation of the left leg at the top of the thigh,' Mr Raptis explains to me and the consultant and the podiatrist in the room – a full house.

As Mr Raptis inspects the wound, I talk to the Learys – partly in order to distract them, in case Mr Raptis starts poking at anything. I ask about Mr Leary's level of pain. I ask who else is at home. They answer without much interest, but when I get to asking how they have arrived at this point, Mrs Leary cuts me off.

'It was that bloody busybody Linda from next door, the boring little bitch,' she splutters with sudden animation and unexpected venom.

It transpires that the tissue in Mr Leary's leg had completely died some time ago, to the point where the neighbour could smell it from next door and found it so repugnant she called the police. The police suspected a dead body and entered the house with force. But, when they went upstairs, Mr and Mrs Leary were in bed, Mrs Leary sitting up and reading a book, both in complete denial of the smell and the serious condition of the leg, despite Mr Leary's pallor. He was brought straight into the hospital by ambulance.

'Denial, fear and . . . anosmia, a.k.a. an inability to smell, maybe?' I say to Mr Raptis when the Learys leave, trying to rationalize their behaviour.

'Just fucking mental cases,' he replies.

Kelli diagnoses

I haven't seen Kelli since the accident, but I did let her know what happened, from my hospital bed. She was concerned, warm, and ended each message with, *Take good care*.

I felt a similar sense of warmth from Dr Lane. 'Don't worry about anything or anyone else but yourself right now,' she kept saying when I mentioned patients I needed to contact. I asked her to speak to Peggy first, as a priority. Her fear of something happening to me had become reality and I knew she would feel abandoned. Dr Lane insisted she would take care of everything and rang Peggy to set up regular 'welfare checks'. I wondered if she had me in her diary under the same heading, because she called at the same time every week.

I am looking forward to seeing Kelli again. I finally feel I have something exciting to bring to therapy – some actual trauma – making my previous micro-traumas of being lied to and feeling like an imposter seem frivolous, and I hope she will call me brave and resilient. I have missed her maternal warmth and unconditional acceptance, albeit sprinkled with a few home truths.

She has moved offices and her new workplace is quite hard to find. I park nearby and start out across a muddy patch of land towards a group of makeshift buildings. A large dog is wandering around outside and I am frozen to the spot. My ridiculous fear of dogs has shattered my credibility on many home visits. Ah, the patient thinks, the psychologist has arrived to cure my phobia, but she's a quivering wreck because of our cute family pet.

I know how to work with phobias. I do it all the time. But

have I worked on my own? No, I have not. I text Kelli and ask her to escort me safely past the dog. Maybe if I didn't have access to Kelli, I would face this alone, but I don't feel shame in front of her.

For years, I would ask my mum about my fear of dogs.

'Did something, anything at all, happen to me as a child to lodge this fear so deep?'

'No, nothing I can think of, darling,' she would say every time.

Then, one afternoon when I was at home during my recovery, my mum was looking out over the front garden and, apropos of nothing, she said, 'You know, Nat, maybe that time I left you on the lawn in a child car seat, strapped in, and that Rottweiler jumped on top of you and pushed you over . . . That might have been it.'

In Kelli's new office, I am relieved to see the familiar chaise longue and, as I settle onto it, I relax. Although the environment is unfamiliar and my experience on the way in has been disquieting, everything seems right. I am here, fully present, bolstered by a feeling of safety and peace. This internal state of security can emerge thanks to the presence of another – and for me it's Kelli.

We talk about my accident and my time in hospital, and I start to recall pieces of the story that I have forgotten about until now, including having a panic attack on the first night in hospital. I remember a nurse coming over to me who was curt and wouldn't let me hold her hand, despite my pleas. Eventually, she compromised by allowing me to cling to her hip, which I gratefully did for quite some time.

Then Kelli starts asking me questions, which at first seem

entirely random. I feel a flash of irritation. I'm seeking compassion and warmth from her, not an interrogation. But, as I piece the questions together, I realize what she's doing: she is bringing my awareness to the parts of my recent experience that I have so far denied. I have been suffering emotionally since the acute physical trauma ended, but I haven't wanted to acknowledge it for fear of being engulfed, overwhelmed.

Together, over the next hour, we start to build a picture of the dysphoria I have been experiencing since leaving hospital – the flatness and numbness, the waking at night in a hot sweat, feeling detached and dissociated at work, then sudden peaks of arousal and a racing heart, or feeling anxious and faint.

Kelli asks how I am coping in the amputee clinic, and I describe a couple of panic episodes that I have tried to ignore, breathing into paper bags in the toilets and, on one occasion, throwing up. She listens patiently, then points out that I have flooded myself. I think about flooding therapy and how, once upon a time, if you were scared of clowns, the therapy would be to fill a caravan with clowns and lock you in it with them, to expose you. Flooding is traumatizing. Today, we want patients to feel mastery over their fears, to gain understanding and insight into how their brain responds to fear, and to build enough resilience to face these fears, a little bit at a time, with the security and support of the therapeutic relationship. We've come a long way.

'How have you been experiencing yourself during this time?' Kelli asks me. 'If you picture yourself in your mind, what do you see?'

It takes only a moment's thought to realize that I still picture myself as fragile, small, limp and lifeless. This is what happens when we are stuck in trauma. We can't move on from the way we felt in ourselves at the time of our pain and distress, so we move forward feeling limited and incapable. We recycle the most acute moments and those small details that hold the most meaning.

Kelli asks me about each tiny detail, gently, slowly.

I talk about the weakness I felt in my neck just after the operation, when it had no muscular strength, and the terror that had pulsed through me when I couldn't lean forward to reach the Rice Krispies left in front of me by a well-meaning nurse.

'What was the fear?' Kelli asks.

She laughs a little, gently, when I say, 'To put it bluntly, it was that my head would literally fall off my body.'

Such a strange sensation, not feeling confident enough to lift the weight of your own head; it's an insight into how babies must feel. These are the moments, my moments, when I felt the most afraid.

In PTSD, re-experiencing is what happens when something triggers and we step into the memory of the traumatic event, as if it is happening to us again, in real time. This response is so attached to our fear and anxiety that it is not integrated into our brain or stored in our memory. It is like a piece of a patchwork that sits outside the quilt of our personal story. It cannot be sewn in, cannot blend in neatly, and so intrudes on our minds, creating the same panic and level of arousal it did at the very moment it initially occurred. Re-experiencing can be so terrifying that people with PTSD usually avoid reminders of their trauma completely. I had one patient who suffered sexual abuse after the perpetrator had been eating an orange, and the smell of oranges became a trigger. To avoid the trigger, he wouldn't go to supermarkets, to restaurants or even on holidays. His avoidance of oranges was life-changing. I, on the other hand, cannot use avoidance techniques. I am working within a medical environment, alongside a surgeon, with patients undergoing amputations and facing life-changing difficulties with mobility and nerve damage.

The most traumatizing memory for me, the bit I keep re-experiencing, happened in the operating theatre. It took me a bit longer than it perhaps should have done to go under the anaesthetic, so I have a memory of being wheeled into theatre. My coping response was to tell myself not to look at the instruments. Don't look. Look straight ahead. I had the sense that I was going to die, and it was then that everything finally faded to black. This moment is being recycled into the present and is the cause of my vomiting and dizziness. Because I now work alongside a surgeon with a table of instruments, and my job is to contain and manage the emotions of those facing life-changing mobility issues and nerve pain, I am, to use the clinical term, freaking the fuck out. I have stepped into a world of triggers. I am locked in the caravan with the clowns.

I know that Kelli will help to get me through the weeks and months to come, that she can help me dissipate the trauma symptoms. I promise her that I will be more compassionate to myself at work, that I will not feel shame about vomiting when the nausea comes over me. And I take away another positive from our session: I now have first-hand insight into trying to push down shame, trying to function with an underlying sense of panic, foreboding and anxiety. This means I can connect a little bit deeper with patients when they are overwhelmed and are trying to ignore it, when they are worried and frightened that entering the therapy room will open the floodgates. I get it.

A 'code C'

We now have a junior doctor shadowing us. If someone told me he was in Year Six at school, I would believe them. So, here we are, in the cycle of patient care, a reminder that I am no longer the junior.

The first patient comes in, a Mr Clarke, and I start by asking the usual questions: What's brought you in today? How is your mood? How are you coping with wound care?

He seems relaxed, jovial and positive: 'Yep, basically left it alone, but seems fine.'

Then Mr Raptis pulls off the bandage and something falls to the floor with a splat. Oh, a beige sponge caught in the bandages, I instantly assume. But, as I look again and peer a little closer, I see the sponge is moving. Oh, maggots.

'Wound care not so good, then,' says Mr Raptis.

I hear the clatter of a medical tray crashing to the floor. In the corner of the room, the junior doctor is keeling over, slumping to the ground. Now I don't feel so bad about my own dizziness and vomiting.

I help him to a seat and send someone off for a 'code C' – jargon we have adopted for when we have juniors in. It means hot chocolate from Costa, with extra sugar.

Ducks in a row

Since returning to work, my ducks are almost back in a row. I have returned to my research, albeit against the advice from my university to wait until I am fully rested. It's my decision and I am thrilled to find I can disagree with authority and the world doesn't end. I have reconnected with Kelli and she is helping me to move forward emotionally and psychologically. I am single and I have coped with so much without a romantic partner, I feel a sense of strength in my singledom that I have never felt before.

The last two ducks on my list are Peggy and Dr Lane. I send Dr Lane a few messages, but there's no reply. She must be frazzled, I think; she was in charge of covering my cancer caseload when I was off.

Peggy is easier to track down and she is understandably furious that I had the audacity to injure myself and nearly die, after I promised I wouldn't let her down. We meet at Kiwi and share chocolate Mini Rolls; I am over the moon to see her eat. I try to work through her anger and rage, but I begin by apologizing for making a promise. This is something that, as a therapist, I should never have done, and I take responsibility for my mistake. Making a promise in the therapeutic relationship is problematic, as it assumes the therapist is aware of the patient's internal world. This relationship can become very important to a patient, making it very precious, and precious things are often fragile.

I tell Peggy, 'As a therapist, I can't promise to never let you down, because I don't fully know what that looks like for you. Maybe me glancing at the clock during our session or using certain words may hold a special meaning for you. Maybe you find it hard to tolerate me using praise, or me touching your arm might remind you of a previous trauma . . . All of these little things could be ways in which I am letting you down. Any of my actions, mistakes or oversights might be your internal cue for danger, based on your previous experiences. All I can do is do my best to relate to you, be curious about how I make mistakes, and take ownership of them.'

She says she found my disappearance very confusing and very hard. She says, 'People always leave. You left me, and I knew I wouldn't have been the first person you called, and maybe you only thought about me after a few days, and it's OK.'

The incident feels like a bit of a rupture between us. But, in my absence, she has found alternative support in the form of group therapy, which she really enjoys, and she has also started a college course. Peggy has grown in her insight; she is now able to look at her thoughts. She knew I wouldn't have called her first, but instead of feeling the pain of this and reacting with rage, she observed this thought and deduced that 'it's OK'. Peggy has moved out of her psychic-equivalence mode, which is when a patient believes something and so it is considered factually true, with no room for perspective – the thought has the same value as physical reality. She is more flexible in her thinking and she has grown in confidence, so within group support she is thriving.

I tell her how proud I am of her and decide not to mention that I am also pleased to see her reach for another Mini Roll. I don't want to open old wounds. I let her know it has been a privilege to get to know her during our time together, and she says she can let me go now and she won't panic when I leave this time. She can cope.

Lost in loss

I know now that I'm suffering from trauma-induced anxiety and flattened mood, due to the exhaustion associated with hypervigilance, lack of sleep and re-experiencing. Mustering any feeling other than apathy or slight irritation is almost impossible. I am socializing less and enjoying calmer and quieter spaces more – I need to be away from people and, as that's not possible during the working day, I'm spending more and more time alone during my evenings and weekends. I still feel the draw to go back to my parents' as often as I can, as it's a safe space. My dad has been urging me to visit, suggesting walks, lunches, seeing family. He is insistent. So, I book a train ticket and look forward to a weekend of cheese on toast and clean linen.

Dr Lane

After a few days of regression into my teenage self, lounging about in a hoodie and eating ice cream in front of the TV, it is Monday again. I get an unexpected call from the hospital. This has happened before, when patients have mixed up appointments or I have messed up and they come in when I am on annual leave. I am filled with dread. Things get much worse when I realize it is Dr Weller, the head of paediatrics, on the other end of the phone.

'Hello, Natalie. I hope you are well. I heard about the

accident – terrible stuff.' Before I can speak, he says, 'I am very sorry to have to inform you that Dr Lane has died; she took her own life a few days ago.'

The denial hits at speed and I say, 'No, no, no . . .' over and over. It's all I can say. I search my mind for answers, for the reality, as this surely can't be it.

Images run through my mind: the overstuffed notebook, her eyes holding my gaze as we laughed together, the dance classes she told me she was booking in as her coping tool, the horses. The pain she must have been trying to cope with underneath it all, that last time we saw each other. The Nokia. Why didn't I ask about the Nokia? Now I will never know. I think of her little boy and how they will have broken the news to him.

I know Dr Lane was well loved. I feel privileged to have gained her time, her energy, her warmth, her wisdom and her humour over the years we worked together. I will now never understand her inner world and the turmoil she must have been fighting daily while she was helping me with mine.

Psychologists might understand the mechanisms and work-ings and symptoms of poor mental health and how to treat it, but this doesn't necessarily mean we know how to take care of our own. Psychologists and doctors are often seen – and need to be seen – as all-knowing, having it together and able to contain the rest of us when we are patients. We need to see them in this way to feel confident in their ability to fix us. But psychologists are as fallible as anyone else in their emotional and relational worlds.

As therapists, our aim is to become part of the patient's processing, a part of their mind that can be compassionate and supportive outside of the therapeutic relationship. What would my therapist say? What would my therapist tell me to do here? These are the questions we want our patients to ask themselves. I now try to do this with Dr Lane. What would she tell me to do? What would her advice be? I picture her standing in front of me with the bursting Filofax, guiding me patiently to the insight and the answer. In the end, I simply can't imagine what advice she would give, but I am struck by the sense of safety I feel as I imagine being in her company. I marvel at how she brought peace to so many others – me included – when all the while she was battling her own devastating inner turmoil. The need to be curious about people has never been clearer to me. Even when they seem in control, we are all coping with something.

Bear witness

After her death, there are whispers in the corridors about Dr Lane being selfish. How could she leave her little boy? people ask. I feel this is the question they want to ask me, but thankfully they don't. They are locating blame in Dr Lane and I find this difficult to receive. I understand that people may feel anger towards the person who is gone, and this is all the more complicated when someone takes their own life, but I find it to be misinformed and judgemental.

The fact is, a mood disorder, such as major depression, distorts the way we think. In this state of mind, people experience a distorted perception of reality. Depression plays tricks. This is biochemical; it is not a decision. The parts of the brain that control cortisol – the stress hormone – and our response to threat can change during depression, and this is influenced both by genetics and early adverse childhood experiences, causing reality to look different. It creates a negative filter and a tendency to view situations in extreme terms. The pain threshold is changed, so that even minor events are experienced as painful. Everything is blurred, distorted, disfigured. Those contemplating taking their own life truly believe negative thoughts like, 'My loved ones will be better off without me,' or 'I am a burden and everything is hopeless and I need the pain to stop,' without necessarily fully acknowledging that this means everything really will stop.

A micro-version of this for an average person is when they 'emotionally see' that they are having a bad day, feel criticized or feel as though they have failed. But this negativity will pass and they will soon look at themselves again with kinder eyes when things are better. This is the real tragedy of suicide. Would that moment of acute pain and hopelessness have passed? Would things have got better? We are all encouraged to focus on the future and a time when difficulties will pass or shift – the phrase 'This too shall pass' comes to mind. With depression, it's about holding out. I wish Dr Lane had been able to hold out.

At the same time, I also think it's important to honour how we are feeling in any given moment – we shouldn't rush through it, but should feel it all the way through. This helps us to gain clarity and work out what our feelings mean, find ways of coping with them and living with them rather than waiting for them to magically go away.

I miss Dr Lane every day. I feel huge waves of guilt that I didn't bond with her more and take more of an interest in her personal life. I was so worried about maintaining a professional boundary that I missed opportunities; maybe I missed her bids for connection. I think about how she held my gaze when we laughed together and I wish we had laughed together more. I still talk to her. She was more than a mentor; she was my friend, and I wish I had told her this when I had the chance.

Speed dating

I am tasked with finding a new supervisor for my NHS work. I already have a university supervisor for my PhD, who is brilliant and straight-talking and someone I respect in a world where, along the way, I have started to lose respect for a great many professionals. I need someone else like that.

Searching for a new supervisor feels like dating. I create imagined versions of each supervisor from their online profile, and a narrative, and a sense of who they are. Then, when we speak and their voice isn't how I imagined it, or they wear a skinny scarf like an aging rockstar, or say things like, 'We're singing from the same hymn sheet,' or 'Let's look under the bonnet,' I check out. Not for me. I have several supervisors for short periods. I am having flings with the psychology community, I realize. I am having commitment issues with my psychologists because Dr Lane can't be replaced and no connection feels the same.

Viva reviver

I'm approaching the end of my PhD training and the end of my research, an 80,000-word piece of original clinical work on self-harm, examining what patients have found helpful and unhelpful about the therapy they have received and the therapy I have practised. This has taken hours of interviewing, which I have enjoyed and found hard in equal measure. The interviews couldn't take the shape and form of a therapy session and it was hard for me not to go into therapist mode but to stay as interviewer. After analysing and reviewing this data, I then have to attend a viva, a verbal examination in which I must defend my work to a panel with vast amounts of experience and much more research credibility than me. During the exam, just two minutes in, I think I have failed, and a feeling of pure deflation comes over me. I feel as though I have just started my driving test and have ploughed into a lamp post, yet I am being forced to finish while my examiner sits in an eerie knowing silence.

At the end of several excruciating hours, in which I bumble and stumble but somehow manage to support and justify my written work, it turns out my examiner is just unreadable and I have passed. My professor is in the room to support me and, when the verdict comes in, I detect a hint of surprise in his eyes, a slight raising of an eyebrow. Or maybe my nerves have made me paranoid. I like to think it's the latter.

Some people say that, when they are awarded the title of doctor, it feels anticlimactic, and does nothing to make them feel accomplished or to shake off the imposter syndrome. It is just a piece of paper and two letters before their name. This is not the case for me. I am fucking over the moon and it feels as big a moment as I had hoped. There is an instant shift in terms of my confidence. This is not to say the imposter syndrome has vanished entirely, but at least people now have to say, 'That "doctor" doesn't seem to have a clue what she's doing.'

I celebrate as soon as I possibly can with Alex and some of our friends in the pub. We drink champagne and I feel like an adult. I've finally done it. I am mature, assured, accomplished. I've made it.

At 7 a.m., I wake up on the floor, naked, dehydrated, with a throbbing headache and fistfuls of half-eaten cheese toastie in my hands, remembering the several mortifying calls I made to confused ex-lovers in the early hours of the morning.

Kelli assembles the pieces

Back in Kelli's office, I unravel the embarrassing details of the night's antics: the phone calls and texts, my humiliation at appearing needy and vulnerable. I talk at speed, clutching a carton of sweet apple juice that's helping to balance my blood sugars.

Kelli sighs. 'We could take a risk today,' she says. 'Would you like to? Because I would like to share my formulation of you during the course of our work together.'

A formulation is a like a map or a jigsaw of a patient, piecing together all their personality traits, characteristics, experiences, defences, challenges and ways of coping. I sometimes share this with my patients to help them gain a better understanding of themselves, but I have two distinct versions: one formulation is marked *Safe to share* and the other formulation is marked *Just for me*. The *Just-for-me* file has notes I've jotted in the sessions that would not be helpful to share with a patient – things like, *Nearly fell asleep here*, or *Might be a case of the 'worried wells' – they've looked this up on Google/TikTok*, or *Dramatic mother*.

Imagine all the annotations Kelli has made on my notes during our sessions, after three years of therapy, throughout my whole PhD training. But, of course, I don't have to imagine; she's going to tell me.

'You have an attachment style that leans towards *avoidant*,' she begins.

Attachment styles have become quite fashionable, with the terms watered down and used in popular culture. There is likely a *Which attachment style am I?* quiz on Facebook.

The safety and responsiveness of the parent–child relationship informs how we understand ourselves, our world and our relationships with others. A psychologist in the seventies, Mary Ainsworth, conducted a famous experiment known as the 'strange situation'. She placed infants in a room with their mothers and studied a number of different scenarios. The mother left the infant alone. The mother left them with a stranger, but returned. The mother ignored the infant completely. By observing the different responses of the children – how quickly they were soothed, whether they even batted an eyelid at being left with a stranger or went batshit as soon as their mother left – Ainsworth was able to determine that children fit into three categories.

They might be secure – certain their mother will come back, that she is safe, wherever she may be, which allows them to go exploring, simply getting on with their baby business. They might be ambivalent (or anxious) – which means they freak out excessively when their mother leaves, so that they can't be soothed by her when she returns and may even hit her, striking out at her face. Or, finally, they might be avoidant, which is summarized as 'they couldn't give a fuck'. They keep to themselves and seem so self-sufficient and adult you feel you could hand them a briefcase and they'd likely ask you to arrange their 4 p.m. meeting.

This experiment might seem odd, and even a little crude, but children have been found to continue their relational behaviour in the ways expected of their category as they grow up. What's more, people's adult styles of romantic love have been found to be directly related to their attachment styles as children. Knowing all this means I understand that, as an adult with an attachment style leaning closer to avoidant, I am considered to have a fear of intimacy and a closed-off attitude to love, prioritizing independence and being a sort of lone wolf.

I am confused. Given my constant scrambling for love, Kelli must be wrong. But, of course, she is ready to back up her findings – a kind of viva in which I'm now the examiner, asking questions to which she has all the answers.

'Your subconscious way of coping with a fear of intimacy is to choose the wrong partners,' she tells me. 'Is it fair to say you have chosen the wrong partners?'

I feel she is being a little smug here, like a prosecution barrister armed with all the evidence and with the bit between her teeth. God, why is she always so bloody right?

'And, in terms of independence, what do you do when you're sick or injured?' she continues remorselessly. 'What do you do when your spine is broken in two places? You go off alone, you keep going, keep quiet, you seek nothing from anybody until it is almost too late.'

I feel my tears brimming and hear Kelli's voice adjust to a

warmer, more caring tone in response. She has broken me and now she can go more gently.

'The thing is,' she tells me, 'you had something to prove. When you were in pain, when Steve left you, you had a frantic need to prove that you could fill the original void, the void he created when he left.'

She's right. I needed to replace the fantasy of the utopia I had imagined in being the 'good doctor's wife', or anybody's wife, as an identity.

'You set about doing this by becoming your own safe place and becoming a doctor in your own right,' Kelli continues, 'replacing the fantasy with your own success as a doctor, to prove your value to yourself. You have achieved this. You are more independent, knowledgeable, assertive . . . You can cope.

'But it's not just about coping, Natalie. That's why these moments of chaos erupt from you, like last night. Last night, when all your defences and inhibitions were down—'

'Because of the tequilas?' I chip in before she can finish.

'Yes, partially because of the tequilas,' Kelli replies, 'but fundamentally because you were seeking connection. And that's OK, Natalie. Stop shaming yourself for it.

'You may think on some level that you don't need intimacy, or that you're scared to have it in case it ends or betrays you, but the truth is that we all need it. We are attachment beings, hardwired for connection and bonding. The point is, Natalie, none of us can cope alone.'

In this *aha* moment, some part of me is profoundly shifted. I feel euphoria and relief as the pieces of my puzzle slot into place. Working with my patients, I've seen how, in times of stress and suffering, we are all susceptible to developing maladaptive, chaotic ways of coping – unhelpful behaviours we feel ashamed about or see as abnormal. I've learned how I can support patients by removing the shame and sense of aloneness in these seemingly odd responses and helping them to find more adaptive ways to cope. I was beginning to gain trust in my ability to do this, but the doctorate has given me the final seal of approval that supporting others in this way is a strength of mine. This is the validation I needed to bolster me. At the beginning, I maladaptively sought a marriage to a doctor to mask my own self-doubt. Now, I don't need it.

My string of relationships with men who were struggling with their own issues was my way of coping. I was focusing on their needs to deflect from my own. I was also seeking connection. But there is no shame in that. Connection is the mother of all coping mechanisms. It's how we regulate our emotions and feel secure within ourselves. The foundation for all our emotional pain is disconnection. Loss, betrayal, despair, rejection – they are all relational. Finally, I can accept the vulnerability and all the chaotic messy bits of Natalie. I allow her to keep seeking, as we all do, connection and safety in the world.

Acknowledgements

I have to start by thanking all of the people who allowed me into their worlds and were patient with me as I developed my craft. I continue to learn from patients every day and I am constantly reminded that they are the experts of themselves.

I would like to thank my dad, whose wisdom is sprinkled throughout the book, for igniting my interest in people-watching as a toddler and believing in me ever since.

I thank my brother for always keeping me humble, and my mum for battling to get me to read as a child.

Thank you to Alex for always seeing the funny side of every heartbreak, breakdown, meltdown and achievement. Thank you for the telling-offs and belly laughs.

Thank you to Ange for lending me her skills to build my website, and entertaining my ideas and Notes app lists over wine and vegan nachos.

A big thank-you to Charlie for always listening and denying me any opportunity to treat myself, ever.

A special mention to Giri and his encouragement to always 'go for it and see what happens'.

I thank Jamie for listening to me cry-read many sections of

the book and sticking it out despite his fear of being 'the next chapter'.

A huge thank-you to Jen, my incredibly thoughtful, supportive and nurturing agent. Jen has helped to make the writing fun and rewarding. She has given me the best advice throughout and she should definitely be a psychologist in her next life.

Thank you so much to the team at Picador for allowing me this opportunity, with a special thanks to my editor, Andrea, who helped shape the narrative and dedicated time and energy to my vision. Special thanks are extended to Gillian for her thoughtful insight and also to Mary for her support and input (and for letting me keep the title).

About the author

Dr Natalie Cawley is a psychotherapist and counselling psychologist with a BSc, MSc and PsychD in psychology and has worked and trained in both the NHS and private practice, within paediatric and adult services. Her experience covers a wide range of health conditions and clinical presentations in the community and within psychiatric hospitals. Her specialism in attachment theory, the driving force behind our psychological and emotional functioning, informs all her therapeutic work. Her hobbies include stand-up comedy – mostly watching, although she has performed a set about bad dates that went better than expected. She lives and works in Manchester and can be contacted via www.nataliecawley.com. *Just About Coping* is her first book.